VERBAL ART IN SAN BLAS

VERBAL ART IN SAN BLAS

Kuna Culture Through its Discourse

Joel Sherzer

UNIVERSITY OF NEW MEXICO PRESS
Albuquerque

LIBRARY OF CONGRESS CATALOGUING–IN–PUBLICATION DATA

Sherzer, Joel.
   Verbal art in San Blas : Kuna culture through its
discourse / Joel Sherzer.
     p. cm.
English and Cuna.
Originally published: Cambridge [England] ; New York :
Cambridge University Press, 1990, in series: Cambridge
studies in oral and literate culture ; 21.
   Includes bibliographical references (p.) and index.
   ISBN–8263–1882–7 (paper)
   1. Cuna language—Discourse analysis.
   2. Cuna literature—History and criticism.
   3. Cuna language—Social aspects. I. Title.
[PM3743. 1.S54 1998]
498'.2—dc21   97–48952
                CIP

CONTENTS

v

Preface

My fieldwork among the Kuna began in 1968 and has involved repeated visits to San Blas, some longer, some shorter, since then. Almost all of the time I have spent in San Blas has been on the island of Sasartii-Mulatuppu, near the Panama-Colombia border. The people of Sasartii-Mulatuppu have always been helpful to me and supportive of my work. I am most grateful to them for this.

The individuals whose verbal performances are presented here were eager to participate in the recording and preservation of their traditional knowledge and verbal art. It gives me great pleasure to be able to bring their desires to fruition. They are Chief (previously Chief's Spokesman) Armando González, Chief Mastayans, Chief Olowitinappi, Chief's Spokesman Olowitinappi (now deceased), Chief Muristo Pérez, and Pranki Pilos. Hortenciano Martínez and Anselmo Urrutia aided me in the delicate process of transcription, translation, and interpretation.

My research among the Kuna was supported by a National Science Foundation grant to the University of Texas, a National Institute of Mental Health small grant, summer grants from the University of Texas Institute of Latin American Studies, and a John Simon Guggenheim Memorial Foundation fellowship. The government of Panama, through Patrimonio Histórico, granted me permission to carry out research in Panama.

I would like to thank my closest colleagues in the study of Kuna language, culture, and society, Mac Chapin and James Howe, for comments on previous versions of the chapters of this book, including questions of textual presentation and translation. Charles Briggs, William Bright, and Dennis Tedlock were official readers for Cambridge University Press and provided most thought-provoking, sensitive, and sensible suggestions. Ruth Finnegan and Dina Sherzer were unofficial readers whose comments were also most helpful.

An earlier version of chapter five appeared in Joel Sherzer and Greg Urban (eds.), *Native South American discourse* (1986). An earlier version of chapter six, without the presentation of the Kuna text, appeared in the *Journal of American Folklore* 92 (1979) and, with the Kuna text, in Brian Swann and Arnold Krupat (eds.), *Recovering the word: Essays on Native American literature* (1987). An earlier version of chapter eight, without the presentation of the Kuna text, appeared in Deborah Tannen (ed.), *Analyzing discourse: Text and talk* (1981).

Guide to pronunciation and notational conventions

The following symbols are used in the representation of the Kuna language:

Vowels
i high front open
e middle front open
a low front open
u high back rounded
o middle back rounded

Consonants
p voiced bilabial stop
pp voiceless bilabial stop
t voiced dental stop
tt voiceless dental stop
k voiced velar stop
kk voiceless velar stop
kw   voiced labiovelar stop
kkw   voiceless labiovelar stop
s voiceless dental spirant
c voiceless palatal affricate
m voiced bilabial nasal
n voiced dental nasal
l voiced lateral
r voiced flap
w voiced bilabial semivowel
y voiced palatal semivowel

Stress is usually on the penultimate syllable.

Expressive features of pronunciation in performance are represented in the texts as follows:

Lengthening of vowels and nasals, indicated by doubling of letters, tripling for extra
   lengthening:
   waaalking along

Loud speech, indicated by capital letters:
   YOU HAVE HEARD, up to here.

Decreasing volume, indicated by > placed before the stretch of speech affected:
   > scarred scarred

Stretched-out, syllabic pronunciation, indicated by dashes between syllables:
   who-of-the-two-of-us-in-deed-might-be-a-bet-ter-per-son?

Vibrating voice, indicated by dashes between letters:
   o-n-l-y t-h-e i-m-p-o-r-t-a-n-t p-e-o-p-l-e

Slowing of tempo, indicated by stretching out of letters and words, without dashes:
   But we are not now like that w e   a r e   t r u e   g o l d e n   p e o p l e   s e e

Faster tempo, indicated by a dotted underline under the words which are spoken faster:
   "Did I not now buy a plate"? you would say.

Rising pitch, indicated by ´ placed before the stretch of speech affected:
   ´ you will sit saying

Falling pitch, indicated by ` placed before the stretch of speech affected:
   ` he says

Whole line is higher in pitch, indicated by ^ placed before the line:
   ^ This chief standing speaking where is he from?

Part of line is higher in pitch, indicated by raising the words of higher pitch:

"Did I not now buy a plate?" you would say.

Line-ending pause, indicated by . at the end of line:

Little by little I was catching on.

Short interlinear pause, indicated by , :

Well, you know it all.

Long interlinear pause, without falling pitch, indicated by extra long space:

"Well   it is to frighten the devil" he says.

1. INTRODUCTION

The Kuna Indians are probably best known for their molas, colorful appliqué and reverse-appliqué blouses made and worn by Kuna women and sold all over the world. They are one of the largest indigenous groups in the South American tropics, numbering more than 30,000 individuals, the majority of whom inhabit San Blas, a string of island villages stretching from near the Canal Zone to the Panama-Colombia border, quite close to the jungle mainland, where they farm. Living on the edge of modern, urban civilization, the Kuna have managed to maintain their cultural uniqueness through a creative integration of old and new, constantly adapting and manipulating traditional patterns to make them fit new situations.

The Kuna language is usually classified as Chibchan, a very broad grouping which encompasses other languages of southern Central America and northern South America. It is not closely related, however, genetically or typologically, to any other Amerindian language. With regard to social and cultural organization, the Kuna are also unique, remarkably different from the other indigenous populations of Panama and neighboring regions. On the other hand, close and deep analysis of Kuna language, culture, and society, and especially their interaction and intersection, reveals certain similarities with other native groups in Central and South America, including some as far away as Brazil.

The Kuna have a rich and dynamic verbal life. Like most tropical forest and lowland South American Indian societies, the Kuna's world is permeated by and in fact organized by means of their discourse – the mythical chants of chiefs; the histories, legends, and stories of traditional leaders; the magical chants and secret charms of curing specialists; the speeches and reports of personal experience of all men and women; and the greetings, leave-takings, conversations, and joking of everyday life. All of this is oral – spoken, chanted, sung, shouted, and listened to.

This book is about the verbal life of the Kuna, presented here in the form of original versions and translations of myths, speeches, stories, and magical chants, together with extensive and intensive social, cultural, and linguistic commentary and analysis. My purpose is to demonstrate concretely how such discourse shapes life and experience in this nonliterate tropical island and forest society, in which all knowledge and information, from history and geography to the latest sports news from Panama City, is orally conceived, perceived, and transmitted. Experience of the physical, natural, and

1

human world – both Kuna and non-Kuna – is expressed and mediated through the discourse presented here. And it is through this discourse that we as outsiders can best appreciate Kuna life – its philosophy, mythology, symbolism, rhetoric, esthetics, and daily preoccupations; what Kuna individuals consider to be serious or sad, tragic or funny.

The verbal performances presented here were all recorded on the island of Sasartii-Mulatuppu, located in the eastern portion of San Blas, near the Colombian border. I first visited this island in 1969 and was immediately drawn into the fascinating world of Kuna discourse. From early in the morning to late at night I saw and heard the talking, chanting, shouting, and laughing of men and women as they conversed, counseled, cured, and joked. As the result of many visits I have made to Sasartii-Mulatuppu since that first one, I have become increasingly sensitive to and appreciative of the artistic properties of Kuna discourse as well as the necessity of approaching Kuna culture and society in terms of this discourse. From both theoretical and methodological perspectives my research is discourse centered. An earlier book, *Kuna Ways of Speaking*, is an exploration of Kuna language and culture from an ethnographic perspective. In it I examine general and specific patterns of language use, in both ritual and everyday life. This second book delves further and deeper into Kuna discourse. Each of the chapters centers on a particular verbal performance and follows the intersecting paths of linguistic, cultural, social, and poetic patterning reflected in and created by it.

The organizing focus of this book is verbal art. The Kuna are superb verbal artists, remarkable performers of the poetic discourse which is so essential to their social and cultural life. The performances presented here are all considered verbally artistic by the Kuna, who perform, listen to, appreciate, and evaluate them. They provide a rich and varied illustration of Kuna verbal practices, including chanted and spoken speech, ritual myth telling and formal speech making, political oratory and magical communication with the spirit world, serious reporting and humorous tale telling. They are the locus of many aspects of Kuna life – ecology, political and religious beliefs, curing and medicine, economic concerns, dealings with the outside world, personal relations, and humor.

While to a certain degree, all Kuna discourse, including everyday conversations and joking, is verbally artistic, it is especially in formal and ritual contexts that the Kuna most consider themselves to be verbally "on stage" and "on display," attempt to heighten the quality of their own verbal artistry, and critically evaluate the artistry of others. One major ritual context is the centrally located gathering house, in which chiefs chant about myths, legends, local history, and personal experiences, political leaders counsel, debate, and report in long and eloquent speeches, and expert story tellers unfold their serious and humorous tales. The other major type of ritual verbal performance involves communication with representatives of the spirit world. This communication, whose purpose is magical and curative, is in the form of long chants, usually performed in the home of the performer or his or her patient.

As it is most often men who are the public performers of verbal art among the Kuna, all of the individuals whose voices are represented here are men. An investigation of genres and ways of speaking in terms of men and women reveals that men are involved in speech that is traditional, ritual, symbolic, esoteric, and public, such as the chanting of chiefs in the gathering house and the performance of curing and magical chants, while women, whose major performance genres are lullabies for children and laments for the dead, deal with matters which are, from the Kuna point of view, more personal, private, and superficial – even though child care and mourning for the dead are clearly basic concerns of social and cultural life. That is, again from the Kuna point of view, it is men who are the public verbal artists. The primary form of women's artistic and communicative expression is not ritual speaking and chanting, but, rather, the decorative and visual mola. It is interesting that one of the primary contexts for the making (as well as the wearing) of molas is the gathering house, the central public meeting place, and the locus of verbally artistic performances by men. Women make their molas there as they listen to men perform.[1]

The performers represented here are all verbal leaders and acknowledged verbal artists. Their verbal performances were recorded in natural settings. They are actual instances of the ongoing flow of Kuna verbal life. Especially because of the formal and ritual contexts in which they were recorded, the heightened attention to verbal artistry involved in their performance, and the performers' sense of being "on stage" and "on display," the form and the content were not determined by or affected by my presence or the presence of the tape recorder. While it is impossible to prove that my presence made no difference, the particular performances and events presented here regularly occur and would have occurred whether or not I was there. The Kuna treated me as an

---

[1]   See Sherzer and Sherzer (1976), Sherzer (1983: 70-71, 176-179, 232-233), and Sherzer (1987).

ordinary member of the audience and my tape recorder as an instrument of recording their oral traditions, something they are most concerned about.

My approach to verbal art is both sociolinguistic and ethnographic. It is sociolinguistic in that I view the grammar of the Kuna language, the different varieties of Kuna, and the human voice as resources which are exploited by speakers in the creation and structuring of actual forms of discourse. It is ethnographic in that I situate this discourse within the social, cultural, and personal contexts in which it occurred. The concept of context, in two senses, plays a crucial role in my interpretations and analyses. Context signifies on the one hand the social and cultural backdrop, the assumptions, beliefs, and symbolic associations that are uniquely Kuna. These include aspects of the local ecology, including plant and animal life; the nature of politics, curing, magic, and other ritual; figurative and allusive uses of language; history; and humor. Context signifies on the other hand the immediate location and situation in which a particular form of discourse occurred and was recorded, including the relations and interactions among those present; recent, relevant local, national, and natural happenings; and the specific goals and meanings of words and actions. In this way Kuna language, culture, and society can be viewed as both traditional and adaptive. The voices represented in these pages reflect the most ancient of tradition while at the same time they creatively mold this tradition to current situations. For this reason, my approach crucially depends on the recording of actual and natural speech events.

One aspect of the recent interest on the part of several disciplines in the detailed and precise analysis of discourse is a focus on structure and style in such a way that it seems difficult if not incorrect to make a distinction between ordinary language on the one hand, and literary and poetic language on the other. All discourse has features that have characteristically and traditionally been considered to be literary, and analysis of poetic structure is often what discourse analysis is all about. So rather than shove off the study of metaphor, foregrounding, cohesion, line and verse structure, dramatization of the voice, and grammatical aspects of style on literary critics, attention to such matters is basic to the work of linguists, anthropologists, and folklorists.[2]

---

2   For consideration of poetic and literary aspects of and approaches to discourse as central to the study of language and speech and the relationship among language, culture, and society, see Bauman's (1977) focus on culturally and socially situated performance as the locus of verbal art; Friedrich's (1979) studies of the symbolic and poetic potentialities of grammar; Gumperz's (1971) studies of code-switching and contextualization, in which such poetic processes as foregrounding and metaphor are

In my analyses and interpretations, I demonstrate the ways in which grammatical, discourse, social, cultural, and personal factors intersect and interact in the creation and structuring of verbal art. The result is a contribution to ethnopoetics – a presentation of the rich, varied, and dynamic nature of Kuna verbal art, intended both to be faithful to the Kuna's own performance and esthetic values and principles and to be accessible and understandable to a wider audience.

An important aspect of Kuna ethnopoetics, as distinct from the published literature of literate societies, which is often conceived of as a body of masterpieces that a few educated people are able to read and enjoy, is the fact that Kuna verbal art is a central, instrumental part of social and cultural life, including politics, curing, magic, and social control. Kuna discourse is serious, humorous, poetic, recreational, and socially and culturally functional, all at the same time.

In addition to being a contribution to Native American verbal art, precisely by providing readers with concrete, illustrative examples, this volume also contributes, theoretically and methodologically, to linguistics, anthropology, folklore, and literary criticism. With regard to linguistics, it offers analyses, from a nonliterate society, of forms of discourse, recorded in actual, natural contexts. These analyses demonstrate not only that discourse has a structure and a patterning of its own, related to but separate from grammar, but furthermore that it draws on and utilizes the resources provided by grammar in ways that shed most interesting light on grammar itself. More generally, there is increasing recognition that discourse is not only the place of the actualization of grammar, but the place of the creation of grammar. The study of discourse is thus anything but marginal to linguistics, it is essential to it.

In addition, there are aspects of linguistic form and linguistic structure that only emerge through the study of language use in verbally artistic discourse. Speech play, humor, and verbal art involve language in its essence, on display. Potentials inherent in language are packed and pushed to their highest limits as they are manipulated by

---

shown to be at the heart of everyday communication; Hymes's (1981) grammatical/cultural/rhetorical analyses of North American Indian narrative, in which it is argued that narrative is central to the creative expression of what culture is all about; Labov's (1972b) analysis of the structure of the quite literary personal narratives that occur within everyday conversational interaction; and the work of Tedlock (1978, 1983) in the analysis and especially the translation of American Indian performance style. This work must be carefully distinguished from Geertzian "interpretive anthropology" in which both "text" and "interpretation" are used metaphorically and in which native voices are seldom heard. See Geertz (1973).

skilled performers. Rather than viewing the structural principles and processes that constitute artistic language as marginal to linguistic research, I would argue, on the basis of the analyses presented here, that they are central, in that crucial and significant aspects of phonology, morphology, syntax, semantics, and style emerge in sharply distilled form in artistic performance. A good example of the intimate relationship between grammar and verbal art is the system of verbal suffixes, used in different ways in different styles and genres. (See chapter two and Sherzer 1989.) The study of verbal art, then, is of utmost relevance to linguistics, methodologically, analytically, and theoretically, a point stressed by two of the pioneers of modern linguistics, Edward Sapir, and Roman Jakobson, but not followed up by mainstream linguistics.

From the perspective of anthropology, the forms of discourse presented here cannot be viewed as marginal to social and cultural life, unimportant sideshows to much more significant main events. Nor on the other hand are they mere mirror reflections of and thus totally determined by and redundant with regard to some abstract ideational cultural patterning or social organization. Quite the contrary. Discourse is the richest point of intersection of the relationship among language, culture, society, and individual expression. In discourse individuals draw on their personal creativity and at the same time on the special and unique resources of the language and culture of their communities, including vocabulary and grammar, norms of interpretation, cultural knowledge and symbolism, systems of genres and style, and rules of effective performance. In so doing, they not only replicate, interpret, and transmit, but actually conceive, create, and recreate their social and cultural reality. The best way to understand Kuna politics is through a political speech; Kuna curing, through the report of a curing specialist; Kuna magic, through a magical chant; Kuna mythology, through the performance of a myth; and Kuna humor, through the telling of a trickster tale.

This book then is not only about verbal art in San Blas, but, simultaneously, as the subtitle indicates, Kuna culture through its discourse. And this is precisely the point. The best way, and I would argue the only valid way, to apprehend Kuna culture is through its discourse and this discourse is verbally artistic. There is thus an intimate relationship between Kuna culture and verbal esthetics. Verbal art and, as I will show, verbal play are at the heart of Kuna culture.

The analysis of discourse, especially the analysis of the structuring of verbally artistic discourse, is a logical continuation of the Boas, Sapir, Whorf tradition in anthropology and linguistics with regard to the relationship between language and culture. While Boas, Sapir, and their students considered texts to be an essential part of linguistic field work and analysis, these texts tended not to be studied as verbal art and were not viewed as the place to look for intersections between language and culture. Rather, the Sapir-Whorf hypothesis, as it has come to be known, is associated with a search for isomorphisms between grammar, conceived of in a narrow, abstract sense, and culture, conceived of as a separate, nonverbal entity. My approach is quite different and is concerned with the poetic and rhetorical organization of discourse as an expression of the intimate intersection of language and culture and with the dynamic actualization of the potentials of language in culturally meaningful and socially situated discourse. It is for this reason that it is essential that the oral performances which I have rendered in the subsequent chapters of this book in the form of written texts, in Kuna and in English translation, be accompanied by my analyses, which root them in the social and cultural contexts in which they were orally performed.

In addition, there are certain contemporary issues in anthropology which are spoken to by the discourse-centered and verbal art-centered approach I espouse and adopt here. One is ideology. Discourse is the locus of the expression of ideology and especially of the playing out and the working out of conflicts, tensions, and changes inherent in ideological systems. In focusing on the expression of ideology in discourse, it is important to pay attention to matters of detail, such as lists and orders within lists, which are most revealing of underlying beliefs. (See chapters three and four.) Related to ideology is a historical perspective in conjunction with the influences of the world economic and political system, both of which can be shown to be perceived by and interpreted by interactants and performers in concrete instances of discourse. (See chapters four and five.) Also related to ideology is political structure and political structure, like ideology, is expressed in various ways in discourse. In particular political discourse is characterized by a fascinating intersection of rhetoric and poetics. In Kuna political discourse, like that of many traditional societies with egalitarian orientations, allusive and metaphorical language are important as is the translation of the esoteric to the intelligible. The particular intersection of and manipulation of metaphor, ritual, public speaking, rhetoric, poetics, humor, and personal experience, out of which Kuna ideology and politics are created, can only be appreciated and analyzed through a careful investigation of a Kuna political speech. (See chapter four.)

Another contemporary concern of anthropology is the role and the place of nature in relation to individuals and society. This concern is particularly relevant to lowland and tropical forest societies such as the Kuna whose environment is shrinking daily. In Kuna discourse we find an expression of a very intimate esthetic relationship between humans and nature, including plants and animals. The Kuna view themselves as the guardians of nature. While they use elements of nature, both actually and symbolically, they also are careful to replenish it. In Kuna discourse, nature is used rhetorically and poetically, to convince and to control magically.

Control of the natural, as well as the human world, is often the role of shamans, whose expertise and power derive from knowledge of and ability to manipulate the spiritual realms which underlie the overtly natural and human. In traditional societies such as the Kuna, falling increasingly under the influence of an impinging modern world, the continuing practice of shamanism is particularly interesting, some would even say subversive. Knowledge about shamanistic practices, both for native Kuna and for us, outside observers, can best be acquired through discourse – the actual esoteric chants used in magical control (chapter eight) as well as discourse describing the learning and teaching practices of shamanism (chapter five).

Another issue in contemporary anthropology is the recognition that social and cultural categories are not static and monolithic but rather dynamic and constantly emerging. One aspect of this is the influence of history and especially, in recent years, of the overarching world economic and political system. But it is a focus on discourse and in particular the multi-voiced, metacommunicative, and culture-creating aspects of discourse that enable us to see the emergent properties of both discourse and culture and society and especially their interaction.

One aspect of approaching culture, society, and discourse as emergent categories is that methodologically we must analyze not abstractions but concrete moments of social and cultural life. For the worlds of the people we study are not made up out of monolithic abstractions, but rather actual moments and instances of discourse. It is in these moments that their social and cultural worlds emerge. The moments, as I label them here, are quite akin to what Dell Hymes (1974) calls speech events. My emphasis on the significance and emergent quality of these moments is related to what Clifford Geertz calls the circumstantial – things that happen to happen in the course of individuals' lives and anthropological field workers' experiences which are packed with significance and must be taken seriously.

Thus topics which are traditionally considered important within anthropology, such as metaphor, ritual, politics, and curing, are studied here in concrete and specific terms as actualized in particular events, moments of Kuna cultural life. In these moments, Kuna concepts and notions of metaphor, ritual, politics, and curing in the abstract are realized in actuality, as Kuna performers, Kuna actors in social life, make their cultural worlds come alive, create them.

In addition, by focusing on moments in the flow of Kuna discourse in the chapters of this book, I find that play, humor, and esthetics emerge as much more significant in Kuna life than they would seem to be if I followed conventional and static anthropological models. Verbal esthetics and verbal humor, I would argue, on the basis of my experience with Kuna, are not just interesting in their own terms, but are central to the anthropological enterprise. For as individuals play, manipulate, esthetically perform, and joke with language, they demonstrate their knowledge of and put on display the essence of their cultural beliefs and practices.

Finally, with regard to folklore and literary studies, as well as anthropology and linguistics, these analyses of Kuna verbal art contribute to our understanding of the nature of the discourse of nonliterate societies. The texts provide an addition to the published corpus of Native American literature and are of value with regard to both content and style. They embody the esthetics of Kuna culture and at the same time make a distinctive contribution to world literature.

Consistent with contemporary trends in folklore, I take the presentation of Kuna performances, their representation and translation on the printed page, quite seriously. All performances are presented as full, complete texts. I draw on recent work dealing with the transcription, translation, and analysis of oral discourse and oral performance while at the same time contributing to issues raised by this work.

The distinctions between oral and written discourse have recently been given considerable attention. While there are literate Kuna, Kuna discourse, and in particular the verbal art that is the focus of this book, is oral. This does not mean that Kuna discourse is **oral** rather than **written** in some simple general or universal sense. There is no single feature that characterizes Kuna discourse as a whole. Rather there is a set or complex of such characteristic features. While some of these features may be uniquely characteristic of oral discourse, especially those involving the dramatization of the voice – the manipulation of pitch, tempo, amplitude, silence, and musicality; others, such as parallelism, formulaic repetition, and metaphor, are also found in written speech. My research clearly indicates that there is not a simple set of features which uniquely characterizes oral discourse, a position in keeping with Finnegan's (1977) pioneering overview of oral literature and critique of simplistic views of its nature. (See also Finnegan 1988.) There are Kuna verbal genres which are absolutely fixed in form and memorized word for word. There are others which are relatively fixed in general form and structure but which individuals creatively manipulate in actual performance. And there are still others which must adhere to a certain formulaic style but within which considerable individual improvisation is permitted and indeed expected and valued. Nor can one sharply dichotomize ordinary and literary Kuna language and speech. Rather, it is necessary to recognize poetic structures and processes in a wide range of forms of Kuna discourse, from everyday and informal to ritual and formal.

Given its nature, as a unique event situated in a unique social, cultural, and individual context, there is always an emergent structure to an oral performance. Each of the oral performances presented and discussed here thus involves a particular interplay of memorized, precomposed, formulaic, and improvised verbal elements and at the same time contributes to theories of oral composition in general. The significance, meaning, and function of a performance is not inherent in or obvious from a text, but must be studied as part of a contextual and especially emergent and emerging structure of performance as a whole.

In these last few pages I have outlined what I see as the significance of the study of discourse, especially verbally artistic discourse and particularly the chapters which follow for several disciplines – linguistics, anthropology, and folklore. What is perhaps even more interesting is that the study of discourse is located at the intersection of a series of waves of contemporary critical thought linking sociology, anthropology, linguistics, philosophy, psychoanalysis, and literary criticism. In each of these disciplines discourse is increasingly viewed, not as marginal, nor even as a means to an object of study, but rather the object of study itself. And whether we are talking about the social construction of reality or the literary construction of fictional worlds, it is by means of the study of discourse, especially approached in dynamic, contextual, and emergent terms, that we can perceive the intimate relationship that exists among social and cultural life, language, and esthetics.

It is impossible to write about the discourse of native South America without relating to the monumental work of Claude Lévi-Strauss, dealing with the languages, cultures, societies, and especially the mythologies of lowland South America. Lévi-Strauss's approach is in many ways diametrically opposed to mine. He is abstract, while I am concrete. He combines bits and pieces of evidence from various secondary sources, while I focus on specific and complete Kuna verbal performances that I personally recorded. His locus is the human mind as a producer of myth, while mine is the intersection of Kuna language, culture, society, and individual creativity as expressed in discourse. Nonetheless, the insights Lévi-Strauss provides into the fascinating world of lowland South American indigenous life are penetrating and challenging; they have influenced my work as they have that of others.

Lévi-Strauss's structuralism focuses on relations among signs whose meanings are limited to material phenomena and social categories. The validity of his analysis depends substantially on the degree to which signs and relations among signs can be abstracted from the flow of narrative and the actualities of verbal performances. More and more, contemporary scholars (and my own work as represented here) understand myths (and all discourse) as culturally and socially contextualized and contextualizing verbal art. We see myth not merely as abstract semiotic categories and/or logical connections, but in terms of particular performances and texts and in terms of dynamic and emergent processes involving interactants – tellers, responders, and audiences.

In particular students of lowland South American discourse have uncovered a number of patterns and processes which cannot be discovered by Lévi-Strauss's approach and which are most revealing of the nature of social, cultural, and verbal life in the area. These include especially the prominence of multiple voices, due to the frequently dialogic structure of performance, the great degree of direct quotation, and the focus on metacommunication; the magical power of combined narrative and metaphorical description; and the omnipresence of humor, especially trickster-like humor, in both fictional worlds and everyday real life interactions.

The chapters of this book move from more general and theoretical to more specific and circumstantial. Chapter two provides an overview of Kuna discourse, focusing on the concept of the poetics of performance as well as the social and cultural contexts in which speaking and chanting occur. Each of the subsequent chapters is organized around particular verbal performances, a representative cross-section of Kuna verbal art, including myth, magic, public speech making, and humorous storytelling. Each analysis includes a description of the setting of the performance and its significance in Kuna culture and society. The structure of the performance, in terms of both overall organization and grammatical and stylistic detail, is discussed. At the end of every chapter I present a text, my written representation and translation of the oral performance I have analyzed. From the point of view of western discourse and western literature, these texts fall into no well-defined genres. They do not look like "our" novels, "our" short stories, "our" poems, or "our" political speeches. Understanding of Kuna verbal genres depends on placing them within that intersection of form, style, context, function, and performance in which Kuna individuals themselves experience them.

Native American languages, cultures, and literatures are incredibly diverse. With regard to oral discourse and verbal art, there is a remarkable range of function as well as form. But while the function of language and speech is not everywhere the same, it has long been noted, by both Native Americans and observers of them, that the **word** (=discourse) is sacred and powerful. It carries the past into the present; incorporates values, ideals, hopes and aspirations; conveys knowledge, history, and truth; and instructs and entertains. And yet, the word is rarely studied in and for itself, or even represented and translated as a scholarly enterprise. Despite the impetus of the Boas and Sapir tradition within Amerindian linguistic and anthropological scholarship, there are surprisingly few collections of Native American verbal art, especially the verbal art of lowland and tropical forest South America. Furthermore, very rarely are we provided with texts in the native, indigenous language as well as in translation and practically never with descriptions of the social and cultural contexts in which actual verbal performances are situated.[3]

The Kuna are exceptional in this regard in that there exists a tradition of collecting and publishing Kuna texts. This tradition began in the 1920s, 1930s, and 1940s with a group of Swedes from the Göteborgs Etnografiska Museum. Their publications are based on a few short field trips, work with a Kuna informant in Sweden during 1931, and texts mailed to Sweden by literate informants. They published extensive textual material, in addition to their survey reports. As valuable as their work is, their texts, translation, and analyses are at times confusing, due to the nature of their methodology

---

[3]   Significant exceptions to these generalizations are Bright (1984), Burns (1983), Gossen (1974), Hymes (1981), Kroeber (1981), Sherzer and Urban (1986), Sherzer and Woodbury (1987), Swann (1983), Swann and Krupat (1987), and Tedlock (1978). Of particular comparative interest here are the studies of the discourse of another lowland South American society, the Kalapalo Indians of Brazil, by Ellen Basso (1985, 1987).

and their lack of understanding of Kuna discourse processes.[4] The collection and publication of texts, both as a means to the analysis of Kuna society and culture and in and for itself, continue in contemporary ethnographic work.[5] I belong to this tradition and contribute to its development in this book.

There are several ways in which this study is unique. It is the first book to present complete, verbal performances, transcribed in the original native language from tape recordings and translated into English, from the broad spectrum of the verbal art of a single Native American society.[6] In particular it offers an in-depth glimpse of the ongoing discourse of lowland South America, one of the least studied regions of the world and yet one which is most rapidly and drastically changing. All performances were recorded in natural, actual contexts, providing the reader with a sense of the intimate relationship that always exists between Kuna verbal art and the particular setting and circumstances in which it occurs. Finally, along with the texts there is a discussion of the social and cultural backdrop, the symbolic meanings, assumptions, and understandings which both anchor the performances for audiences and contribute to their creative artistry.

No Kuna verbal artist has ever won the Nobel prize. And none will. This is because of the western industrial world's lack of knowledge of and appreciation for the nonliterate cultures of the world and its prejudice against even considering that oral literature can have a value comparable to a Cervantes, a Shakespeare, or a Beckett. Furthermore, texts such as those presented here have not been available and accessible to literate, western audiences. And yet, every day, literally from early morning to late at night, Kuna men and women are creating and performing literary works of great esthetic quality. This literature demands the same degree of seriousness we apply to the analysis of Shakespeare, from combined literary critical, linguistic, and anthropological perspectives.

---

[4]   See Holmer and Wassén (1947), Holmer and Wassén (1958), Holmer and Wassén (1963), Nordenskiöld (1938), and Wassén (1938). Holmer and Wassén (1947) is the basis of Lévi-Strauss's (1949) well-known analysis of the language of a Kuna curing ritual. Kramer (1970) is based on published and unpublished materials collected by the Swedish group.
[5]   See Chapin (1970), Howe (1986), Howe, Sherzer, and Chapin (1980), and Sherzer (1983).
[6]   Burns (1983) presents a broad range of Yucatec Maya oral literature translated into English. Gossen (1974) presents the full range of Chamula oral tradition, but the texts are for the most part excerpts from complete performances. The same is true of my earlier book on the Kuna (Sherzer 1983).

The recording and analysis of discourse is an urgent and critical task in tropical forest South America in that many societies are rapidly disappearing. The Kuna themselves, while seeming to thrive, maintain a fragile balance, there being a constant danger that increased contacts with the outside as well as economic necessities will destroy their culture, or many aspects of it.

Anthropologists, linguists, and folklorists have often been criticized, by natives as well as by professional scholars, for elaborating theories, methods, and analyses which never allow the voices of actual native people to emerge, to speak out for themselves. (See Tedlock 1983: 321-338.) Most of the published literature on American Indian cultures and societies in particular consists of interpretations by anthropologists, folklorists, historians, and linguists which transform and explain Native American culture for Euro-American readers, recasting traditional Indian concepts and practices into the idioms and categories of western civilization.

As an alternative to this tradition my approach provides the perspectives of native members of an American Indian society in their own words. This book is a presentation and representation of Kuna voices. These voices demonstrate the creativity, the complexity, the dynamics, the diversity, the subtlety, the imagination, the humor, and especially the beauty of Kuna verbal life. They provide insights into the experiences and perceptions of Kuna individuals by revealing subtleties of Kuna ideas about causality, time, history, being, and religious belief – the entire implicit and explicit epistemology of a culture.

This book is the result of many hours of meticulous work – being present at verbal events and recording them, listening to tape recordings over and over and fretting about a pause or a falling intonation, and endlessly discussing the meaning of a word, the connotations of a phrase, or the symbolic significance of an allusion with Kuna performers and assistants. This has been my role, my entrance onto the scene of Kuna verbal life, my interaction with native performers, audiences and interpreters. Obviously since my role involves transcription and translation, choice and placement of materials, analysis and interpretation, I am very much present in this book. At the same time, I would never claim and would consider it quite pretentious to claim that this book is about me and them, the anthropologist-linguist-folklorist-whiteman-visitor's dialogue with the Kuna Indians. Quite the contrary. I have made every effort, in my field work and beyond, to avoid intrusions that alter performances or make me a major actor in the story. It is the Kuna who are on stage in this book and that is as it should be.

Essential to my task as combined linguist, anthropologist, folklorist, and student of literature as I gradually acquired an intimate feel for the intersection of Kuna language, culture, and verbal art, has been the collaboration with sensitive, intelligent, informed, and patient performers and assistants, always a most rewarding and indeed often extraordinary experience, as the fascinating world of Kuna verbal esthetics was revealed to me. The preparation of this book has been a labor of love which I hope comes through on these pages. The challenge I have undertaken is to demonstrate how sophisticated, complex, and rich the verbal art of a traditional, nonliterate society such as the Kuna can be and how valuable to linguistics, anthropology, folklore, and literature a careful study of them can be.

A salient feature of Kuna speaking and chanting is that retelling, interpreting, and translating are incorporated into performances themselves. In this book, I humbly add my voice to those of the Kuna as a reteller, transcriber, interpreter, and translator of Kuna verbal art.

2. THE POETICS OF KUNA VERBAL ART

In spite of considerable theorizing on the subject, concrete published information concerning the nature of oral discourse is sparse and fragmentary, especially from a cross-cultural perspective. In particular there is a need for empirical studies of the oral performances of verbal art of nonliterate societies from various parts of the world. Because of the vitality of Kuna verbal life, which includes a diversity of linguistic varieties, styles, and genres, from colloquial and everyday to formal and ritual, in both spoken and chanted form, Kuna society provides an excellent setting, indeed a living laboratory, for the study of oral discourse, its performance and its poetics.

My purpose here is to describe the major features of Kuna poetics, in order to set the scene for the discussions of particular performances, texts, and analyses which follow in subsequent chapters. Investigation of Kuna poetics requires attention to the interplay of linguistic and sociolinguistic structures and processes along with such aspects of the dramatization of the voice as pause, intonation, volume, and musicality.

Grammar of poetry and poetry of grammar

My discussion of Kuna poetics begins with conventional features of grammatical analysis. The complex and varied set of Kuna poetic styles and forms is created by means of an overlapping of phonological, morphological, syntactic, lexical, and semantic systems, each of which provides a set of potentials which are exploited in actual performance. Phonological processes nicely illustrate this situation. The most basic feature of Kuna phonology, from the point of view of verbal art, is the existence of vowels, which are deleted under certain conditions, bringing together consonants that in turn undergo changes. It is in everyday, colloquial Kuna that the most vowel deletion occurs.[1] For example

---

[1] There is no contradiction between my use of the analytic category "everyday, colloquial Kuna," a grammatical style, and my earlier statement (in chapter one) that ordinary language and poetic language intersect one another. Colloquial Kuna as an analytic category can be precisely determined and specified in phonology, morphology, syntax, and semantics. In actual discourse it is found in many genres, from everyday to ritual, and has poetic and rhetorical effects depending on the context. In addition to grammar per se, there are features of language use, such as metaphor, cohesion, line and verse structure, and dramatization of the voice, all aspects of the poetry of discourse, which are found in all genres of speech, again from everyday to ritual, in distinct and separate ways in each. Attention to such matters, traditionally viewed as the work of literary critics, I argue here, is central and basic to linguistics and anthropology.

(1) *walappa* (three pole-like objects) becomes by vowel deletion

(2) *walppaa* and by consonantal changes

(3) *warpaa*

Form (3) is common in colloquial speech. Form (2) is never used, in any linguistic variety or style. Form (1) is used in colloquial speech for rhetorical emphasis, for example when insisting or when angry. It is also used in storytelling and public speech making for emphasis. It is most common in ritual gathering-house and magical chanting. The presence of potentially deletable vowels functions together with melodic shape to confer an incantatory feeling to ritual performances. The process of vowel deletion is a basic feature distinguishing verbal genres, especially everyday from ritual. Words in ritual varieties and styles of Kuna are typically fuller and longer than the same words in colloquial Kuna. Vowel deletion is not a purely linguistic process, but is rather involved in an intersection of sociolinguistic, rhetorical-poetic, and musical patterning.

Similarly in morphological structure, there is an interplay of sociolinguistic patterning and poetic patterns and processes. The most characteristic feature of Kuna morphology is verbal suffixation. There are many verbal suffixes and an essential aspect of Kuna grammar is a statement of their order and cooccurrence possibilities. Theoretically, a large number of suffixes can be attached to any verb. In actual practice, in colloquial speech, the number of suffixes per verb is relatively few, often two or three. In more formal and ritual verbal styles and genres, more verbal suffixes are employed. Overall word length, marked by both inclusion of potentially deletable vowels and the number of suffixes on words, thus serves as a sociolinguistic marker of formal and ritual speaking and is an important aspect of the poetic quality associated with this speaking and chanting. In addition, while all of the nominal and verbal affixes which occur in colloquial Kuna are found in the ritual varieties and styles as well, some of these have a greater frequency and an apparent greater range of meaning in particular varieties, styles, and genres. An example is the suffix *-ye*, which in colloquial Kuna is a verbal or nominal suffix indicating an optative-like feeling and a vocative on nouns, especially in repetition and insistence. It occurs with great frequency in the language of magic and curing, perhaps stressing the optative mood of the magical chants which are performed in this linguistic variety, but also as a place filler, giving the performer time to remember the next line of these memorized chants. *-ye* can be viewed as a verbally artistic embellisher as well; it is sometimes repeated two or three times. In magical chants, *-ye* frequently occurs at the ends of lines, and thus serves, along with other devices, as a poetic line marker. There are also prefixes and suffixes which, along with certain words, serve primarily as markers of the various Kuna linguistic varieties and styles. Examples are the verb suffixes *-kua* and *-yar*, which occur mainly in magical-curing chanting. Although some of these affixes and words have specific referential meanings and/or grammatical functions, an important feature of their meaning is as a sociolinguistic marker of particular styles or verbal genres. And they also often function as part of the poetic line and verse marking system.[2]

The use of *-ye*, as well as other affixes, in the poetic structuring of Kuna verbal art, involves a process probably widespread in oral discourse. It seems appropriate to call this process the **poeticization of grammar**. This process involves an element or feature of grammar either losing its grammatical function as it takes on a poetic function or adding a poetic function to its already existing referential and grammatical functions. Another example, also from magical chanting, has to do with the verbal suffixes of position, *-mai* (in a horizontal position) and *-nai* (in a hanging position). In a performance that I recorded of *The way of the basil plant*, a chant used to insure magically success in hunting, these suffixes alternate in the consecutive coupled lines of four verses. These same four two-line verses also alternate the verb stem formative *-makke* (with final vowel) and its shorter alternate form *-mak* (without final vowel). Both the *-mai/-nai* alternation and the *-makke/-mak* alternation contribute to the poetics of these verses in the Jakobsonian sense of projecting a paradigm syntagmatically. (See Jakobson 1960; Sherzer 1977.) The *-mai/-nai* distinction is crucial to both the poetics and the efficacy of the magical chant, *The way of the snake*, presented and analyzed in chapter eight. The verbal suffixes of position are also part of the figurative and metaphorical language of gathering-house discourse, as is discussed in chapter four.

Parallelism

Attention to grammatical structure more generally takes us to a central feature of Kuna verbal art that is also extremely common in oral and written ritual and poetic language

---

2   For a fuller statement of Kuna morphology and especially verbal suffixation in relation to the sociolinguistic differentiation of verbal genres, see Sherzer (1989).

around the world, grammatical and semantic parallelism. Parallelism is the patterned repetition, with variation, of sounds, forms, and meanings. It involves the interplay of invariants and variants, of recurrences and differences. There are many types of parallelism in Kuna verbal art, involving morphology, syntax, and semantics. Extensive and pervasive parallelism is especially characteristic of ritual speaking and chanting, an important aspect of the poetry of ritual genres.

Parallelism is closely tied to line organization and structure in that it sets up correspondences based on and cutting across lines and units composed of lines, such as verses. Sometimes adjacent lines are identical, with the exception of the deletion of a single word. Sometimes adjacent lines differ only in non-referential morphemes, such as stem formatives. Sometimes a series of lines differ only in that a single word is replaced by others with slightly different meaning within a same semantic field. The result of all of these types of parallelism is a slow-moving narration, advancing by slight changes in referential content, added to repeated information. Extreme attention is paid to minute and precise detail.

Sometimes the pattern underlying the parallel structure is not a single line, but rather an entire set of lines, a verse, or a stanza, a frame which is repeated over and over with changes in one or more words. In *The way of the snake*, a magical chant used to raise a dangerous snake in the air, a parallel verse structure is used to enumerate all of the parts of the snake's body. (See chapter eight.)

The parallelistic structure of curing and magical chants in particular involves all levels, from the most macro – repetition of whole verse and stanza patterns – to the most micro – repetition of words and morphemes. The result is an overlapping and integration of various parallelistic patterns, a verbal polyphony composed of a tenacious array of cohesive and contrapuntal forms and meanings.[3]

In addition to poetic function, these various types of parallelism have other functions as well. It is important for Kuna ritual chants to be long, length being an aspect of their magical power as well as their esthetic quality. Parallelism slows and lengthens the performance of the text. Performers' knowledge, especially of such

---

[3] See Jakobson (1966) for a discussion of the powerful role of parallelism in the structuring of poetry, in both oral and written traditions. Of comparative interest is Fox (1988), which deals with the very central and crucial role of parallelism in the ritual discourse of the cultures of eastern Indonesia. Closer to the Kuna, parallelism has long been noted as a characteristic feature of the verbal art of Mesoamerica, from pre-Columbian times to the present.

matters as taxonomic classification, is displayed through the parallel listing of items. The repetition involved in parallelism contributes to the incantatory aura of chanting. And, finally, parallelism seems to be a mnemonic aid to the retention and performance of memorized chants.

Vocabulary

Turning now to vocabulary, there is once again an intersection of sociolinguistic and poetic organization. Vocabulary differentiation is the primary diagnostic marker of the different Kuna linguistic varieties, styles, and genres. Each variety, style, and genre has associated with it its own lexicon, with some overlaps among them. There are thus many objects and activities, especially plants and animals and other aspects of Kuna ecology, many important items in Kuna culture, and significant cultural activities which are labeled not by a single lexical item, but several or even many. In addition to the colloquial, everyday Kuna word, there is often a different word used in each of the ritual varieties, styles, and genres.

In addition to its sociolinguistic function of marking and differentiating linguistic varieties, styles, and genres, Kuna lexical diversity is at the heart of another aspect of Kuna verbal art – figurative and metaphorical speech. Figurative vocabulary is found especially in ritual varieties and genres of Kuna. When lexical items in ritual varieties of Kuna are based on words in colloquial Kuna that have a different meaning, the effect is figurative and metaphorical. Many examples will be discussed in the subsequent chapters of this book.

It is especially in gathering-house chanting and speaking that figurative and metaphorical speech abounds. One of the most characteristic markers of a good gathering-house speaker is the use of metaphorical language. This not only pleases the audience which appreciates the oral poetry involved, but also convinces and wins it over to a point of view, by means of a poetic rhetoric. In gathering-house discourse, metaphorical vocabulary sets and semantic fields are open to individual development and adaptation. The basic organizing principle of the speech represented in chapter four is the performer's creative elaboration of metaphors.

Narrative

Another important aspect of Kuna verbal art is narrative, the verbal reformulation of a set of events, real or fictional.[4] Since my intention here is to provide an overview of Kuna poetic devices, I will not describe Kuna narrative structure in great depth, but rather point to several of its outstanding and special features, leaving details for subsequent chapters in which particular texts are discussed. Kuna narratives are told in either the first person or the third person, that is, they either recount personal experiences or those of others. In either case, they may be descriptions of new events, not known to the audience, or descriptions of known events which are retold. One striking aspect of Kuna discourse and verbal art, which is shared with other native lowland South American groups, is the constant retelling of the same narrative, in different contexts and in different ways, for different purposes. This includes the incorporation of narratives within narratives, tellings within tellings. This process is crucial to the speech analyzed in chapter five.

Whether first person or third person, fact or fiction, myth or history, spoken or chanted, ritual or everyday, Kuna narratives are appreciated for their length. Length is achieved by various poetic devices, including repetition and parallelism. Narrative length is also created by means of extreme attention to fine detail, including such matters as waking up, going to sleep, travel to and from places, and reported conversations. (See especially chapter five.) These details are often presented in the form of formulaic expressions or literary topoi, especially in ritual genres. The formulaic expressions and literary topoi, like parallelism, serve different functions. In addition to increasing the length of a narrative, they aid the memorization (of fixed texts) or the creative performance (of improvised texts), and they provide artistic embellishment.

Another characteristic of Kuna narration is humor, omnipresent in Kuna verbal life. Humor is notoriously difficult to translate from one language and culture to another. Kuna humor is intimately dependent on and integrated with actual verbal performance, in conjunction with knowledge, assumptions, and experiences shared by narrators and audiences. The manipulation of the voice in performance is crucial, especially the stereotyped imitation of various noises and the mocking imitation and quotation of the

---

[4] This definition, while purposely simple and general, is in accord with most recent literature. See Mitchell (1981) and Prince (1973).

speech of others. Surprising juxtapositions of events, humorous in themselves, are made even funnier through being expressed by means of juxtapositions in the dramatization of the voice – fast vs. slow, loud vs. soft, high pitch vs. low pitch, and staccato vs. fluid. Humor is also highlighted by describing experiences in great and exaggerated detail and by considerable repetition. Humor, joking, play, and verbal tricking are the subject of chapter seven.

The Kuna believe both that in verbal performance there is power and that different kinds of verbal activities produce different kinds of power.   In magical chants, narratives have the power to activate the audience of spirits who listen to them. Upon hearing a chant and because of hearing and understanding it, the spirits do, detail by detail, everything that the narrative contained within the chant describes. Magical chants are thus performative, in the sense of the philosopher J. L. Austin and his followers. (See chapter eight.) Narratives addressed to humans involve other kinds of power. A narrative report, especially a public one in the gathering house, is a validation of one's experience, for the immediate audience and for the entire community. The detailed report of the experience of learning ritual knowledge concretizes this knowledge and grants the performer the right to exercise the role of ritual specialist. (See chapter five.) In gathering-house discourse more generally, narratives are exemplary, moral lessons, a crucial feature of the exhortative nature and indeed power of this discourse.

The structuring of verbal art in performance: the line
In addition to its special, sometimes esoteric language, its metaphors, its parallelism, and its narrative structure, Kuna discourse is poetic because it is organized in terms of lines. At the heart of Kuna poetics is the poetic line. The line is in many ways the most basic unit of all forms of Kuna discourse, from the most informal and colloquial to the most formal and ritual. It is independent of and yet related to grammatical units such as phonemes, morphemes, and sentences and is the most overtly marked discourse unit linguistically and, in chanting, musically.

Discovery of lines requires attention to very different features than those traditionally associated with the European poetic tradition, especially rhyme and meter. Kuna line structure and organization incorporates and integrates all of the features of Kuna poetics that I have just discussed, especially phonological and morphological patterning, parallelism, and features of the dramatization of the voice such as pause, intonation, and musical melody, as well as aspects of the social organization of speech such as turn taking. It is furthermore extremely useful for a diagnostic comparison and typological classification of Kuna verbal genres.

In each of the Kuna verbal styles and genres, it is possible to recognize the existence of lines. These lines are marked by a set of distinct devices. Not all of the devices are operative in every case. In addition, the devices have other functions besides marking lines. As a result there is not always congruence among them. In fact, a most interesting aspect of the various line-marking devices in Kuna is the ways in which speakers play them off against each other, creating contrasts and tensions among them. The four principal line-marking devices are:

(1) Lines are marked grammatically by means of an elaborate set of initial and final words and affixes. Among the various other functions of these elements is metacommunication; they signify such notions as "say," "see," "hear," and "truly." They are furthermore simultaneously sociolinguistic markers in that different verbal styles and genres have distinct sets of these elements.

(2) Especially in more formal and ritual styles, lines are marked by extensive syntactic and semantic parallelism. This parallelism is organized in terms of line structure and in turn contributes to this structure.

(3) Lines are marked by intonation patterns; in particular in spoken speech by the structuring of pauses and the rising and falling of pitch, as well as tempo, and in chanting by melodic shapes involving volume, duration, and tempo, along with pauses and, in some genres, the structured use of coughs or cough-like noises.

(4) Lines are marked according to a coparticipant dialogic interactional structure in which an addressee responds with one of a set of ratifiers after each line. This pattern is common in many styles of speaking; it is formalized in certain forms of ritual chanting.[5]

Attention to line structuring in Kuna speech thus reveals an intersection of referential and nonreferential, grammatical, sociolinguistic, social interactional, and musical factors and patterns. In addition, the study of line structure reveals function and pattern in the traditional components of grammar (phonology, morphology, syntax,

---

[5]   Such ritualized dialogues seem to be fairly common in tropical forest South America. Fock (1963) suggests an areal distribution. See also Sherzer (1983: 196-200) and Urban (1986). Burns (1980) describes a somewhat different pattern among the Yucatec Mayan.

semantics, and lexicon) that are otherwise impossible to discover.

In the most ritual styles and genres of Kuna, which are frequently chanted, there is the greatest tendency for there to be a combined, cooperating, congruent, and reinforcing use of all the line-marking devices. In gathering-house chanting, myths, legends, and personal experiences are performed to an audience in the form of a ritual dialogue between two chiefs, the second chief responding to the chanted utterances of the first. Lines are often grouped together into clearly marked verses (using the terminology of Hymes 1977). The responding chief chants *teki* (so it is) after each verse, thus quite clearly marking verse endings. Verses typically consist of two lines. Lines and especially verses drop in pitch at the end and final vowels are lengthened. There is a decrease in volume and tempo at the ends of lines and verses. The responding chief begins to chant during the lengthened final vowel of the principal chanting chief, who in turn begins his next line during the lengthened *i* of *teki*. There is thus never silence, since each chanter begins his turn by overlapping the long, held vowel of the previous voice.

It is the combination of falling pitch, vowel lengthening, decreasing volume and tempo, and alternation of chanters which I have used as the criterion for the determination of lines and verses in my transcriptions of gathering-house chanting. In addition, verses often begin with the word *sunna* (truly) or the phrase *al inso* (thus) and end with the word *soke* (say, it is said), *oparye* (utter, it is uttered), or *tayleye* (see). The first line of a verse often ends with the phrase, sometimes combined into a single word, *tayle soke l ittole* (see it is said it is heard). Syntactic and semantic parallelism also contributes to the structuring of lines and verses. Performers can create poetic counterpoint by playing off the line-initial and line-final words and phrases and the parallelistic patterns against the intonational, musical, and interactional markers of lines. (See chapter three for examples of gathering-house chanting and further discussion of its properties.)

Curing and magical chanting, performed by specialists to representatives of the spirit world, is in a linguistic variety quite distinct from chiefs' chanting. In addition to falling pitch, final vowel lengthening, and decreasing volume and tempo, lines in this genre are marked primarily by the suffix *-ye*. There is a notable pause between lines and for some performers a slight cough or cough-like noise between structured groups of lines, which I call a verse (again utilizing the terminology of Hymes 1977). There is extensive line parallelism, involving a layering of phonological, morphological, syntactic, and semantic features. In some performances the various line-marking devices overlap isomorphically, resulting in an incantatory regularity. At times, however, performers introduce some contrast and counterpoint, especially between verbal and musical parallelism, still against the backdrop of considerable regularity. (Chapter eight presents an example of a magical chant.)

The most formal of speaking styles is that of the chief's spokesman, who follows a chief's chant, retells the chant, and interprets it for the gathered audience. In spokesman's speeches, there are short but clearly audible pauses between lines, coupled with a falling pitch contour and a slowing of tempo. Longer pauses set off a larger unit of several lines, a unit that again I label a verse, even though it is marked rather differently than are verses in ritual chanting. The words *tek* (well), *inso* (thus), and *taylekuti* (indeed) are common line openers of spokesmen's speeches and are often bunched together. A very common line-final marker in this style is *pittosursoke* (don't you hear it is said), often coming at the ends of verses. Spokesmen introduce various contrasts and tensions among the different line and verse-marking devices. (See chapter three, in which a spokesman's speech is presented, along with the chief's chant which it interprets; chapters four and five present public speeches performed in a formal style that shares many features with that of chief's spokesmen's speeches.)

Stories, both serious and humorous, are told publicly in a less formal style than that of the speeches of chief's spokesmen. Typical line openers are *teki* (well), *takkarku* (so), and *emite* (now); line-final markers, *soke* (say, it is said), *napir soke* (it is true), and *soysunto* (he, she said in truth). There is not a clear demarcation of verses. There is even less congruence, that is, there is even more contrast, among the various line markers than in the more formal spokesmen's speeches. In particular, pause structure and grammatical elements and words, both resources for the marking of lines, are often used contrapuntally in order to create a rhythm of performance characteristic of storytelling, involving dramatic interplay of long and short, slow and fast lines as the narration proceeds. (See chapter six for a presentation and analysis of *The hot pepper story* and chapter seven for a presentation and analysis of *The Agouti story*.)

Since lines are so basic to Kuna discourse, and especially to representation and translation of this discourse, each chapter of this book includes a discussion of line structure in the texts presented. Lines are not named units in Kuna. Nonetheless there is strong evidence for the Kuna's perception of them. In addition to the evidence presented here, the teaching of the most esoteric ritual chants, those used in magic and curing, by specialist-teachers to students, is line by line.

The existence of poetic contrasts and tensions between the different line-marking devices should not be an unfamiliar phenomenon for students of written poetry, any more than for students of oral literature. In fact we might appropriately speak of two esthetic principles in Kuna verbal life, one which involves harmonious synchrony and symmetry and the other which involves dynamic contrast and tension. Both have been noted among Native Americans.[6] Kuna speakers and chanters draw on both of these esthetic principles in their individual structuring of verbal forms. I use the term structuring rather than structure in order to stress the dynamic process which is involved. Against the backdrop of linguistic and cultural traditions, speakers and chanters develop individual creative styles. The fact that different verbal genres or different speakers can utilize distinct poetic organizations is very much in keeping with Kuna social, cultural, and verbal life, which is characterized by a remarkable organization of diversity (see Sherzer 1970 and Howe and Sherzer 1975).

It is important to make clear that the concept of "line" is both a label for what occurs in actual Kuna oral performances and a label for the visual representation that I have made in my written, textual versions of Kuna performances on the printed pages of this book. The line is thus a combined emic, analytic, and transcriptional category. Thus while I have argued quite strongly for the validity of the existence of lines, as basic to Kuna discourse, with linguistic, sociological, and even psychological reality, here is a place where I as writer-analyst, transcriber, and translator of Kuna discourse enter centrally and crucially into the picture. That is, while I have argued, hopefully convincingly, that Kuna performers segment and organize their performances by means of an intersection of overlapping devices – pause, vowel length, alternations in pitch and loudness, parallelism, and placement of words and phrases, an intersection that I have called "line," it is I who represent this intersection on the printed page as actual, visual lines. If I am successful, the result is a meeting of my methods with Kuna performance practices.

---

[6]   For dynamic lack of symmetry and synchrony as an esthetic principle in North America, see Philips (1974) on the structure of Warm Springs communicative events and Barbara Tedlock (1986) on Zuni pottery and other visual expressive forms.

Transcription, representation, and translation

In my transcriptions, representations, and translations of Kuna discourse, I follow a contemporary current in Native American discourse analysis and translation in being as faithful as possible to actual performances. This work is part of an ongoing experimentation in the representation and accompanying translation of Native American verbal art that began with a pioneering article by Dell Hymes (1965), and continued with the insistence of both Hymes and Dennis Tedlock on the importance of the matter through extensive exploration of models, the founding of the journal *Alcheringa: Ethnopoetics* (1970) which focused on the representation and translation of Native American as well as other oral verbal art traditions, and the ongoing work of both Hymes and Tedlock, as well as a growing number of others, including Ellen Basso, Victoria Bricker, William Bright, Alan Burns, Gary Gossen, Bruce Mannheim, Sally McLendon, Greg Urban, Anthony Woodbury, and myself.

Breaking with an earlier generation, these researchers, myself included, believe that Native American oral discourse and especially verbal art is best analyzed and represented as linear poetry rather than block prose. In particular, I pay considerable attention to such features of poetic organization as line and verse structure, intonation, pause patterning, and other oral features of the dramatization of the voice so characteristic of and so essential to Kuna verbal performances. I have faithfully retained, in the transcription of the original performances and the translations, the many Kuna words and phrases signifying such concepts as "say," "see," "hear," "then," "therefore," "thus," and "so," elements which I will show to be highly significant in the poetic organization of these texts.

One important aspect of our cultural and linguistic competence as members of the contemporary western world is to be able to listen to or read instances of discourse, whether a story, a political speech, or a newspaper article, and understand and interpret it. This means comprehending a totality of elements, from sound patterns, through tense and aspect, to narrative logic. The same is true for the Kuna. For this reason, my task here, in transcribing, representing, and translating Kuna discourse is twofold – first to capture the Kuna ways of experiencing this discourse and second to render the Kuna experience meaningful for a non-Kuna audience, in particular for an English-reading audience.

Recent research has demonstrated that there are many different organizing principles and patterns involved in the structuring of Native American discourse. The discovery of each new element of patterning raises the possibility of a different way of transcribing a text, or representing it on a printed page. One solution is to choose one type of patterning and make it the governing principle for the transcription and representation of the text. Dell Hymes, working from texts taken down in dictation by previous generations of scholars and without the availability of tape recordings, uses grammatical, semantic, and content analysis as the basis for his transcription and representation of discourse from Chinookan and other languages of western North America. (Hymes 1981.) Dennis Tedlock, using tape recordings, pays attention to expressive features of the voice, especially pause and pitch patterns, in his representation of Zuni and narratives. (Tedlock 1978, 1983.) In his work with Quiché discourse, while he continues to focus on expressive features of the voice, his segmentation derives as well from consideration of all aspects of discourse I have discussed here. (Tedlock 1987.) William Bright and Sally McLendon, investigating Karok and Eastern Pomo, have noted a fair degree of convergence between discourse units determined by grammatical and lexical features and discourse units determined by pauses and intonation. In their emphasis on convergence, they tend to be more concerned with normative behavior (characteristic of a particular genre) than the non-convergences that emerge as moments of individual artistry. (Bright 1979, McLendon 1981.)   Anthony Woodbury studies the interplay of convergences and non-convergences in the emergent structure of Central Yupik Eskimo discourse. (Woodbury 1985, 1987.)   It is important to recognize in all this work that grammatical and lexical features, like pause and pitch, can be expressive and esthetic, just as pause and pitch, like grammar and lexicon, can at times not serve expressive and esthetic ends. A significant part of the linguistic and stylistic analysis of verbal art I propose and engage in here is precisely to figure this all out.

My investigation of Kuna discourse has revealed that each of the line and verse-marking devices, grammatical, intonational, musical, and social interactional, is highly elaborated and developed in and of itself, and enters into different types of relationships with the others, sometimes congruent, synchronic, and isomorphic, sometimes creating contrasts, tensions, and counterpoint. Given this situation, it might then seem appropriate to provide several written representations of the same performance, according to each of the different organizational criteria I have discovered. But this would miss the poetics of Kuna performances as I have tried to capture and represent them here. Therefore I have opted for a single transcription and representation of each text which aims at capturing as much as possible of what members of a Kuna audience actually feel in listening to a performance. In both the representation of the original Kuna and the translation I have attempted to portray visually the dramatization of the voice, so essential to the poetics of these oral performances – the interplay of sound and silence, of words and pauses, of loudness and softness, of fast speech and slow speech, the stylized imitations of voices and noises, the tightenings, loosenings, and vibrations of the vocal apparatus, and the patterned repetitions and variations of grammatical elements, words, and phrases.

In each of the texts presented in this book, transcriptional and representational issues are discussed. Lines are the basic units. In certain texts, larger units, such as verses and episodes, are also demarcated. I have determined lines according to pauses coupled with falling pitch, in spoken speech; according to musical pattern and shape, (a combination of pitch, tempo, and volume), as well as pause, in chanted speech. Lines are numbered consecutively, for convenient reference, and end with a period. Long pauses without falling pitch are transcribed as blank spaces between words within lines. Short, interlinear pauses are represented with a comma. In this way, the various Kuna line-marking and line-framing devices, including the elaborate set of words, phrases, and affixes, parallelistic patterns, and multi-participant verbal interaction, can clearly be seen as interacting with, intersecting with, and playing off against pause and intonation, sometimes congruently, sometimes contrapuntally.

Other expressive devices represented in the text are lengthening of sounds (indicated by doubling of letters), loud speech (indicated by capital letters), decreasing volume (indicated by > placed before the stretch of speech in question), stretched-out, syllabic pronunciation (indicated by dashes between syllables), vibrating voice (indicated by dashes between letters), slowing of tempo (indicated by stretching out of letters and words), faster tempo (indicated by a dotted underline under the words which are spoken faster), rising pitch (indicated by ´ placed before the stretch of speech in question), falling pitch (indicated by ` placed before the stretch of speech in question), a whole line higher in pitch (indicated by ^ placed before the line), and part of a line higher in pitch (indicated by raising the words of higher pitch).

While my transcriptions capture certain expressive devices, I have opted not to transcribe at a surface phonetic level, but rather at a middle range abstract phonemic level, marking words and their boundaries quite clearly. The distinction between word boundary and morpheme boundary is a difficult one in Kuna. I have used grammatical and semantic criteria more than phonetic ones in separating words. This means that in some cases words are transcribed as separate entities that in actual performance have merged phonetically, a quite common occurrence in Kuna, which is a language in which independent words quite easily become fused together and in which phonetic/phonological processes and semantic/psychological feel are two different, not always congruent dimensions. My transcriptions thus combine drawing attention to such relatively surface expressive features of the voice as pause, pitch, loudness, and softness with a recognition of a deeper, more abstract concept of individual words.

The quite common Kuna practice of quoting oneself and other speakers and of inserting or embedding quotations within quotations poses another problem for transcription, especially since quotations are not consistently marked by expressive features in oral performances. Quotation marks (single and double) are used whenever a speaker quotes another or himself, resulting at times in a considerable degree of quotes within quotes. Quotations are typically framed with verbs of saying, although there is not always a one-to-one relationship between the number of verbs of saying and the number or levels of embedded quotations. When verbs of perception, such as see or think, are used to frame lines or other utterances, quotation marks are not used, even though the textual pattern is at times quite similar to the case of verbs of saying.

Translators of American Indian discourse have followed one of several tendencies. Either they produce translations that are extremely literal and for this reason difficult to read and appreciate, even if, as in the case of the morpheme-by-morpheme translations used conventionally by linguists, they are of linguistic and ethnographic value. Or they have tried to make their texts seem "Indian," drawing on stereotypes of Indian English. Or they have used the native texts as a source for the creation of a new artistic work of their own, in keeping with their personal and their period's esthetic canons and preferences.

More generally, translators from one language to another must move along a continuum between being faithful and literal with regard to the original text and capturing the spirit of the original in a different language.[7] When two texts are relatively close (in culture, time, language, etc.), it is possible to maintain a literalness between them while at the same time being fairly faithful to the spirit. But the more

---

[7]   See Arrowsmith (1961), Carne-Ross (1961), and Jakobson (1959) for a discussion of these issues.

distant two texts are (again in culture, time, language, etc.), the more difficult translation becomes. It is important to recognize that translation involves language, in the sense of grammar and vocabulary, style, including formal patterning, and culture, especially the unstated or understated assumptions and presuppositions which hearers or readers of native performances and texts take for granted and which readers of translations typically are unaware of.

The Kuna case, that is, translation of Kuna discourse into English, like that of other Native American situations, is complicated by several factors. In addition to all of the issues and difficulties involved in translation, thoughtfully noted by such experts on the subject as William Arrowsmith, D. S. Carne-Ross, and Roman Jakobson, I am translating from oral discourse (Kuna) into written discourse (English) and therefore must proceed by first rendering oral performances in Kuna into written transcriptions in Kuna. Issues of translation then are intimately bound up with issues of transcription and representation on the printed page. The formal properties and patterning of oral Kuna performances, alternation of sound and silence, fast and slow and loud and soft speech, and repetitions and parallelism, so essential to Kuna poetics and rhetoric, must be captured in my written, English translations. And then there are vast differences between the languages and cultures involved. Kuna is a polysynthetic language in which words consist of several suffixes following a stem. Verbal suffixation is particularly complicated and constitutes the basis of stylistic differentiation. In English, syntactic patterning, including word order, plays a much greater role than in Kuna. With regard to culture, my translations must capture the poetic and rhetorical subtleties, the symbolism, the allusions and presuppositions, and the play and humor of Kuna verbal life.

The great translational distance between Kuna and English might seem to call for extreme liberty on my part. I accept this to a certain degree. But at the same time, in my determination to maintain the Kuna spirit, I lean in the direction of literalness, thus demanding more work, but I hope rewards as well, on the part of the reader.

Theorists of translation recognize that in order to capture the spirit, the tone and feel of the original it is perfectly acceptable and even expected to retain certain words and expressions from the original, or translate them absolutely literally. From French, examples abound – *excusez-moi, monsieur, mon Dieu, s'il vous plait*. It is part of reader's competence as individuals in the western world to associate such words and phrases with French language, culture, and life. They make the effort in reading to incorporate these foreign words into their comprehension and in a certain sense feel they are reading French.

For readers of this book, there is a greater effort to be made. It is not part of ordinary reader's competence, however educated and cultured they may be, to know certain Kuna words and phrases, however common and typical they may be in Kuna life. At the same time, just as if I were translating from French, I feel it necessary to retain certain words, phrases, and expressions in literal translation from Kuna. Primary among these are "say," "hear," "see," "it is said," "therefore," "then," "thus," and "so," words which permeate and punctuate Kuna conversations, speeches, stories, and literally all Kuna verbal life. While they may at first seem awkward for the, in this case uneducated, reader, appreciation of Kuna verbal life will gradually result from reading these texts, punctuated and adorned with these, literally translated, Kuna words and phrases, as they are punctuated and adorned with formal patterns of pause (represented by spaces on the printed page), repetition and parallelism, and quotation and quotation within quotation.

It has often been noted that different translations and types of translation serve different purposes. As with regard to transcription and representation of the original Kuna performance, it might seem useful to provide several different translations, according to different criteria. However, again, I have opted for a single one. In my goal of being as literal as possible and to provide a feel for the Kuna style of speechmaking and chanting (see extended discussion in chapter one), I adhere strictly to the line structure of the original performances, as I have represented it. There is thus a tight correspondence between the Kuna representation and the English translation.

The line-framing words and phrases are translated with a set of equivalent English expressions – say, it is said, utter, it is uttered, see, hear, don't you hear, well, then, thus, indeed, now, certainly, in fact, truly, so, and therefore. They are placed in the location in which they occurred in the Kuna performance – word initially, medially, or finally. And when they are bunched together in Kuna, I have similarly bunched them together in the English translation. In this way, the role of these words and phrases and their interaction with pause structure in the creation of the rhythm of performance is rendered in English.

Kuna word order is different from English. Sentences typically begin with the subject followed by the object followed by the verb, as distinct from English, in which the typical order is subject-verb-object. I have translated the ordinary Kuna word order with the equivalent ordinary English word order. When Kuna uses a contrastive order, I have used a contrastive order in English.

The Kuna tense-aspect system, marked by combinations of verbal suffixes, is quite different from English. In particular, much attention is paid to details of direction of movement, positions of actors, and timing of events. In order to retain the Kuna system as faithfully as possible, my translation at times focuses more on aspect than on tense. Native English readers may occasionally be surprised by a seeming shifting in and out of particular time frames and by sudden alterations in point of view.

Kuna vocabulary is characterized by extreme variety and subtlety, reflecting and expressing the ideational, ecological, material, metaphorical, and sociolinguistic worlds of the Kuna. As far as possible, I have translated Kuna informal, slang, formal, and ritual words with English equivalents – house/abode, kill/finish off, deceive/fool, trip up, etc. Onomatopoetic words (*mok, tacak*, etc.) are rendered exactly as in Kuna, so as to retain the Kuna sense of sound, so essential to performance.

My translations may seem to readers unfamiliar with Native American discourse to lack logic and coherence with regard to space and time, to be too repetitive, or to move along too quickly. But the logic and coherence of these texts must be understood as Kuna cultural logic and coherence and not be approached with western eyes and ears. My intention in my translations is not only to respond to my audience's reading practices, but to educate, expand, and enlarge these reading practices as well, by including within them the world of nonliterate, Native America, and especially Kuna verbal esthetics. A kind of "reader's criticism" is thus imposed on the reader, who might at first feel uncomfortable and need to work in order to get the feel for and appreciate the texts they are reading. For part of the appreciation of the texts I present here involves the opportunity to enter into Kuna logic and through this logic to acquire a sense of Kuna knowledge and thought.

At the same time, aspects of each text which depend on knowledge of Kuna language, culture, and society, from allusions to metaphors, are explained in my discussion. The meaning of a story, myth, or magical chant is not necessarily inherent in the words contained within it, just as it does not lie totally outside them. Meaning rather emerges from the interactions between the text and its contexts, and my analyses and interpretations deal with these interactions.

One intrusion of me as author of this book into Kuna verbal art is the choice of the placement of the texts of Kuna performances. As will soon become obvious to the reader, I have placed these texts at the end of every chapter, a placement I feel works best. In earlier drafts and published versions of some of these chapters as well as in oral presentations, I have placed the texts elsewhere, at the beginning or within my own texts. A good argument can be made for each placement.

As distinct from an oral performance, this is a published book. Readers are thus free to read it in any order they choose, or in several orders, just as the author was free to organize it in several ways before it was published. Readers can for example first read the text of a Kuna performance and then read my text about it. Or they can first read my text and then read the text of the Kuna performance (the order I have provided). Or they can intersperse, reading back and forth and between portions of my text and portions of the text of the Kuna performance. All this is one of the advantages of a published book.

Similarly, readers can read the Kuna text and the English text on facing pages, as I have presented them here and as three readers have suggested, or they can treat them as separate units, first reading all the Kuna and then all the English, a presentational format I have used elsewhere as have other represeners and translators of Native American discourse.

The point is that the placement of texts at particular locations within chapters and in particular ways, like transcription, representation, and translation more generally, is the result of experimentation by an author, as well as interaction between the author and the performances and social and cultural contexts on which this experimentation is necessarily based.

In conclusion to this extended discussion of the ways in which I have represented and translated Kuna verbal performances, I want to stress the importance of paying serious attention to this question. For there is a close relationship between transcription, representation, translation, and theoretical and methodological issues in the study of oral discourse and verbal art.[8] All the more so in this book with its discourse, performance, and text-centered approach. Consideration of transcription conventions and how to represent Kuna discourse on the printed page, in Kuna and in English translation, are by no means secondary or marginal to my endeavor. Quite the contrary. I spend so much space discussing these issues precisely because they are so

---

[8]   For recent overviews of issues in and illustrations of representation, translation, and analysis of Native American discourse, see Sherzer and Urban (1986) and Sherzer and Woodbury (1987).

central. I have opted for a transcription and representation which highlights expressive oral devices but in which grammatical, lexical, and semantic features of Kuna poetics and rhetoric emerge as well and for a translation which is as close to Kuna as possible while still being accessible and understandable to English readers. The result, I hope, reveals the structural complexity and the rich beauty of Kuna verbal art.

In subsequent chapters issues of transcription, representation, and translation will be discussed again, with regard to particular performances and particular texts. The combined task of transcription, representation, and translation of Kuna verbal art involves questions of theory, method, and analysis and requires that I integrate my skills as linguist, anthropologist, and literary critic.

Kuna discourse, because of its ongoing diversity and vitality, provides a virtual laboratory for the study of Native American verbal art in particular and for an exploration of the complex nature of oral discourse more generally. This chapter has introduced the structuring principles and processes involved in the performance of Kuna verbal art. These structuring principles and processes constitute the poetics of performance. I move now to specific performances and particular texts.

3. WHITE PROPHET: A KUNA MYTH CHANTED, SPOKEN, AND TRANSLATED

Translation is omnipresent in the Kuna world. And the Kuna are superb on the spot translators. Their translations are never abbreviated or perfunctory. They are remarkable reformulations, always repeating all of the minute and technical details of the original, including such matters as time of day, geography, what people saw, what they ate, how they slept, what emotions they had, and, of course, what they said. Translation, verbal performance, transmission of tradition, and memory are intimately linked. Translation means both repetition and reformulation. The translator is respectful of the original and at the same time an individually creative performer himself or herself.

In many everyday interactions, as family members and friends sit together and report on personal experiences, gossip about others, converse, and joke, there is constant retelling, reformulation, and indeed translation, from speaker to speaker, from style to style, from genre to genre, and from a serious to a playful and humorous mode.

As in many societies around the world the existence in Kuna of special, esoteric, ritual, and ceremonial languages and forms of discourse renders possible and in fact requires translation. These translations, as well as the contexts in which they occur, are quite varied. Ritual specialists who learn magical and curing chants first learn the chant and only after they have memorized it are taught its translated meaning in everyday Kuna. (See chapter five.) In the performance of these chants for curative and magical purposes, however, there is no translation. The spirit-addressees of these chants do not need one, since the esoteric language is their language and they understand it. Humans present do not constitute an official audience; these chants are not directly intended for them and no translation is offered them. (See chapter eight.)

On the other hand, Kuna myths, legends, stories, and personal reports which are performed by chiefs in the gathering house for Kuna audiences are always followed by translations in more colloquial, everyday Kuna. Such translations are performances in and of themselves, formal, constituent parts of the entire speech event. In fact, the chanting of chiefs and the spoken reformulation by chief's spokesmen no doubt constitute the most spectacular of all Kuna performances of translation. The gathering house, which the Kuna also call the "listening house," the "performance house," and "God's house," is also the house of languages and the house of translation. It is here where visiting dignitaries, both Panamanian and Kuna political leaders, make speeches in Spanish and in Kuna, and where, immediately afterward, these speeches are translated, for both visitors and gathered audience. And it is here where approximately every other evening, chiefs chant and spokesmen translate.

The structure of this event highlights and focuses on translation. At dusk, after a day of work and relaxation, individuals bathe and then gradually walk to the gathering house. Chiefs, their spokesmen, and other village dignitaries arrive first. The chiefs lie in hammocks in the center of the gathering house and the others sit on long benches on either side of the hammocks. They talk and joke among themselves. Women arrive carrying small tables, kerosine lamps, and a sewing basket. They sit close to the chiefs, behind the long benches, sewing their molas as they listen to the performances. The entire event is often viewed as being for precisely this purpose. The men of the village sit behind the women, close to the walls of the gathering house. After any other village business that needs to be attended to, the official event of the evening begins. First one of the chiefs of the village or a visiting chief from another village chants. This chant is in the form of a dialogue between two chiefs, the principal performer and a second, called the *apinsuet* (responder), who chants *teki* (so it is) after each verse of the principal performer. The two chiefs are now in the *nai* (hanging or perched) position in their hammocks, looking neither at the audience nor at each other, but rather maintaining a meditative middle distance, seeming almost lost in their own thoughts and dialogic performance.[1] The chant is in an esoteric language, phonologically, morphologically, syntactically, and semantically different from ordinary Kuna. It is characterized by the use of metaphorical and allusive language. The members of the audience understand the chant to varying degrees, depending on their knowledge of the ritual language used and the amount of attention they pay to the event.

When the chief has finished chanting, the spokesman rises from his bench to his feet and speaks directly to the audience in a speech using more ordinary colloquial Kuna, but in a formal speech-making style. The spokesman, in his performance, serves not only as translator, but as reteller, reformulator, interpreter, and editor as well. Performance, translation, and interpretation, for the Kuna spokesman, are very close to being one and the same, in contrast to our own western tradition, in which they

---

[1] The dialogic performance of ritual discourse is widespread in lowland South America and seems to have areal-typological links that go beyond this region. (See Sherzer 1983: 196-200 and Urban 1986).

are kept distinct, in spite of all the tension and overlaps among the roles of poet, translator, and critic discussed in the literature on translation.

It is important to stress that this performance, by the chief and by the spokesman, is a naturally occurring event – chanting and subsequent spoken interpretations are one of the central rituals of Kuna life. Even if the audience understands some or all of the chief's chant, it is always followed by the spokesman's interpretation. The event as a whole involves a translation that moves from chanting to speaking, from esoteric to intelligible, from ritual to everyday, and from the realm of the Gods and Kuna legendary heroes to the realm of contemporary Kuna humans.

The chief's and the spokesman's versions of a myth, legend, or story are twin performances, twin texts that are related and yet different. There are striking differences in the oral and aural quality of the same narrative content, reaffirming both the power of language and the verbal abilities of individual performers. The chief's chant is performed as a dialogue, while the spokesman's speech is a monologue. The esoteric chant, which begins softly, almost in a whisper, gradually reaches a crescendo, with the chief booming out his verses. There is never a moment of hesitation and never a moment of silence, as the chief continuously chants his verses and his responder overlaps them with ratifications, in a performance that typically lasts two or more hours. The overlapping voices of the two performing chiefs dominate the gathering house and create a mystical, religious atmosphere. As he rhythmically explains, translates, and quotes what the chief has just chanted, the spokesman transforms the atmosphere of the gathering house from religious to didactic. He, like the chief, never hesitates. He is fluent and speaks with conviction. It is clear that while he is translating and reformulating the chief's words, this is his own speech, his own individual creation, his own personal performance.

It is instructive to ask why the Kuna translate the chief's chant for the audience? Why is it necessary for the spokesman to retell, reformulate, and explain the words of the chief? There are several intersecting reasons. Intelligibility and comprehensibility are very important to the Kuna. While the chief's chant is partially intelligible and comprehensible to the audience, the spokesman's retelling is much more so and much more direct. Furthermore, the repetition involved in a second telling is a way of doubly stressing the moralistic message of the chief as well as adding to it that of the spokesman. Then there is the esthetics of the event, clearly pleasurable to the audience. This esthetics involves a most interesting juxtaposition of similarity and difference.

There is similarity in referential content; the story told by both chief and spokesman is essentially the same. But there is difference as well in that first the story is chanted, then spoken; first told as a dialogue, then as a monologue; first is in an esoteric and partially or barely intelligible medium and then in a form intelligible and accessible to the audience. The audience appreciates both styles, both performances, and especially their juxtaposition within a single event. Gathering-house chanting and speaking are also a display of knowledge and artistry, on the part of both chief and spokesman. And the juxtaposition of the two adds a bit of rivalry and competitive tension which heightens the esthetics of the performance. Finally, performers and audience enjoy taking part in the maintenance of tradition through performance. And the translation from the chief's to the spokesman's version is essential to this maintenance.

The myth of White Prophet

The chief's chant and spokesman's translation which I present here are from the myth of *nele sipu* (White Prophet), recorded on April 9, 1970 in the Mulatuppu gathering house. The myth was chanted by Olowitinappi, a chief from the western region of San Blas who at the time was visiting the island of Sasartii-Mulatuppu. It is one of several Kuna myths which are frequently performed in western San Blas and while known in general terms by ritual specialists in the east, chiefs and spokesmen on eastern islands such as Sasartii-Mulatuppu for the most part do not include them in their performance repertoires. This is one of the the fascinating aspects of this particular event, since the Mulatuppu spokesman, Armando,[2] must translate, reformulate, and explain a myth he is not particularly familiar with and under usual circumstances never performs.

The myth of White Prophet describes the wonders of life in the Kuna afterworld. Its moralistic purpose is to remind the gathered audience, especially the women, to behave properly in this world. The description and counsel are all encoded in the words of White Prophet, one of the first great leaders of the Kuna, who is taken on a preview tour of the afterworld.[3]

The myth is not a fixed text. Each performer has a certain degree of freedom in manipulating its structure in actual performance. In this sense, the chanting by chiefs

---

[2]   This is the same Armando who serves as primary addressee of and commentator on the humorous Agouti story presented in chapter seven.
[3]   The presentation of narrative in the words of others is a very characteristic feature of Kuna discourse, with areal-typological links throughout lowland South America. (See chapter five.)

differs from the performance of magical chants, also often myth-like, which are much more fixed in form. (See chapter eight.) The spokesman, Armando, by providing his own retelling, by adding still another version to the chief's version, although based on and derived from the chief's performance which has just occurred, both maintains the tradition of the myth and contributes to its open and flexible structure.

Twin performances: a structural comparison

In comparing the twin performances of the myth of White Prophet, it is useful to distinguish two aspects of its structure and structuring – first the macrostructure, the overall general organization and second the microstructure, especially the structuring of lines and verses. With regard to macrostructure, the two performances of White Prophet are practically identical. The chanted version opens with a statement of the health of the performing chief, a ritual greeting with which chiefs always open their chants. Then both chanted and spoken versions have the same general structure. First there is an opening, a reflexive description of the event itself (the spokesman's spoken version begins with this) – the arrival of the members of the village to the gathering house, organized according to named roles in the community. After this reflexive description, the story proper begins with a story preface, announcing the myth of White Prophet. Then the body of the story, the visit of White Prophet to four levels of the afterworld. The description of each level delimits an episode in the structuring of the story: (1) the level of reborn sweepings; (2) the level of reborn birds; (3) the level of reborn *paypa* birds; and (4) the longest episode, the level of the human afterworld.[4] There is strong moralistic tone to these descriptions. Everything in this world comes to life again in the afterworld, often in golden form. For this reason the audience is exhorted to care for what it finds here and await the better life it will have later. For example, in episode one, the women are told to clean up this world carefully, as what we sweep up here comes to life in the afterworld. And indeed a striking feature of Kuna villages is the sight of groups of women sweeping the streets, especially around the gathering house, and especially when there are chiefs such as Olowitinappi visiting in residence, until they are impeccably clean and tidy. Each performance ends with a

---

[4]   I find the term "episode" appropriate for these segments or units within the text; they share features with both act and scene of Hymes's (1977) terminology.

coda – a list of renowned Kuna chiefs of the past who also chanted about White Prophet. For comparative purposes the portions of the performance I present here are the opening and the first episode of the myth, as chanted by Chief Olowitinappi and as interpreted by Spokesman Armando.

In the opening, the listing of the arrival of individuals to the gathering house is most interesting, both for its expression of Kuna ideology, especially as enacted in this particular event, and for its role in the structuring of the performance and text of the myth. First the men of the village are listed, beginning with political leaders, chiefs, then spokesmen, then policemen, the three roles in Kuna political/gathering-house structure, in hierarchical order (verses 2 and 3 of Olowitinappi's chant, verses 2 and 3 of Armando's interpretation). Both Chief Olowitinappi and Spokesman Armando specify all three of these roles by name. Then comes a listing of other ritual specialists. The chief and the spokesman enumerate this list slightly differently. The chief first lists cacao men and hot pepper birds in a single verse (5). Cacao men are knowers of *The way of cacao*; hot pepper birds (an almost playful euphemism for man) are knowers of *The way of the hot pepper*. These two very commonly-known chants are used to cure fever. The chief then mentions medicine men in general (verse 6); these are herbalists who cure with plants found in the nearby Darien jungle. In the same verse are mentioned the *kantules*, the masters of ceremony and verbal performers at girls' puberty rites. Then come the knowers of *The way of the wind*, a chant used to cure epilepsy (verse 7). The spokesman's list of ritual specialists is much shorter; it is limited to first the hot pepper men (verse 4) and then the medicine men (verse 5).

The final class of individuals the chief lists are the women, beginning with two kin terms which figuratively stand for all women in general, aunts and nieces (verse 9). Then he mentions two specialized women's roles, bird catchers, which signify midwives, again using the word bird as a metaphor-euphemism, this time for babies, and hammock makers (verse 10). Then come two metonyms for women in general, mola makers and bead stringers (verse 11). Finally there is another set of ritual specialists, the hair cutters at girls' puberty rites (verse 12). The spokesman begins with women in general (verse 11), then hammock makers (verse 12), mola makers (verse 13), bead stringers (verse 14), and two puberty rites specialists, hair cutters and water sprinklers (verse 15).

The order of this listing, by both chief and spokesman, is not haphazard. It is a simultaneous expression of Kuna ideological structure and the spatial organization of the event. Men are listed before women, and political leaders before curing and other ritual specialists. Political leaders are ranked hierarchically and curing and other ritual specialists are mingled in a more egalitarian way. Women are described in more figurative terms than men. This is the Kuna view of its own society. Men lead and protect women who are considered fragile; political structure is hierarchical; yet the curing system and ultimately Kuna society as a whole is egalitarian – anyone can potentially fill any role, if he or she is willing to do the work necessary. Spatially, the description moves from the center of the gathering house outward, from chiefs through spokesmen and ritual specialists to women, precisely as they are situated in this particular event.

This event and the performance and text contained within it, including its spatial structure, is an excellent illustration of the discourse-centered approach to language and culture I advocate here. For this prelude to a myth constitutes more than a mere list of individuals. It is a reflection of and indeed a creation and recreation of Kuna ideology and world view, expressed both textually and visually.

The chief and the spokesman both employ certain Kuna conventional literary devices in the structuring of their performances. One of these, the use of figurative and euphemistic language, especially in the naming of groups of individuals and social roles, is typical of gathering-house discourse. It is often much more allusive than in this particular performance. (See chapter four.) The use of kin terms to refer to non-kin, sometimes metaphorically and playfully, is also quite typically Kuna. (See chapter seven for the use of kin terms between animals in trickster tales.) In this performance, the kin terms *papa* (father) and *nana* (mother) are used to represent the Kuna concept of the deity. God is also called *tios* in Kuna, a word borrowed from Spanish *Dios*.

Another Kuna literary device, quite prominent in these performances, is the frequent repetition of certain words and phrases, as introductory and concluding units, as linking elements, or as aspects of description. These expressions, which are also often somewhat metaphorical, share features with both the topoi characteristic of European medieval literature (Curtius 1953) and the formulas characteristic of Greek and Slavic oral literature (Lord 1960). I will refer to these expressions here as literary formulas, with the understanding that they are both a particularly and characteristically Kuna phenomenon and at the same time an instance of a more general process in oral discourse, and ultimately a member of a class of processes, such as parallelism, whose underlying principle is repetition.

Notice that metrical factors are crucial to the Parry-Lord definition of the formula (see Lord 1960), much more so than is the case for Kuna discourse in which, like in most Native American discourse, pause and intonation pattern play a much greater role than phonological metrics.[5] The claim that literary formulas or parallelism in particular or repetition more generally are characteristic of oral discourse should not be interpreted to mean that there is no oral discourse which does not have these features; there is; or that written discourse never has these features; it does. In fact these same features which are characteristic of oral discourse are also characteristic of poetic discourse, both oral and written. (See Finnegan 1977.)

Here are some examples of literary formulas. In the opening of the myth, the chief chants of the "golden benches that Father placed here" in the verses that conclude his listings of classes of persons present in the gathering house. He ends the opening with a series of literary formulas, describing "golden papers" (verse 13), "angel people" (verse 15), and a "golden listening wire" (verses 16 and 17) to record performances. The gathering house is called by one of its many literary names, the "listening place."

In the first episode, the chief pairs literary formulas in parallel couplets, a frequent process in Kuna ritual discourse. Thus in verse (3), first "Father placed the sweeping's mother here," then "Father placed the sweeping's father here." In verse (5) it is first stated that "Father created a place of many golden flags" and then that he "created a place of many golden bells." The golden streets "shine brilliantly then they are all like gold," another Kuna literary formula. The spokesman talks of the "golden road" and the "golden flags." He does not repeat the golden bells from the chief's chant.

The literary formulas and metaphors intersect with the parallelistic structure of the chant and its spoken interpretation in that they are often presented in parallel lines and verses. An excellent example is the parallel repetition, three times, of the sitting of individuals on gathering-house benches, in the chief's chanting of the opening of the myth, verses (4), (8), and (13):

    (4)   *siknonimarye* "have come to sit."

    (8)   *upononimarte* "have come to enter."

   (13) *ampakkunonimarte* "have come to congregate."

---

[5]   See Stolz and Shannon (1976) for discussions of the applicability of the concept of the formula to various oral literatures around the world.

A different verb stem is used each time – *sike* (sit), *upoe* (enter), and *ampakkue* (congregate) – and the suffix *-ye* (subjunctive, optative) alternates with the narrative suffix *-te* (then).   As is so typical of Kuna verbal performance and cultural life in general, parallelism with variation simultaneously expresses tradition and innovation, the harmony of repetition together with the pleasure of difference.

Both the list of village dignitaries in the gathering house (in the opening) and the sights seen by White Prophet (in the first episode), in the performances of the chief and the spokesman, constitute paradigms of items which are inserted into fixed line and verse patterns.   The principle at work here, namely the projection of a paradigm syntagmatically, is of course the well-known Jakobsonian definition of poetry.

A discussion of line and verse parallelism takes us into more microlevels of textual patterning.   A comparison of the chief's and the spokesman's performances of the myth of White Prophet at a more micro level reveals both similarities and differences. Differences have mainly to do with the very different styles used in these performances, with the very different resources which the performers have at their disposal.   Most strikingly, the chief's version is chanted; the spokesman's, spoken.   As a result, the incantatory nature of the chief's performance, a crucial aspect of its religiously sacred and ritual quality, is not rendered in the spokesman's reformulation.   In addition, the chief's version is more esoteric, phonologically, syntactically, semantically, and with regard to metaphor and allusion; while the spokesman's reformulation is more intelligible, comprehensible, and accessible to the audience.   The spokesman's version involves one degree of reporting more than the chief's.   The spokesman quotes the words of the chief quoting White Prophet, while the chief quotes White Prophet directly.

The styles of the chanted and spoken versions of the myth of White Prophet contrast most clearly in the structuring of lines and verses.   Let us examine first the chanted version.   In Olowitinappi's chanting, lines and verses are quite clearly marked by a reinforcing combination of melodic shape, pause pattern, and ratification by the second chief.   It is these devices which I have used to determine lines and verses in my representation and translation.   Grammatical and lexical line-framing devices tend to coincide with musical, intonational, and social interactional markers of lines and verses. Verses often begin with *al inso* (thus) or *al inso sunna* (thus truly) and end with *oparye* (utter) or *soke* (say) and/or with the suffixes *-ye* or *-te*.   The first line of a verse often ends with the suffix *-te*.   Some first lines end with the word *takku*, derived from *takke* (see). Others end with *soke* (say). The ritual aura of the chanted version is reinforced by the isomorphism in line and verse structure and the stacking of parallel lines and verses.[6]

There are certain contrasts and tensions created between the various line and verse-marking devices however. Notice for example the interplay of one, two, and three-line verses in my representation. While the usual pattern is a two-line verse, verses 4, 5, 6, 7, 8, 9, 10, 11, and 14 in the opening and verses 1, 6, and 9 in the first episode break this pattern by having only one line. Three-line verses are rare but also occur, as in verse 15 in the opening and verse 8 in the first episode. Verse 1 of the first episode is particularly striking in that it includes in the middle of a line the long verb final vowel *-ee* and the word *takku*, both of which are practically always line final markers. Another usual line final marker, *soke*, appears in the middle of verse 9 of this episode. While predications usually occur within single lines, in verse 5 of the first episode, *papa*, which is the first word of the second sentence of this verse, occurs as the last word of the first line, producing a contrast between sentence structure and line structure. Similarly, quotations often occur within single lines, but they can also cut across lines (as in verse 2 of the first episode) or even across verses (as in verses 3 and 4 of the first episode).

Turning now to Armando's spoken version of the myth of White Prophet, although there is a fair degree of congruence among the various line and verse-marking devices, there tends to be less than in the chanted version. Poetic contrasts and tensions are created in various ways: the interplay of one, two, and three-line verses; the insertion of the line initial marker *taylekuti* (as a line initial marker it is used conjointly with *tek*, *inso*, or *emi*) in the middle of lines; and the use of line-framing words all by themselves to constitute a line without referential content (as in verses 5, 10, and 11 of the first episode). The greater degree of counterpoint in the spoken version of the myth, as compared with the chanted version, is in keeping with the less ritual, more colloquial style of a performance that is intended more for humans than for Gods.

Another way to compare and contrast the twin performances of the myth of White Prophet, which sheds most interesting light on the Kuna practice of translation, is by focusing on line-by-line and verse-by-verse correspondences between the chanted and

---

[6] I borrow the concept of stacking from Gossen (1974: 155-156). It is a process in Native American discourse which is especially prevalent in Mesoamerica and lowland South America.

spoken versions. The chanted version of the opening is structured into seventeen verses; the spoken version, sixteen. The chanted version of the first episode is structured into eleven verses; the spoken version, fourteen. While the basic content is the same, each version includes referential details not found in the other. Thus in the opening the chief and spokesman provide slightly different lists of individuals who arrive in the gathering house. And they mention God at different moments in their listing. On the other hand, certain verses correspond exactly or almost exactly with regard to referential content while differing strikingly in poetic structuring. Here are some examples.

(1)   The first verses, chanted and spoken, of the opening. Differences include the verse-initial *al emite* (now), the line-initial *sunna* (truly), and the lengthened line-final vowels of the chief, in contrast with the line-final *taylekutina* (indeed) and the verse-final *takken soke* (see it is said) of the spokesman; the chief's use of *tummakana* (literally "big ones") and the spokesman's use of *tule nuy nikka* (people with names) to express the meaning "important people;" and the chief's use of the verb *noni* (come) as a verb stem, while the spokesman uses the verb stem *upo* (enter) and suffixes *noni* to it.

(2)   The second verses, chanted and spoken of the opening. Here the major differences are the lengthened line-final vowels of the chief; the use of the words *tayle* (indeed) and *takkenye* (see) by the spokesman, words which are sometimes but not in this case line-final markers; and the spokesman's concluding metacommunicative phrase.

(3)   Verse 11 of the chanted version of the first episode and verse 14 of the spoken version. Here lexical correspondences are quite close. Differences involve the chief's verse-initial *al inso teki* (thus so) and verse-final *oparye* (I utter) and the spokesman's verse-initial *inso taylekuti* (thus indeed) and verse-final *pittosursoke* (don't you hear it is said). The spokesman also inserts *takken soke* (see it is said), usually a verse-final marker, into the middle of line 2.

Translation, memory, and performance

In many societies in the world in which esoteric, ritual languages are in use, verbal performances in these ritual languages constitute the means by which traditions are maintained, knowledge is memorized, and memorized knowledge is displayed. In eastern Indonesia, public rituals involve as their centerpiece the performance of long, esoteric chants to the Gods and spirits. The most characteristic feature of these chants is their intertwined metaphorical and parallelistic structure. (See Fox 1988.) Translation from the ritual and the sacred to the colloquial and everyday, that is, from the ancient past to the modern present is frequently of the utmost importance in the maintaining of tradition. In Bali, also in Indonesia, there are many events – masked dances, dance-dramas, and puppet performances – which involve as a central feature translation from an ancient language to a modern language, from esoteric content to intelligible content, from ritual to everyday, and from singing or chanting to speaking. But much more than for the Kuna, Balinese translation involves satire and humor and playful translations intersect disjunctively with serious ritual content. As fond as the Kuna are of play and humor, gathering-house translations of myth are not the place for them.

It has been noted that in traditional hierarchically organized societies, especially in Africa and Oceania, political leaders, for fear of risking power, tend to speak through representatives or spokesmen. On the other hand, in traditional egalitarian oriented societies, leaders themselves engage in political oratory, often using metaphorical, allusive, or veiled speech. (See Brenneis and Myers 1984.) The Kuna combine an egalitarian orientation with a somewhat hierarchical political system. It is interesting that Kuna speaking practices reflect this combination in that both chiefs and spokesmen are named roles and both are expected to and do engage in highly poetic political oratory, often metaphorical and allusive. (See also chapter four.)

The concept of translation, which is a key element in the relationship between chief and spokesman, and which is omnipresent and most significant in Kuna verbal life more generally, is most dramatically and spectacularly in evidence in events such as the twin performances of the myth of White Prophet. In his role as repeater, translator, interpreter, explainer, and editor of the chief's performance, the spokesman moves the original along several dimensions and continua – from chanted to spoken, from ritual to everyday, and from esoteric to intelligible.

The two different performances of the myth of White Prophet, that of Chief Olowitinappi and that of Spokesman Armando, provide us with an enactment through actual practice of the Kuna view of the translational relationship between chiefly ritual chanting and colloquial spoken retellings. The two performances, the two versions, the twin texts, as I have called them here, occurring naturally within a single event, make possible controlled comparisons, contrasting different poetic and discourse organizations, structures, and styles, in spoken and chanted speech.

This focus on translation also provides us with insights into the nature and actual practice of memory among the Kuna and takes us into general and theoretical questions relating memory, the maintenance, transmission, and demonstration of knowledge, and verbal performance, in traditional oral societies. These questions have been discussed by scholars dealing with societies, times, and places as far removed from one another as ancient Greece and Rome, medieval and renaissance Europe, and contemporary Africa and the American Southwest. There is considerable discussion and indeed debate with regard to the nature of orality and to what degree and in what ways memorization takes place. (See Finnegan 1977, Lord 1960, and Yates 1966.)

The myth performance which I represent and discuss here is most fascinating and relevant to this debate in that from the Kuna point of view the same memorized myth is performed in two different ways within the same event. The performance of ritual chanting and subsequent spoken translation involves a structural edifice that is both poetic and mnemonic, providing devices that enable chiefs to remember and fluently chant their myth and spokesmen to fluently translate and reformulate them on the spot. Armando's performance/interpretation of the myth of White Prophet is remarkable in that the chanter, Olowitinappi, was a visiting chief from a distant region and the chant was not one particularly familiar to Armando.

The chief and the spokesman have two different problematics with regard to memory and performance, The chief must perform a myth that he remembers, that he has memorized in a general sense of knowing the story. While he is faithful to the myth, he is free to present it as he chooses. At the same time he must maintain absolute chanted fluency for two or more hours. He achieves this fluency by means of a combined intersection of several poetic mnemonic devices and processes – literary formulas, line and verse parallelism, and an edifice of line and verse-initial and final words and phrases that serve as frames for referential content. All of these devices provide a rhythm and flow to the chant, ways to maintain continuity, and time to remember while chanting.

The parallelistic listing of dignitaries in the opening of the myth is reminiscent of the ancient Greek taste for genealogies and their mythological representation. (See Calame 1987.) The Kuna passion for listing of people, within the frames provided by literary formulas and parallel lines and verses, mapped onto a narrative and having ideological purposes, has echoes not only in ancient Greece, but in many places in the world, from New Guinea to Africa. (See Blount 1975 and Stanek 1983, among many others.) The use of lists in order to generate forms of discourse is so widespread in the world that it clearly constitutes a universal principle of oral discourse, of course as an instance of the most general universal principle, repetition. (See Finnegan 1977: 127-133.) In addition to the societies I have mentioned here, western European medieval literature reflects this principle as well. In France's earliest epic literature, kinship and familial origins are used strategically to create what have been called "genealogical narratives." Lineages serve to organize entire literary modes. (Bloch 1983: 79-93.) In the Kuna listing represented here, the chief also uses a mnemonic process well known to students of classical European traditions, the use of the visual setting in which the performance is situated in structuring the verbal text which is produced within it. (See Yates 1966.) The result is a mytho-narrative representation of social-spatial organization, with ideological force. All of this is strengthened in the body of the myth which relates this world to the afterworld.

The spokesman, Armando, on the other hand, performs a myth which he has just heard. His performance is his version of the chief's version. His memory is not only of a general story of a myth, but, in addition and especially, of a myth just told. While he is free to summarize and elaborate as he chooses, emphasizing a bit more here, focusing a bit less there, changing the order of a list or adding to or deleting from it, he must be faithful to the chief and in fact will be criticized if he is not. This is particularly the case if he is too general and does not specify and reformulate the details of the chief's chant but rather fills the air with empty meaningless fillers, the line and verse-framing words and phrases.

The spokesman is more of a reteller than an explainer. He does not ever completely decipher the metaphors and allusions of the chief's chant; rather he renders them in another form. The spokesman is often an apprentice; he learns by listening to the chief and by performing his version of what he has just listened to. In a certain sense, all Kuna chiefs and spokesmen are always apprentices, listening to others perform and translating and interpreting what they have heard within their own performances. This is why both chief and spokesman mention the chiefs before them who have chanted the myth of White Prophet, the line of teachers, students, apprentices, and interpreters in which they locate themselves. (See also chapter six.) Notice that performers of magical chants, which are considered to be fixed texts and not interpretations, do not include lists of other performers in their chants. (See chapter eight.) On the other hand, reports of their learning experience typically do trace the line of teachers and students. (See chapter five.)

Like the chief, the spokesman makes use of structural and structuring principles which enable him to memorize the chant he has just heard and perform an accurate and complete rendering of it in his translation. These include literary formulas, parallelism, line and verse framing devices, the use of space, and quotation. In the text presented here, the spokesman's version has the same general structure as the chief's, includes the same actions and categories of action, and expounds the same general ideology, while differing in some of the details.

While the twin myth performances I have studied here have interesting echoes from Indonesia to Greece and western Europe, they speak most directly to issues in the study of myth within lowland South America. Claude Lévi-Strauss (1964-1971) studies variations of the same myth, in different South American Indian societies, in order to create his own abstracted version of the basic structure of myth. My approach here, on the other hand, has been to record, transcribe, and analyze different versions, actually performances, of the same myth, within a single society, occurring as constituent parts of a single event, in order to more fully comprehend Kuna theories and practices of the poetics of performance, the creation and artistic structuring of meaning through discourse.

In the performances and texts I have presented and examined here there is a constant interplay of shared tradition and individual creativity, of memorization, composition, and improvisation. Since the various poetic, mnemonic, and ideological devices intersect and intertwine continuously throughout the two performances, they have a truly emergent and emerging structure, at the same time offering a rather impressive instance of the memory of traditional verbal knowledge. The myth of White Prophet has a general structure which is shared by all knowers and performers, a structure which involves content, style, and canons of performance appropriate to the genres they perform – for chief's, chanting, and for spokesmen, formal speech making. This structure enables memorization and replication of similarities in performance. At the same time and against this backdrop of shared tradition, the diversity of linguistic-poetic devices – grammatical, semantic, lexical, intonational, musical, and social-interactional – provides a set of resources which are drawn on in different ways by performers who are thus able to produce line and verse patterns, meanings, and metaphors which, while steeped in the traditions of Kuna verbal art, are also their own unique and personal creation.

The text

Here then is the opening and the first episode of the myth of White Prophet, as chanted by Olowitinappi and as spoken by Armando. In the representation of the chanted version, verses are primarily determined by the regular turn taking between Olowitinappi and the responding chief, Mantiwekinya. Verses are also characterized by a regular melodic shape. Verses are numbered consecutively. All lines end with a period; in the English translation the first letter is capitalized. The lines of the responding chief are indented.

In Armando's spoken interpretation of the myth, I have used the slowing of tempo, coupled with falling pitch, and short and long pauses, to determine lines and verses. As in the chief's chant, verses are numbered consecutively. An extra space separates verses.

SAYLA OLOWITINAPPI NAMAKKE

Opening

al emite tule tummakanakwalee.

sunna nase nonimaryee.

    tekii.

tule saylakanakwal arkarmalakwalee.

na nase nonimaryee.

    tekii.

tule polisiakanakwaletee.

nase nonimaryee.

    tekii.

papa olokansupilli mesisakwatse na siknonimaryee.

    tekii.

al inso sunna sia tulekan kapur sikkwimala panse nonimaryee.   5

    tekii.

tule inatulekanakwar tule kanturkanakwar nase nonimaryee.

    tekii.

al inso tule purwa ikar wisimalatti noniteee sokee.

    tekii.

papa oloittokunnekaki olokansuseka l upononimartee.

    tekii.

sikwa l ammamalakwar siamalakwale panse l upononitee.

    tekii.

tule sikkwikaemala nase noni kacisopemalatee.   10

    tekii.

tule mornattulekan noni wini onimalat nonitee.

    tekii.

amma iete panse nonimartee.

iemalakwar nase nonimaryee.

    tekii.

pela olokansuse pani ampakkunonimartee.

CHIEF OLOWITINAPPI CHANTS

Opening

Now all the great people.

Truly have come together.

    So it is.

The people who are chiefs who are spokesmen.

Have indeed come together.

    So it is.

The people who are policemen then.

Have come together.

    So it is.

They have indeed come to sit in the golden benches that Father placed here.

    So it is.

Thus truly cacao men and hot pepper birds you have come to me.   5

    So it is.

The people who are medicine men the people who are *kantules* have come together.

    So it is.

Thus the people who are knowers of *The way of the wind* have come I say.

    So it is.

They have come to enter the golden benches in Father's golden listening house then.

    So it is.

For a short while aunts and nieces you have come to enter to me then.

    So it is.

The people who catch birds have come together those who make hammocks then.   10

    So it is.

The people who are mola people have come and those who string beads have come then.

    So it is

Aunts who are hair cutters you have come to me then.

The hair cutters have come together.

    So it is.

You have all come to congregate in the golden benches then.

olokarta nikkapukkwamaryee.

    tekii.

papati oloniptolapa tule tummakan otenonimartee.

    tekii.

tule ankermala aktenoni.   15

paliwitturmar aktenoni.

an palittokeka kumartee.

    tekii.

papati l ittoket neka upepepartee.

olokalalatupa opaksa nasiktee.

    tekii.

papa oloittokuna upepepartee.

na olotupa otenoniyee.

    tekii.

First episode

al inso sunna "teki pillikwense aytettee" takku l ipitikuyen oparye.

    tekii.

al inso " 'weti oloturwakkapillitee.'

tule l anka sokeen" oparye.

    tekii.

"papati weki turwa nana mesistee.

papa weki turwa papa mesisyee.

    tekii.

oloturwakkapillisetee" soke.

"turwatulekana turkupukkwayeen" oparye.

    tekii.

"The golden papers[7] are present.

So it is.

And Father came from among the golden dwellers above to lower down the great people then.

So it is.

The angel people have come to descend. 15

The holy people[8] have come to descend.

They are here in order to listen to us then.

So it is.

And father from the front of the listening house then.

Hung a golden listening wire across[9] then.

So it is.

Father from the front of the listening place then.

Indeed came to lower a golden wire.

So it is.

First episode

Thus truly "well one level down [I] descended then" see I utter.

So it is.

Thus " 'This is the level of the golden sweepings then.'

The man[10] said to me" I utter.

So it is.

"And father placed the sweepings' mother here then.

Father placed the sweepings' father here.

So it is.

At the level of the golden sweepings then" it is said.

"The sweepings people come to life" I utter.

So it is.

---

7 List of inhabitants including the record of their conduct
8 angels
9 to heaven
10 guide

"oloturwakkaki papa olopanter pukkipnekatee papa.   5

olokappan pukkipnekkuyee.

    tekii.

oloturwakka olonekinpa tarmakkemaite l olopikuyen" oparyee.

    tekii.

"ammamarye nue l an palittokotee" takku.

nele sipu namakketeen oparye.

    tekii.

"ammamarye nue neka turwioeye" soketee.

"melle pani siotee.

turwapilli miotee."

    tekii.

al insoti "kakka yalapar" soke "nue pani turwapilli urpotee" sokee.

    tekii.

al inso "wese turwatulekana turkupukkwatee."   10

nele sipu namakketee.

    tekii.

al inso teki "neka taktetee takku.

pillikwense palakte nonipartee" oparye.

    tekii.

ARKAR ARMANDO SUNMAKKE

Opening

"tule nuy nikka nikka taylekutina.

we neyse upononi" takken soke.

"tule saylakanakwar tayle nase nonimala, tule arkarkanakwar takkenye," sayla anmar

owiso takken.

"tule taylekuti polisiakanakwar" takken soke.

"In the place of the golden sweepings Father created a place of many golden flags
then Father. 5
Created a place of many golden bells.
 So it is.
The golden streets of the place of the golden sweepings shine brilliantly then they are
all like gold" I utter.
 So it is.
"Aunts listen to me well."
White Prophet chanted I utter.
 So it is.
"Aunts clean your houses well" it is said then.
"Don't you leave them around then.
You must throw away the sweepings then."
 So it is.
And thus "along the mouth of the river" it is said "you must place the sweepings then"
it is said.
 So it is.
Thus "there the sweepings people come to life then." 10
White Prophet chanted then.
 So it is.
Thus so "he saw this place then indeed.
He descended again one level then " I utter.
 So it is.

SPOKESMAN ARMANDO SPEAKS

Opening
"The people with names with names indeed.
Have come to enter this house" see it is said.

"The people who are chiefs indeed have come together, the people who are spokesmen
see," the chief informs us see.

"The people indeed who are policemen" see it is said.

"tule kapur tule kanakwar tayle nase upononimala.
we neyse kup" ittosursoke soy takken.

inso taylekutina.
"inaturkanakwar tayle nase nonimar" takken soke.
"pap ittoet neyse" pittosursoke takken.

"papti taylekuti anka ittoet nek mettenatmala.

e nuy piekar" pittosurso pittosursokene.

" 'ipakwenpa tayleku panse wis korpukkwa taylekuti nanamaloe.'
papti kottenat" takken soke.

"nan tummatti kottenat" pittosursoke soy takken.

"papti taylekuti we nekki taylekutina.
anka kan nuekan taylekuti urpisnatmala.
aa kanse an ampakunonimarye," anmarka soy pittosursokene.

"inso taylekuti punmar upononikki.
nuy nikka nikka tayleku panse upononimarye."
sayla anmar owiso pittosursokene.

inso taylekutina.
"kwena kwena panse pe upononima taylelekuti.
tule kaci wisimalat noni" takken soke.

"tule moray tulekan tayleku nonikki.
we neyse" pittosursoy takken.

5

10

"The people who are hot pepper men indeed have come to enter together.
Into this house" don't you hear it is said it is said see.

Thus indeed.   5
"The medicine men indeed have come together" see it is said.
"To Father's listening house" don't you hear it is said see.

"And Father indeed left us this listening house as he departed.

So that we may pronounce his name" don't you hear it is said don't you hear it is said.

" 'You must go around[11] indeed calling to me a little indeed from time to time.'
Father himself called as he departed" see it is said.

"And Great Mother called as she departed" don't you hear it is said it is said see.

"And Father indeed in this house indeed.   10
Left us indeed good benches.
To those benches we have come to congregate," he says to us don't you hear it is said.

"Thus indeed the sisters have come to enter.
You who have names indeed have come to enter here to me."
The chief informs us don't you hear it is said.

Thus indeed.
"One by one you have come to enter to me indeed.
The people who know hammocks have come" see it is said.

"The mola people these people indeed have come.
To this house" don't you hear it is said see.

---

[11] live your lives

inso taylekutin win onimalat noni takken soke.

"iemalat nonikki, timimmimalat noniye," sayla anmal oisomar takken.   15

"pela taylekuti nuy nikkatpi" pittosursoke soy takkenye.

First episode
tek inso taylekuti "pillikwense taylekuti nerti aytetee."
kusun pittosursokeye.

"ney pillikwense aytes taylekutina.
oloturwana pillise aytetapye," anmar oiso takken.

inso taylekutina " 'we nap nekki pani neyturwitimala.
aakwat pillikwense pattemaye,' " anmar oiso pittosursokeye.

"'aaki taylekuti turwakan taylekuti mai'" takken soke.

emit taylekutina.   5
" 'aase turkupuyye,' " soy pe ittosursokeye.

inso taylekutina " 'pe neyturwioet nue mio' takken soke.

'mer tipa miar saoye' nerti nek owisos" pittosursokeye.

" 'aaki taylekutina.
papti taylekutin nek urpitappi.
nek nuet, taylekuti papti kal urpis' " takken soke.

Thus indeed "those who string beads have come" see it is said.

"The haircutters have come, the water sprinklers have come," the chief informs us   15
see.

"All of them indeed each have names" don't you hear it is said it is said see.

First episode
Well thus indeed "one level down indeed the prophet descended."
That is how it really was don't you hear it is said.

"To the first level of the earth he descended indeed.
To the level of the golden sweepings he descended there" he[12] informs us see.

Thus indeed " 'what you sweep for me on this earth.
It falls to the first level' " he informs us don't you hear it is said.

" 'There indeed are the sweepings indeed' " see it is said.

Now indeed.   5
" 'There they come to life,' " it is said don't you hear it is said.

Thus indeed " 'you must throw away the sweepings well' see it is said.

'Don't be throwing them in the sea' the prophet informed" don't you hear it is said.

" 'There indeed.
And Father indeed left a home there.
A good home, indeed Father left for them' " see it is said.

[12]   the chief

" 'olo ikar nuet tayle kar mesisa.
neyti kuye' " soy pittosur sokken.

inso taylekuti.   10
" 'olo panter pukkipney takkenye,' anmar oiso" pittosursokene.

inso taylekuti.
" 'papti pel immar akkalomasokku, ney nutaymait mai' " takken soke.

" 'immal icomasurye,' anmarka soy" takken.

en taylekutin " 'a tule puymarye,' soy" pittosursokeye.

inso taylekuti "nerti tey ney taysa.
pal aytes" takken soke "pillikwense.
natsun" pittosursokeye.

" 'He placed a good golden road indeed for them.
That is how the place is' " it is said don't you hear it is said.

Thus indeed. 10
" 'It is a place of many golden flags see,' he informs us" don't you hear it is said.

Thus indeed.
" 'And since Father is changing all things, the one who puts the place in order is
there' " see it is said.

" 'He does not harm things,' he says to us" see.

Now indeed " 'there they are these[13] people,' he says" don't you hear it is said.

Thus indeed "the prophet saw the place that way.
He descended again" see it is said "one level.
He departed" don't you hear it is said.

[13] sweepings

4. COUNSELING A NEW CHIEF: A FUGUE OF METAPHORS

On April 24, 1971, the village of Sasartii, one of two villages on the island of Sasartii-Mulatuppu, inaugurated a new chief, Takkin Hakkin. Takkin had been chosen several days before as a replacement for the previous chief, who was suddenly thrown out of office for misbehavior. As is Kuna custom, the inauguration occurred during a long public gathering in the village gathering house. This gathering began in the early evening and continued on late into the night. Speaker after speaker counseled the new chief. The first speaker was Kawiti, a renowned chief from Tupwala, an island one-half hour away from Sasartii-Mulatuppu by five horse power motor boat. Kawiti was invited especially for this event. There was much fanfare as his boat arrived. Kawiti came along with other Tupwala leaders and their wives, representatives of their village. The boat, made out of a jungle tree, was quite crowded and animated. A Panamanian flag raised high in the air on a pole symbolized the significance of the arriving delegation and could be seen at a great distance. The other speakers at Takkin's inauguration were chiefs and political leaders from Sasartii and Mulatuppu. The speeches were lengthy, each one lasting approximately one hour. The speech which is the focus of this chapter was given by Muristo Pérez, who at the time was the first chief of Mulatuppu. Muristo also happens to be Takkin's older brother. Muristo's speech was the second of the evening. It followed that of the invited visitor Kawiti. The occasion was both festive and serious – festive because of the invited guests and the pleasure of publicly celebrating Kuna tradition, serious because of the formal and ritual nature of Kuna gatherings and the importance of this event in particular. While the speeches were intended for the ears of the new chief Takkin, they also provided opportunities for the speech makers themselves to demonstrate their own abilities – knowledge of Kuna tradition and skill in performing publicly. In the case of inaugurating and in particular counseling a new political leader such as chief, speakers demonstrate their knowledge of traditional, conventional metaphors for political structure and their ability to adapt and mold these metaphors creatively and individually, as well as to introduce new ones.

Muristo's speech is dramatic and lively. Delivered with no written notes in a fluently booming voice, it is an eloquent example of the Kuna art of persuasion. It is full of, and in fact organized in terms of, overlapping and intersecting metaphors and other allusive, illustrative material, all aimed at counseling, not only the new chief, but also the community as a whole, and offering Muristo's traditionalist yet dynamic view of the world.

Structure of performance and (con)textual assumptions

The counsel for a new chief is one of many forms of verbal counsel in use among the Kuna. In fact verbal counsel, called *unaet*, is the name for a variety of speech events which cut across ritual and everyday life and constitutes one of the major Kuna patterns of speaking (See Sherzer, 1983: 200-201.) Gathering-house counsels are performed either to the community at large or to groups or individuals within it. All persons about to embark on a new role or activity receive a public counsel from chiefs and other gathering officials. Students are counseled before school begins and couples are counseled as part of their marriage ceremony. In addition, counsels in the gathering house are also used to remind various individuals of the way to behave in roles they already fill. Chiefs periodically counsel women in general, curing specialists, or midwives, stressing that they should perform their duties properly. And all gathering chanting, whether about history, myth, personal experience, or metaphor, is ultimately counsel in that it exemplifies, figuratively represents, and reminds the audience of proper modes of Kuna behavior.

Counsels are also an important form of punishment in disputes brought before public gatherings. Once the case has been decided, after thorough discussion, long counsels are performed by chiefs and other gathering leaders, either as an accompaniment to other punishments, such as fines, or as the sole punishment. In addition to focusing on a particular wrongdoing, these counsels stress the importance of proper moral behavior more generally and are rhetorically and poetically developed. And since they are public, they are aimed as much at the gathering-house audience as at the person directly accused of wrongdoing.

The ritual magical chant performed by a curing specialist consists of counsel from the specialist to representatives of the spirit world about how to achieve the action desired by the performer. These magical chants are often punctuated with lines stating explicitly that the specialist is counseling the spirits. The spirits, in turn, often counsel other spirits on how to behave, as a result of having been counseled by the performing specialist. The various chants used to activate medicine and render it effective are called "medicine counsel." In both counsels directed to spirits and those of the gathering house, social control, rhetoric, and verbal art are intimately linked. (See chapter eight.)

In everyday speech, counsel is common as well. A child's father counsels her or him at the beginning of the school year; if the child attends school in a village away from home, her or his temporary guardian gives advice periodically on proper behavior and always gives advice in the case of wrongdoing. Similarly, before young men leave for work in Panama City or the Canal Zone, they are counseled by their fathers. It is important to note that physical violence is avoided among the Kuna; there are very strong sanctions against it. Parents do not spank their children. Physical fighting is very rare and always becomes the subject of an evening discussion in the gathering house, in which the protagonists are severely reprimanded and fined.

Given the avoidance of physical means of social control, counsel plays a very important role in the regulation of behavior in everyday as well as ritual life. It is particularly interesting that both the verbal advice given in advance of an activity and the verbal punishment levied after wrongdoing are grouped together as counsel. This combination is a reflection of the Kuna belief in the potential of all beings, human and spirit, for mischievous, immoral, or even evil behavior. Counsels are constantly needed, not just after a misdeed has been committed but before it might occur and so that it does not occur. Kuna counsels, ritual and everyday, are a fascinating reflection of and embodiment of the Kuna conception of the power of words. In a performative way, counsels cause actions to occur, facilitate actions, and constitute actions themselves.

Counsels reinforce Kuna culture by explicitly talking about different aspects of it and deploring the losses and changes of recent times. They are highly rhetorical speech events, aiming at persuasion and insisting on learning and teaching. They are also highly esthetic speech events, especially when performed in formal and ritual contexts. As is the case of all of the forms of discourse represented here, counsels combine rhetoric and poetics, the maintenance of cultural tradition and the affirmation of individual creativity.

The counsel for a new chief is most dramatic and spectacular. The new chief has been chosen in advance, but on this occasion, seated in the gathering house, he pretends not to know anything about it. Suddenly the policemen of the village grab him and his wife and lead them to the center of the gathering house where they are made to sit on small benches in front of the chiefs' hammocks. Pretending to be blind, they listen as chiefs and other leaders speak or chant counsels to them which provide them with new sight and encourage them to perform their new roles well.

Counsels for new chiefs consist of a series of extended metaphors dealing with chiefs, their duties, and their appropriate behavior. The most effective public speakers, the most adept and respected of political leaders, develop and elaborate these metaphors to fit appropriately the particular individual being inaugurated and the circumstances surrounding his choice, including current events in the community. There are many metaphors for chiefs and related political officials and political organization more generally, as well as many possibilities for adapting them and developing them. (See Howe 1977, 1986 and Sherzer 1983.) These metaphors draw on both Kuna ecology and Kuna cultural practices, such as house building. They are not esoteric, but rather quite concrete, made up out of the realities of everyday life. As they are developed these metaphors are created out of and create their own literary topoi and formulas. (See Curtius 1953, Lord 1960, and discussion in chapter three.)

One common metaphor is a description of the different poles utilized in the construction of a Kuna house, their size and location. These represent the different roles in village political organization; the central pole represents the chief, secondary poles represent the chief's spokesmen, and other poles represent other officials. The thin bamboo walls represent the ordinary people of the village. This symbolism can be further developed, creatively and individually, so that a central pole which is rotten represents a bad chief who must be removed from office or a pole which had its rotten part cut away represents a chief who has been reinstated. Muristo uses this metaphor to a certain degree, but does not develop it elaborately, as did another of the speakers who followed him that evening.

Another metaphor is ecological. Chiefs are represented by powerful trees in the jungle, different types of trees representing different types of chiefs, including especially their different personalities. Muristo develops this metaphor as one of the central elements of his speech. It is an expression of the intimate relationship that exists between the Kuna and their surrounding natural environment and is an enactment in verbal performance of both the respect and the esthetic appreciation the Kuna have for the natural world. They consider themselves to be the guardians of nature, which they use both literally and symbolically.

Still another metaphor concerns a chief's behavior. Chiefs are supposed to control their tempers and not show anger. In particular, outside of the gathering house, the physical setting in which they exercise their role, they should not publicly take notice of things which occur and with which they might disagree. Furthermore, they should not pay attention to criticism from members of the community. Criticism of members of the community is represented by the throwing of mud balls and darts, and a chief's needed ability to hold his temper is symbolized by a large trunk in which he can store things. While Muristo talks quite a bit in his speech about appropriate behavior for chiefs, he does not employ this particular metaphor.

Muristo's speech shares features with all counsels for new chiefs and at the same time reflects his own views and his own particular speaking style. He creates and structures his speech by drawing on conventional Kuna metaphors which he adapts and molds for this particular occasion and to which he adds various short narratives, descriptions which, like the metaphors, allusively refer to leadership in the Kuna community. These metaphors, narratives, and allusions intersect, overlap, and chase one another throughout the text, much like the structure of a musical fugue. The overall structure of the text is as follows:

1. (lines 1-30). Reflexive, metacommunicative description of the event of which   this speech is a part, including a list of the individuals in attendance (lines 1-19) and the importance of the island of Mulatuppu governing itself (lines 20-30).
2. (lines 31-76). Discussion and description of the selection of a new chief, in part metaphorically symbolized by trees and poles (lines 31-62).
3. (lines 65-76). Description of what God (called *papa* "father") does for the Kuna here.
4. (lines 77-112). Direct, explicit discussion of Muristo's younger brother, Takkin, and himself as leaders.
5. (lines 113-116). Description of steering a boat, a metaphor for leadership.
6. (lines 120-162). Discussion of individual conduct, including such examples of bad behavior as molesting women and stealing.
7. (lines 163-181). Use of poles and animals as metaphors for humans and their behavior.
8. (lines 182-192). Description of the world left by God, in the words of God himself.
9. (lines 193-214). Description of Muristo growing up, as an allusive representation of becoming a chief.
10. (lines 215-306). Use of plants, trees, and animals as metaphors for chiefs and their behavior.

11. (lines 307-344). General discussion of the importance of proper behavior, not just for chiefs, but for other leaders and their relatives as well. This section concludes (lines 329-344) with a description of how Muristo counsels his own family. The private counseling of family members is thus embedded into the public counseling of a new chief.

12. (lines 345-371). Description of the two brothers, Muristo and Takkin, working together and the possibility of jealousies and criticisms from individuals in the village. Within this description, animals are used as illustrative examples (lines 354-359).

13. (lines 372-378). Description of trees, metaphors for chiefs.

14. (lines 379-387). Description of Muristo's own career.

15. (lines 388-439). Description and discussion of changing customs.

16. (lines 440-444). Coda.

Certain textual assumptions and details need to be explained before proceeding to the main thrust of this paper and the central organizing and structuring principle of Muristo's speech, metaphors and allusions.

The reflexive and metacommunicative description with which Muristo opens his speech is quite typical of Kuna speaking practices and especially of formal and ritual speechmaking and chanting. The Kuna are fond of explicitly stating, often in great detail, when and where the event they are involved in is taking place, who is speaking to whom, what actions are occurring, what topic and content are expressed, and why all this is being done. (See Sherzer, 1983: 207-213.) Like the opening of the performance of the myth of White Prophet (see chapter three), Muristo names the individuals who are in attendance in the gathering house, by means of a listing of roles. This is a conventional Kuna literary device, simultaneously rhetorical, poetic, and ideological, akin to the Greek and Yugoslavian formula and the medieval topos and very common in oral discourse around the world. (See Bloch 1983, Calame 1987, Curtius 1953, Finnegan 1977, Lord 1960, Yates 1966.)

It is important to recognize that Muristo is not reporting or explaining a situation to individuals who do not know or understand what he is talking about. Quite the contrary. The people he is talking about are his audience, sitting right there in front of him. By listing in detail those present he uses language to authenticate the very event that is taking place, at the very moment that it is taking place. The list constitutes an overture and preamble to the full speech of which it is the opening part. It is poetic, in the Jakobsonian sense, in that it projects the paradigm of Kuna roles onto a syntagmatic sequence of lines. It is ideological and rhetorical in that it leads into a political statement and an expression of a world view which is a major organizing principle of the speech as a whole.

Muristo's verbal picture of those in attendance in the gathering house is presented in a different order than that used by Chief Olowitinappi in the myth of White Prophet. (See chapter three.) Muristo begins with ritual, curing specialists who go to the forest to search for herbal medicines – knowers of *The way of balsa wood*, the most ritual of all curing chants, that used to combat village-wide epidemics and the infestation of evil spirits everywhere and knowers of *The way of the hot pepper* and *The way of cacao*, two very commonly performed curing chants. Such individuals know the forest well, its plants and its trees. This leads him directly into his primary metaphor –chiefs as trees in the forest, for these specialists in forest ecology are thus specialists in trees and are thus furthermore specialists in the selection of chiefs. Ideologically Muristo brings together two major Kuna ritual realms, the political and the curing, within the figurative frame of tropical forest ecology.

After listing curing specialists, Muristo lists two political, gathering-house leaders, in ascending order of importance and power – chiefs' spokesmen and chiefs. Then come hunters and killers of tarpon, both metonyms for men in general, though some men are better hunters than others and become renown for this ability. Women are listed first as ritual specialists, in terms of two of the ritual roles that women fulfill in girls' puberty rites – hair cutters and leg crossers, then in general, by means of two metonyms for women – mola sewers and mola cutters.

Muristo continues his list, as part of his discussion and description of the selection of a new chief, by circling back to forest specialists, hunters, medicine men in general, knowers of a particular curing chant, *The way of the wind*, and gatherers of particular herbal medicines, thus once again leading directly into his metaphor: When men, especially curing specialists, search medicine in the jungle, they find trees, that is they discover and select chiefs. He concludes the list by again naming political leaders – policemen, chiefs' spokesmen, and chiefs, in ascending order of power, prestige, and importance.

Muristo's ideological thrust in his metacommunicative listing is thus not, as in the case of Chief Olowitinappi (see chapter three), hierarchical, from top to bottom, from men to women. Rather, Muristo presents a view of an intersection and mingling of ritual roles and realms, political, curing, and puberty, leading his audience to an egalitarian view of Kuna life in which people are chosen for leadership roles by hard-working members of the community and are expected to be open and generous, models of behavior for everyone to follow.

In lines one and two Muristo says that he prefers speaking in a standing position to being in a hanging position in the hammock. Kuna chiefs perform chants from a perched or hanging position in their hammocks, located in the center of the public gathering house. Only chiefs are permitted to sit or lie in these hammocks and in fact being in a hammock is both a symbolic and a literal expression and manifestation of being a chief. When a chief speaks (rather than chants) he may do so either from the hammock or standing. When standing, he assumes the same position as the chiefs' spokesman, who always stands when speaking. Muristo often expresses his belief that when speaking to and counseling the members of his community, the standing position is more appropriate. This may be because it is more democratic – all individuals other than chiefs always rise and stand when they speak. It may also be because he feels more forceful in the standing position. More generally, the Kuna associate four body positions with such actions as speaking and these are encoded in the language as a grammatical category, marked by four positional verbal suffixes – -*mai* (lying, in a horizontal position, as in a hammock), -*nai* (in a perched or hanging position, when in a hammock the feet are barely touching the ground), -*kwici* (standing), and -*sii* (sitting). Examples of the use of these suffixes from the text are:

> -*mai* (line 263): *sucu tulakan se pattemai* (the butterfly people land on it [literally: land in a horizontal position on it]);
> -*nai* (line 238): *akkwaser namaynai* (the spider is chanting [literally: chanting-in a hanging, perched position]);
> -*kwici* (line 364): *we sayla pialit sunmakkwici we?* (that chief speaking where is he from? [literally: speaking-standing]);
> -*sii* (line 80): *emit an ittosii* (now he is listening to me [literally: listening-sitting]).

The positional suffixes, like the chanting/speaking distinction, furthermore both express and symbolize the place of individuals in the community, in particular as this is visualized in the gathering house – chiefs lying in hammocks when attending the gathering (as in line 47), hanging in hammocks when chanting or speaking; chiefs' spokesmen in particular but any individual in general standing when speaking; and the members of the community at large sitting and listening to the performances, speeches, and chants of chiefs, village leaders, and others. (The positional suffixes are also discussed below in relation to metaphors and with regard to the representation and translation of the text.)

The Kuna often use kin terms to represent various roles in Kuna society. In gathering-house chanting and speaking nephews (line 97) commonly represent young men in general, and uncles (line 383), older men. The brothers-in-law in line 56 represent chiefs and the parents-in-law in line 57 represent chiefs' spokesmen. (See chapter three for further examples.)

The old farm in line 58 is a piece of land that has lain fallow for many years. The Kuna practice slash and burn agriculture on the mainland near their island villages and thus leave parcels of land unplanted for several years after use. Land further from the village is likely to be left unplanted longer.

Lines 88-107 and elsewhere in the text focus on particular forms of improper behavior, including such personal, domestic matters as abandoning and beating one's wife and molesting women and such broader, societal matters as stealing the crops of others. These are precisely things that chiefs should never do. In fact chiefs should provide a moral example of proper behavior. Yet at the same time chiefs sometimes behave improperly or are accused of behaving improperly. And if accusations take the form of gossip and are never brought publicly to the gathering house, a chief might never know that he is being accused.

A chief is responsible for both his own and his family's behavior. This behavior can conflict with ritual requirements and requisites for becoming a chief, namely knowledge of Kuna tradition and willingness and ability to perform it publicly. Thus a chief can be removed from office for his bad behavior and reinstalled for his traditional knowledge and verbal abilities. This explains line 96: How many times have I become chief? Line 107 (I myself indeed go about with a black cloth indeed over my own eyes) stresses the need for others to judge us since we are blind to our own behavior. But of course this enables jealousies to develop into gossip and the spread of rumors.

The application of stinging nettles in line 145 is a traditional Kuna way of publicly punishing wrongdoing; it is applied by the policemen of the village and used in conjunction with a verbal counsel by chiefs and other public leaders.

Jealousies and rivalries, between and among chiefs and other leaders, are common in this egalitarian society (lines 149-157 and 345-371). And gossip and the spread of rumors can bring leaders down. This situation gives rise to one of many related conflicts and tensions that are expressed in this speech. On the one hand there is the Kuna ideology that theirs is an idyllic society where everyone is generous and everyone gets along with everyone else. On the other hand jealousies and rivalries do exist, between brothers-in-law, between husbands, wives, and parents-in-law, between ritual specialists, and between political leaders. (See chapter five for a gathering-house speech which includes a lengthy discussion of rivalries between curing specialists.) The Kuna try at every turn to minimize the eruption of these jealousies and rivalries and there exist many mechanisms to deal with them, including an explicit discussion of them in speeches such as this. Line 302 states, somewhat allusively, that ritual performances, by chiefs and spokesmen, themselves are competitions. And in fact, especially when more than one chief and more than one spokesman are performing, evening chanting and speaking have a tournament-like quality to them, Kuna verbal equivalents of the medieval jousting tournaments of medieval Europe.

Lines 222-223 refer to the fact that the Kuna do not like quiet. It is contrary to their esthetic view of and feel for the world. Rather they consider much talk, much laughter, and much noise to be the normal and appropriate state of things.

An important aspect of this text, as will be discussed in greater detail below in relation to metaphors, is the Kuna belief that all objects, plants, and animals have souls and behave in the spirit world just like humans, including speaking to one another. Animals and trees in fact actually used to be people. This is why the birds in line 283 are called curassow people and *ukkur* people and the animals in line 354 are called collared peccary people and whited-lipped peccary people. And trees, one of the central foci of the metaphors of this speech, are explicitly called people in lines 253-254. Just like chiefs today, trees used to listen to one another chant traditions, exchanged knowledge and information, and competed with one another (lines 256, 257, 287-289, 302).

The "we" in line 246 refers to Muristo together with his younger brother Takkin, now the first chiefs of neighboring villages on the same island.

Lines 381-383 concern the ways in which chiefs are selected among the Kuna. It is often the case that a chief progresses to his office through all of the gathering-house roles, in succession – owner of the stick (policeman), chiefs' spokesman, chief. In this way he learns, teaches, and competes with traditional knowledge and verbal prowess, publicly demonstrating his abilities as he rises through the system. Takkin, for example, had been first spokesman of Sasartii before being selected as chief. Muristo on the other hand states in line 381 that he did not follow this path. The elders, especially village leaders (called important people in line 382), select chiefs and other gathering-house officials (lines 382-383). The precise way in which this is done varies considerably from village to village.

In lines 391-392 Muristo reminds the women to attend the gathering house. Gatherings in which chiefs chant are believed to be for women and they are constantly encouraged to attend. In many villages they are required to do so.

In lines 413-436 Muristo discusses various items that the Kuna used to produce natively but no longer do. Hammocks, hats, pants, and shirts were made by breaking up a native tree, the *ikkor* tree, and then weaving. Now these items are imported from Panama City, purchased either in Panama City itself or in small stores which are found in increasing numbers on the islands of San Blas. Similarly in times past the Kuna used gourds and earthen utensils. Now increasingly, and apparently in Muristo's view unfortunately, they buy plates. These and many other Kuna traditions that have been lost, or Muristo fears will be lost, are remembered in the chants of chiefs if nowhere else, as Muristo states in line 438, and are used in the verbal counsels which chiefs perform to their villages, just as Muristo is using them in his speech, in his performed verbal counsel.

More generally, in his discussion of changing customs (lines 388-439), Muristo expresses certain conflicts and tensions that are an increasing part of Kuna life as it adapts to the constantly changing and increasingly complicated world around it. The Kuna are an oft-cited case, especially in native South America, of a highly adaptive society, maintaining tradition and yet altering socially and culturally in order to meet the needs of population pressures, encroachments of surrounding aboriginal and non-aboriginal groups, migrations of their own community members within and without Kuna territory, and influences from nation-states, Colombia, Panama, and the United States in particular. Few lowland South American societies, indeed few native groups in the Americas, indeed few traditional societies in the entire world have fared better.

But the tensions, conflicts, and pressures of recent years, especially of an ever-impinging world system, are increasingly apparent, as more and more Kuna men and also women migrate to Panama City, become part of the Panamanian working and non-working urban slum society, and sometimes return to their villages poor and relatively landless; as village populations explode; as the Panamanian government expands its influences in San Blas; as Kuna traditions are gradually lost; and as more and more a cash-based economy introduces non-Kuna goods into the Kuna world. Muristo speaks to all this. His text is a spelling out and in part a working out of many of these issues, both implicitly and explicitly. (The speech represented in chapter five also discusses the dangers of outside influences, in a different way and in historical perspective.)

Muristo concludes his speech (line 442) by saying that "we are many more speakers." And indeed there were, speaker after speaker, late into the night.

Rhetoric and poetics

The rhetoric of Muristo's speech is highly political. It is very pro-Kuna and very pro-traditional Kuna customs. It is also very pro-individual village, in particular Mulatuppu and its right and need to govern itself.

This political rhetoric is expressed by means of an intersection of Kuna poetic devices. (See chapter two.) In fact, as Parkin (1984) has pointed out with regard to political language more generally, Kuna persuasion, that is rhetoric, may sometimes be an esthetic device in and of itself, having no other end than its own satisfactory performance. More particularly, several poetic devices are highlighted in Muristo's speech. One of these is parallelism. Throughout Muristo's speech there is a repetition with variation of words, phrases, and lines. Striking among these is the listing of people present in the gathering house in the opening of the speech (lines 4-21, 31-39, 45-47), the listing of animals left by God (lines 163-170, 224-229) the listing of things in the local ecology that must be cared for by the Kuna (lines 184-186), and the listing of people related to the chief who must demonstrate model behavior (lines 317-319). Each of these lists provides a paradigm which, through parallelism, is projected syntagmatically (Roman Jakobson's definition of the essence or basis of poetry). Parallelism is mnemonic as well as rhetorical and poetic. It enables speakers such as Muristo to perform fluent, convincing, and often long speeches.

Line-framing (opening and closing) words and phrases constitute a second major rhetorical-poetic device at work in Muristo's speech. Formal line framing intersects and interacts with parallelism in various ways. The line-framing words and phrases themselves can be presented parallelistically, as in the series of lines (402-405, 407,

409, 410, etc.) ending in *takken* (see) or *takken soke* (see it is said). The line-framing words and phrases also often provide the brackets within which the syntactic and semantic parallelism of lines is highlighted.

A third Kuna rhetorical-poetic device employed by Muristo is the quoting of himself and others. This quoting of past occasions confers a sense of reality and authenticity to the words and points of view expressed by Muristo on this particular occasion. It is quite common for Kuna speakers to embed quotes within quotes (as in lines 334-340), and for Kuna audiences thus to follow simultaneously both the story or narrative line and the line of quoted voices doing the telling and narration. A certain esthetic tension is created by the complexity of the intersection of line-framing devices, narrative line, and the use of quoted voices. (See chapter five for an example of extreme degrees of quotation and quotation within quotation.)

The central and organizing rhetorical-poetic device of Muristo's counsel is metaphor. Metaphors, which clearly have esthetic value, bear a most interesting and ambiguous relationship to rhetoric. For, as Parkin notes, tropes are used by speakers both to identify and to hide gaps and possibilities in their arguments. I turn now to Muristo's use of metaphor.

Metaphors and allusions
In order to understand Muristo's creative use of traditional Kuna metaphors, it is first important to elaborate on the Kuna concept of metaphor. When the Kuna use A metaphorically to represent B, it is just as true that B represents A. Thus not only is a chief like a tree, but a tree is like a chief. Furthermore, descriptions are to be taken both literally and metaphorically. When a chief chants or speaks about the physical structure of a Kuna house, he is commenting both on the house itself and on Kuna political organization. And, as he develops the metaphor in personal ways, he throws a new and often poetic light on his audience's understanding of house construction, political organization, and their interrelationship. When Muristo describes the *ikwa* tree and the *isper* tree and their various properties, he is not only talking about chiefs, he is also quite literally describing the Kuna forest, with which his audience is intimately familiar.

As metaphors are developed in detailed ways, there is not necessarily a point by point interpretation for every detail. In fact, as part of the artistry of Kuna speaking and chanting, metaphors can blend into description for description's sake and vice versa. Since animals were once people, and have souls like people, they are often called people and descriptions of them combine their human and their animal characteristics. Metaphors anthropomorphize nature and naturalize humans. But descriptions such as that of small birds and hummingbird people (line 180), the singing, whistling, and pecking of various birds in the mountains (lines 220, 225-229), and the shouting of the collared peccary, white-lipped peccary, sloth, monkey, and tapir people (lines 354-358) are not intended to represent necessarily and arbitrarily particular individuals or classes of individuals. They rather reflect and express Muristo's love of the Kuna ecology and his audience's appreciation of descriptions of it. The same is the case for the listing of plants that the Kuna grow and eat, such as corn and plantains (lines 216-219) and squash, taro, and yams (lines 299-301). Metaphors, like line and verse-framing devices, are ornamentation, an aspect of the poetic beauty of Kuna chanting and speaking. While Muristo's description of the birds, animals, and insects that come to eat the fruit of the *isper* and *ikwa* trees (lines 262-279, 282-284) broadly represents the community being nourished by their chiefs, there is not necessarily an interpretation for each detail in the description, such as the butterflies, the *ukkur* birds, or the deer in particular. At the same time, there are general relations and similarities between certain animals and certain people and no doubt part of the pleasure Kuna audiences get from performances is the imaginative associations they can make in their own minds as they listen to creative uses of metaphors, such as Muristo's in this speech.

It is quite typical for there to be not one but many metaphors for the same thing. In this speech a chief is represented by steering a boat, hanging or lying in a hammock, brothers-in-law, various animals, the central pole of a house, and trees in the nearby jungle. These different metaphors and sets of metaphors for chief are not isomorphic repetitions. Rather, they intersect, relate to, and comment on one another. Kuna metaphors for chief and other political leaders are powerful and beautiful precisely because they are complex and intertwining. (See Howe 1986: 64.)

Kuna figurative vocabulary is not, then, a static set of lexical replacements. Quite the contrary. It constitutes an active system of semantic relationships. This situation enables a speaker to relate, compare, manipulate, and interpret metaphors in his own way for his audience. This is precisely what Muristo does. In addition, Muristo develops metaphors into narratives, building stories which, especially since they are pages out of everyday Kuna life, make the metaphors come alive most vividly and concretely. Let us now examine more closely the metaphors Muristo uses and see what he does with them.

A dominant, repeated metaphor in Muristo's speech concerns poles and trees. Of the various poles used in the construction of a Kuna house, one is the most central, the largest, the strongest, and the most supporting. This is true as well in the gathering house which, while much larger, is built on the model of all traditional Kuna houses. Just as the central pole supports the house, the chief, from his position in the center of the gathering house, right next to the central pole, supports his village. It is this central pole that Muristo says (in line 42) "we are raising," "we are planting." For the pole must be raised up and planted in the ground. Muristo develops this conventional Kuna metaphor, central house pole = chief, by discussing the kind of tree that might be used for the pole. He asks the hunters who go far into the jungle, where the trees are oldest, biggest, and strongest, to look for an *ina kale* tree and if they find one to come and tell him. The *ina kale* tree is a very strong tree which if often used for a house pole. He asks the medicinal specialists, who also often go far into the jungle, to tell him if they see a *sapkwa sis* tree. The *sapkwa sis* tree is very strong and lasts a long time. Muristo notes that after the selection of the proper tree, the tree must be carefully inspected and cleaned. For if it starts to rot, it must be removed and replaced with another, just as bad chiefs must be removed and replaced with others.

Muristo thus combines one metaphor, that of house pole representing chief, with another metaphor, trees representing chief. There are various trees that Muristo selects to discuss, each with its own qualities. In addition to the *ina kale* tree, known for its strength, and the *sapkwa sis* tree, known for both its strength and longevity, Muristo compares and contrasts the *ikwa* tree and the *isper* tree. Each has its strengths and its weaknesses. The *ikwa* tree is a hard, strong, long-lasting tree. However, its fruit is difficult to obtain and its bark is hard. It is therefore difficult to use. The *isper* tree is not as hard as the *ikwa*. Its fruit is easier to obtain, its wood is softer. Muristo prefers the generous *isper* tree to the stingy *ikwa* tree; an open, sharing, democratic chief to a closed, autocratic chief. He wants his brother to be an *isper* tree.

Muristo relates the tree metaphor to another metaphor created out of the Kuna ecology, that of animals, again in various ways. The animals that come and partake of the fruit of the *isper* tree, the butterflies, the deer, the *ukkur* and *suir* birds, are the common, ordinary people of the village, including especially women and children. The animals that constitute the restricted set that the stingy *ikwa* tree feeds, the white-lipped peccary, the tapir, and the squirrel, are the important people of the village, the gathering-house officials, the chiefs, chiefs' spokesmen, and owners of sticks (policemen), and the medicinal, curing, and other ritual specialists.

Animal metaphors are related to tree and pole metaphors in another way. If a pole is not good, if it becomes rotten, then it attracts animals and bugs of various kinds who make it even more rotten. The rotten pole is a bad chief. But the animals themselves, the *usis* bug, the spider, the cockroach, and the scorpion, chanting inside, are also bad chiefs. Other aspects of Muristo's description render the metaphorical possibilities even more complex. The chanting animals are in the *-nai* position, that used for chiefs chanting in their hammock. Furthermore *tior* (scorpion) is called *tatakwa* (grandfather). Five metaphors are combined here – a chief is a tree, a chief is an animal, a chief is a kinsman, a chief is a chanter, and a chief is in the *-nai* (hanging) position. It is this kind of intricate mosaic of signification that characterizes Muristo's structuring of metaphors into a delicate yet complex text.

A completely different metaphor Muristo uses to represent chiefs is that of steering a boat. As in the case of the tree and animal metaphors, Muristo develops the boat metaphor into a short narrative (lines 113-116). The captain of a boat is like a chief, trying to keep the boat moving along, always in danger of bumping into something. A boat is a conventional Kuna metaphor for hammock which in turn represents the role of chief. Muristo thus relates boats, hammocks, and chiefs in his various narratives.

The hammock metaphor brings us back again to the use of the verbal positional suffixes as metaphors. For two of the suffixes, *-mai* (lying) and *-nai* (hanging) refer to positions in the hammock, and, by association, to the positions chiefs take in their hammocks in the center of the gathering house. The positionals, which all by themselves can be metaphors – *-mai, -nai* (chiefs); *-kwici* (chiefs, chiefs' spokesmen); *-sii* (chiefs' spokesmen, ritual leaders, ordinary villagers) – are furthermore associated with and sharpen other metaphors.[1] When trees are *-kwici* (standing), they are like chiefs or spokesmen speaking; when they are *-sii* (sitting), they are like village leaders sitting on benches in the center of the gathering house. When animals are *-nai* (hanging), they are like chiefs chanting in their hammocks. Once again we see the possibilities for connecting, combining, and intersecting metaphors, actualized in this speech in the complex ways Muristo structures his text.

---

[1]   Notice the overlaps in metaphorical representation – *-mai* and *-nai* both represent chief; *-kwici* represents both chief and spokesmen; etc. This kind of overlap is characteristic of Kuna metaphors in general and Muristo's use of them in particular. See chapter eight for a different and magical use of the verbal positional suffixes.

Along with conventional, traditional Kuna metaphors which he molds, adapts, and develops into narratives, Muristo intersperses in his speech a series of personal narratives which, like the metaphors, are to be taken both as literal descriptions and as allusive commentary on the nature of political leadership. One of these personal narratives, which is picked up at several points in the speech, describes Muristo and his brother as little babies, delicate, fragile, but growing, and always cared for by their mother (lines 199-211). Similarly chiefs, as is reiterated throughout Muristo's speech, both literally and metaphorically, are fragile. They can be strong or weak, good or bad, and they must be inspected and protected even as they protect others.

Just as Muristo combines and relates metaphors, he combines and relates allusive narratives and anecdotes. In fact his speech is a web of intersecting metaphors and allusions. The description of babies growing up is combined with the boat metaphor (line 204) which in turn itself represents the hammock metaphor. A description of babies at the end of the speech leads into a commentary on changing customs and the loss of traditions. This in turn is related to the use of native trees and plants, which all through the speech have represented chiefs and chieftainship.

While the study of metaphor clearly takes us into both rhetoric and literary criticism, it has also figured prominently in cultural anthropology, in particular in the work of those scholars who view symbols as central to the definition of culture. There are various ways that symbols in general and metaphors in particular have been approached by anthropologists. Each of these approaches can be related to Muristo's speech and my interpretation of it.

Especially in approaches to symbols influenced by such psychologists as Freud and Jung, attention is paid to universal symbols, symbols which are found in many, if not all societies in the world. (See Langer 1942, Jung 1964.) One good example of such symbols is the metaphorical use of basic areas of vocabulary, such as body parts and color terms. The use of the head to represent a leader or chief is quite common around the world. The Kuna word for chief, *sayla*, in fact, is also the word for head. The Kuna also use a body part to represent the chief's spokesman, in this case *arkar*, which means rib. While color is commonly used metaphorically in societies around the world (see Turner 1966), the Kuna do not tend to use color terms figuratively in verbal discourse, though color is basic to the primary Kuna visual form of esthetic expression, the women's molas. (See Sherzer and Sherzer 1976.) In Muristo's speech, the one figurative use of color is the description of the black cloth he wears over his eyes (line 107) to represent his inability to see his own behavior and recognize his own faults. In fact, color is not prominent in the speech, metaphorically or otherwise.

Another approach to metaphors and cultural symbols more generally focuses on particular cultures and often elaborate and esoteric symbolism known only to ritual specialists and to be decoded like a puzzle by a researcher. (See Douglas 1970, Turner 1967.) Symbolic anthropologists extract major symbols from ritual and narrative contexts and weave their own discourse around them. They tend to deal with the domain of religion where symbols are most esoteric and secretive and to make claims to have entered unconscious realms. A research methodology is implied by a concern with such esoteric symbolism, namely apprenticeship to the ritual specialist whose view of the culture in question comes to take a central place in the anthropologist's representation of that culture to the wider world. Many anthropologists view symbols, whether of the more universal and general or the more particular and esoteric type, as reflections of social organization. (See Douglas 1975.) This stance is particularly characteristic of British social anthropologists who also view other forms of expressive and esthetic behavior that I have been examining here, such as play and humor, in terms of a reflection of social organization. (See chapter seven.)

My thinking has also been influenced by Clifford Geertz's interpretive anthropology (Geertz 1973). Interpretive anthropologists are more likely than symbolic anthropologists to pay attention to the connectedness that symbols already have, through various contexts which they examine. They tend to be interested in politics, where symbols are quite public. The concept of text is largely a metaphor for Geertz and other interpretive anthropologists,[2] whereas I have made specific Kuna texts, the overt representation of Kuna discourse, the focus of every chapter in this book. But my approach to texts shares Geertz's goal of arriving at a thick description, which peels away bit by bit and layer by layer the complex and overlapping meanings expressed in culturally symbolic behavior and pays attention to circumstantial aspects of social and cultural life, focusing on small matters and moments which often seem unimportant to anthropologists used to studying more traditional, broader areas, such as social organization and economic structures.

[2]   Geertz (1960) is a notable exception.

Still another approach to metaphor and figurative language more generally, and one which is close in theory and method to my perspective in this book, is concerned with the social and rhetorical functions of literary forms, such as proverbs and myths. This approach, which has been influenced by the writings of Kenneth Burke, is well represented in a book whose title encapsulates its viewpoint – *The Social Use of Metaphor: Essays on the Anthropology of Rhetoric* (Sapir and Crocker 1977).

Thus while incorporating to some degree the various approaches to metaphor I have discussed here, the discourse-centered approach I take to Muristo's speech highlights the ways in which Kuna metaphors are created and recreated, actualized and developed, and expressed and explained in a particular moment of Kuna verbal life. The metaphors in Muristo's text constitute an enactment of the role of metaphor in Kuna social and cultural life. As distinct from the esoteric metaphors employed by curing and magical specialists (see chapter eight), the metaphors for chief are understood by the large audience present during Muristo's speech, which greatly appreciated the artistry of Muristo's weaving the metaphors together in his own unique and creative way.

Of particular relevance to my discussion here is recent work in political anthropology in which rhetorical and poetic aspects of political discourse have become a central concern. (See Bloch 1975, Brenneis and Myers 1984, Paine 1981, Parkin 1984, and, especially, Howe 1986, which is about the Kuna.) It has been observed that societies which profess egalitarian ideologies, coupled with a desire to avoid confrontation, particularly in two distinct parts of the world in which such matters have been carefully studied, lowland South America and the Pacific, have a tendency to channel and express conflicts and competition into artistic and often indirect and allusive speech. Metaphor and other forms of figurative language have attracted considerable attention in this regard. Kuna discourse, as it is represented in all of the chapters of this book and in particular Muristo's speech which is presented and discussed here, clearly fit this pattern. The political discourse of the societies reported on in Brenneis and Myers, together with that of the Kuna, clearly runs counter to Bloch's (1975) claim that the language of political ritual and oratory in traditional societies is always restricted and rigid in form. Muristo's speech demonstrates how creative, adaptable, flexible, and emergent political oratory can be, particularly in societies, such as the Kuna, with an egalitarian ethic.

More generally and again of relevance to Muristo's speech, there is increasing recognition among anthropologists that traditional societies can no longer be viewed as isolated static wholes which replicate themselves generation after generation. Rather, all societies, including traditional ones, are characterized by conflicts, tensions, contradictions, and changes which derive from both internal and external pressures. External pressures, the result of a wider and wider reaching world economic and political system, impinge more and more on the lives of all peoples, everywhere in the world. (See Moore 1987, Sahlins 1981, 1985, Wolf 1982.) In all of this discourse is central, as the emergent and emerging place and space of, the expression of, and the working out of constantly changing metaphors and interpretations of metaphors which so often represent tradition as well as adaptation, the idyllic view societies have of themselves as well as the conflicts and tensions which are always a part of their lives.

Of the various contradictions inherent in Kuna life (see Howe 1986: 254-257 and Sherzer 1983: 65-71 and 229-234) the ones most explicitly and dramatically expressed in Muristo's speech are Kuna society as egalitarian vs. Kuna society as hierarchical, Kuna society as harmonious and Kuna individuals as cooperative vs. Kuna society as conflictual and Kuna individuals as backbiting and selfish, Kuna society as idyllically continuing its traditions vs. Kuna society as continually prey to the unfortunate influences of the outside world, chiefs as generous vs. chiefs as stingy, and chiefs as models of appropriate and moral behavior vs. chiefs as inevitably prone to wrongdoing. And finally, the entire speech can be seen as an expression of the contradiction and contrast between the allusive world of artistic metaphor and the actual world of concrete everyday reality and behavior.

The Kuna gathering house is a place where chiefs and other village leaders publicly perform verbal traditions and discuss current events at great length. It is a political place, a social place, and a religious place. It is the place where the Kuna art of oratory is most centrally and publicly on display. Kuna speechmaking is a highly creative and highly adaptive process. The many metaphors which are available to speakers for use in gathering-house discourse enable them to finely tune their speeches and chants in accordance with affairs of the moment and their own positions concerning them. Since metaphors can be developed and interpreted in different ways and new ones can be created, speakers can use them both to clarify their points of view and to be ambiguous when necessary.

Muristo's speech is an excellent example of the use of metaphors in the Kuna gathering house. The metaphors Muristo uses, like the narratives he constructs, are resources, part of the overall structuring of his speech. And as the metaphors and narratives combine with one another, comment on one another, intersect, overlap, and chase each other like a musical fugue, Muristo not only counsels his brother, the new chief; he also counsels his audience, by reminding and instructing its members about Kuna traditions and publicly worrying about changes in these traditions in the contexts of influences from the wider world. And he gains renown as a public speaker. Muristo is the kind of chief he counsels his brother to be. The text of his speech, while illustrating and embodying Kuna political discourse, is also a masterpiece of verbal art.

The text

The basic unit of Muristo's speech is the line, determined in my representation by a combination of falling pitch and long following pause. Lines begin flush left and end in a period. They are numbered consecutively. Short interlinear pauses are indicated with a comma. Long pauses without falling pitch are represented as spaces within lines. Line structure is usually reinforced, though sometimes contrapuntally contradicted, by the extensive use of line-framing words and phrases such as *emite*, *tayleku*, *teki*, *teysokku*, *takken*, *takken soke*, and *pittosursin*, as well as a certain degree of grammatical and semantic parallelism. Muristo is quite adept at dramatizing his voice, speaking slower, faster, louder, and softer for oral effects. Slowing of tempo is indicated by stretching out of letters and words. Faster tempo is indicated by a dotted underline under the words which are spoken faster. Loud speech is indicated in capital letters. When a whole line is higher in pitch, ^ is placed before the line. When part of a line is higher in pitch, this is indicated by raising the words of higher pitch. Three conventional Kuna expressive performance devices which Muristo employs frequently are lengthening of vowels and consonants (indicated in both Kuna and English by doubling the letter which represents the sound in question), stretched-out speech (indicated by dashes between syllables), and vibrating the voice (indicated by dashes between letters).

The translation is relatively literal, though accessible to an English audience. The line-framing words and phrases are always translated into English, using appropriate equivalents – now, well, thus, indeed, certainly, therefore, it is said, etc. It is impossible to completely translate the complicated Kuna system of verbal aspect, but I have attempted to do so to the degree that meaningful translation into English permits. In particular, the Kuna verbal suffixes of position – *-mai* (lying), *-nai* (hanging), *-kwici* (standing), *-sii* (sitting) – crucial to an understanding of the text, are included in the translation whenever feasible. Quotation marks are used, in both the Kuna and the English versions, to indicate the quite common Kuna device of embedding and dramatizing the voices of others within one's own speech. Words and phrases whose reference or significance are not obvious or understandable for those not familiar with the Kuna system of meanings are explained within brackets or in notes.

kwici peka sao.

nail akku sunmayle an ittotaet.

teyta.

emite   anmar nase kocato a.

ukkurwal ikar wisit   noni takken soke a.   5

kapul ikar wisit   noni takken soke.

sia ikar wisit, takken soke.

sappurpa taylekuti, yer makkemalat.

sappur nanamalat.

nase kocamar takken soke.   10

arkarkana tayleku nase koca takkenta.

saylakan takken soke.

tule mir makket takken soke.

nase upononimar takkenta.

punmar nonimo takken soke.   15

iet noni takken soke.

nako pakket noni takken soke.

mor makket noni takken soke.

mor sikket noni takken soke.

we tayleku nekkwepur tayleku Mulatup siit.   20

yer an tula merkupuymala.

ittole takkenta.

emi tayleku an kwicit, Mulatup tola.

Mulatup tor kanki anmar pukkwa.

tule pait anka ney seosurmala.   25

tule pait Mulatup nek kannokosuli.

anmar tukkin tayleku nekkwepur kannoerkepe.

"Mulatup nekkwepur kannoerkepye," soylema takkenta.

"emite tayleku teki nase kocamalal ittolesokkua."

naka soysamar takken soke.   30

tule sappur yer makket tayleku pannapa pe naoe, ipi war mai pe taytao? ina kale war

nuet mai appakkar pe takko sua anka soynonikkoe.

kil ina tulet tayleku pannapaisar tayleku ti tuypa tayleku arpakwici.

"sapkwa sis war mai taytakotipa.

I'll do it for you in a standing position.
I find speaking from the hammock unpleasant.
So.
Now   we have been called together ah.
The knowers of *The way of the balsa wood*   have come see it is said ah.   5
The knowers of *The way of the hot pepper*   have come see it is said.
The knowers of *The way of cacao* see it is said.
Those who in the jungle indeed, hunt well.
Those who go about in the jungle.
They have been called together see it is said.   10
The chiefs' spokesmen indeed have been called together see.
The chiefs see it is said.
The people who kill tarpon see it is said.
They have entered together see.
The sisters have come too see it is said.   15
The haircutters have come see it is said.
The leg crossers have come see it is said
Those who sew molas have come see it is said.
Those who cut molas have come see it is said.
This indeed is the village indeed of Mulatuppu.   20
Well we are the inhabitants.
Listen see.
Now indeed I am standing, a Mulatuppu person.
We are the Mulatuppu people seated in our benches.
Another person will not govern us.   25
Another person will not care for Mulatuppu.
We ourselves indeed must care for our village.
"Must care for the village of Mulatuppu," it is said see.
"Now indeed then this is why we have been called together listen it is said."
We said to ourselves see it is said.   30
You people who hunt well in the jungle indeed if you go far, what tree might you
see there? if perhaps you suddenly see a good *ina kale* tree there come tell me.
If Uncle medicine man indeed is working far away indeed at the source of the river.
"If he happens to see a *sapkwa sis* tree there.

soynonikkoye," soylemekis takken soke.

tayleku teki tayleku nase kocamala kilu purwal ikar wisit.   35

anpa se kocamoka.

pannapaisal ina amiet, tampomalat amiet.

acu inamal amiet.

ti ispemal amiet.

"a suar warkwen nuet mai, takkalir tayleku suurmakkoye," soyles takken soke.   40

emite taylekuti, anna suurmaysamar takken soke a.

emiski pulakwa onaymar tiymarsunye, anna se kormar takken soysunto.

iki tayleku an tiymalotipaye? pinsale pittosursin.

kirmarye tayleku pe ani pukkwa ina wisit pukkwat.

suar ipkanye tayleku pe ani pukkwa.   45

arkarkan pukkwa.

saylakan mamanae.

pule tayleku ina kale war tayleku nueti?

pina maraletsuli?

an amismartipane?   50

pule tayleku wala swilitikki tayleku simur kwen sisuli?

an surmaysamartipane?

akkusa tayleku nainu tikkaliki taylekuti, suar war kwicit an surmasmar sokele.

pirkakwen unnila nao suumakkwici tayletakoe.

kannal unke tayletako takken soke.   55

kannar kannar anpesukan oarpatii.

sakkamar oarpati, anmar kutakerye.

nuekkwa tayleku pannapaisar nainu serkanki tayleku anmar surmaysa taylekua.

kwa sunnapi tayleku simur kwen niysuli.

pina maraletsuli.   60

Come say it," it is said see it is said.

Indeed then indeed the uncles who know *The way of the wind* have been called together.   35

They have also been called together.

Those who go far to get medicine, those who get cooling off medicine.

Those who get dog medicine.

Those who get mirrors.[3]

"If they see a good tree there, indeed they should clean it," it was said see it is said.   40

Now indeed, we ourselves cleaned it see it is said ah.

Now together we are raising it we are planting it, for this we have been called together see it is said.

How indeed might we plant it? we don't know don't you hear.

Uncles indeed I have many medicine knowers among you.

I have many indeed owners of sticks.[4]   45

There are many chiefs' spokesmen.

There are many chiefs lying here in their hammocks.

How good indeed is indeed the *ina kale* tree?

Has its core not been split?

How might the one we got be?   50

How smooth indeed is the pole indeed does it have knots?

Were we able to clean it well?

Is this tree indeed standing on a nearby farm a good one indeed, did we clean it well it is said?

Sometimes it lasts only one year and rots standing see.

It has to be removed again see it is said.   55

This makes the brothers-in-law work again and again.

This makes the parents-in-law work, let us hope that this does not happen to us.

Let us hope indeed that we went far enough away in an old farm indeed and we cleaned a good one indeed.

Very hard wood indeed that doesn't have knots.

Whose core has not been split.   60

---

3   medicine found in rivers
4   Kuna policemen

anmar tikerti tayleku pirkapaar saale.
tiylekwici, kuto takken soke.
ipika tek an pey soy takken soke?
emi tayleku anmar san nanaet anna wiculi.
pap tummatti nipa tule tule tummat mai.   65
api warkwennakwa purpa nuet tuleka ukket mai.
pap purpaparpi tayleku anmar nanatii, oippotako pap purpa naoe.
an wetar taytakoe, pap purpaparpi immal anse opallekwici.
yauy per tekii.
"anmar pap nukkinpi, mas ittopuy" takken an soke.   70
tule pait nukkinsur takken.
niptorpa tayleku oloya nekki mai.
an taymai.
an iemasuli.
weki anka napney mettenanmala.   75
ku takken soke.
emite taylekuti, an kwenat takken an soke.
paitsur pe ittosursinta.
tiwar panna pannat tayleku punmar nonimoka.
emit an ittosii.   80
anki pinsasun takken "e kwenat soke" takken soke.
pap kala kwenat pittosursinta.
nan kala kwenat takken soke.
taylekuti nan nu tukku pina tayleku, kalakwen posatti.
emite aparse tayleku tiylesokkar takken soke.   85
em an kwicit tiyles kwicimo takkenta.
kirmar apar, kirmar nukkin pe ittosursinta.
iki an nanatii an nanaet?
an oyotii?
anna wicur pittosursin.   90
ye an ome pipo, ye an ome sarsoe.
sappurpa nat soker tayleku ome pipotii.

If we plant this one indeed it will last for years.

Standing planted, that is how it will do see it is said.

Why then do I tell you this see it is said?

Now indeed we do not know our own behavior.

And great Father above the person the great person who is there.   65

He alone gives a good soul to the Kuna people.

Following Father's soul only indeed we go about, when we wake up we go along Father's soul.

If we come to see collared peccary, it is by Father's soul only that such things are given to us.

All the sea turtles then.

In Father's name only, we taste food see I say.   70

In no one else's name see.

Up above indeed is a golden place.

He sees us.

He does not forget us.

He left us this world as he departed.   75

That is how it is see it is said.

Now indeed, my brother see I say.

He is not another don't you hear.

From distant rivers indeed sisters also came.

Now he is sitting listening to me.   80

He is thinking about me see "he is my brother" he says see it is said.

We are brothers with the same father don't you hear.

We are brothers with the same mother see it is said.

Indeed we cried as one indeed, at the tip of our mother's breast.

Now he is about to be planted indeed in the middle see it is said.   85

Now I am standing I too was planted standing here see.

Among the uncles, in the name of the uncles don't you hear.

How have I gone about have I behaved?

Have I set an example?

I myself do not know don't you hear.   90

If I hit my wife, if I struck my wife.

If I hit my wife it is said indeed in the jungle.

kannar kannar ome mettii.

ome ipe nek eyarmatpaloe.

kannar na ome mosar ney sopnai.   95

an ilapikwa kuetki, an saylaka kustipata?

kek kusar taylekuti niymarye tayleku kirmarye, pe anki pinsa takken soke?

"sayla peece tayleku itti notii.

saylaka kus" takken soke.

"saylaka kusatki tayleku kep wis nukusye."   100

teki tayleku macikwa tunkuarku tayleku tek an nanatisulile.

sun soylepar takken soke.

"itti sayla tayleku toitara   ome mitii.

ome mettii, an taysasurye."

pemar pinsa pittosursin.   105

anti an akku itto takkenta.

anti tukkin tayleku na tukkinni tayleku mor sicit nasiyti pe ittosursinta.

tulati an taypukkwat pelakwaplemakkar neymakapa an taypuy takken soke.

apa emite tayleku kwenatka tayleku kakkakwen immar wis pikwicunna.

anti pat itu kwicisokku.   110

immarti sokoye, soke takketpa   kirmar pe anse koca takken soke.

emi tayleku kal ikar uylesokkalitki tayleku karta tummmati ka kusokkar takken soke.

em pe takkena ulu tummat na takken an soke.

akku anmar attay takkenta.

wesik anpa natpar takken, wesik anpa wesik anpapar takken.   115

akku an attaysokku solaki kwicikuosokkua, kaptanka kwiskus

sokele   ni warkwen nate pirkakwen nate ur kasi yotii.

kuter wileko takken soke.

kannar tayleku unkenai.

If again and again I would abandon my wife.

If I destroyed my wife's house.

So that when I got back to my wife I had to rebuild the house. 95

How many times have I become, have I become chief?

It was not that way indeed Nephews indeed Uncles, what do you think about me?

see it is said.

"This chief indeed used to break the rules badly.

When he became chief" see it is said.

"When he became chief indeed then he got a bit better." 100

Well indeed as a boy growing up indeed well I did not used to be like that.

Truly it can be said again see it is said.

"This chief indeed   never threw out his wife.

We never saw him, abandon his wife."

You think don't you hear. 105

And as for me I don't know see.

I myself indeed myself indeed wear a black cloth[5] don't you hear.

And all the inhabitants see us people from elsewhere also see us see it is said.

For this reason now indeed I am standing pronouncing indeed a few words to my
brother.

And since I already am standing before him. 110

The uncles called me, it is said see   in order to say these things see it is said.

Now indeed a way is about to be given to him indeed biiig news is about to occur
to him see it is said.

Now you see a big boat see I say.

We cannot make it out see.

There it goes still again see, there again there it goes still again see. 115

Since I cannot make things out as I stand at the stern, as I stood as captain it is
said   one month went by, one year went by and the keel of the boat would hit
something.

If this happens it will be a shame see it is said.

You are being removed indeed again.

5   over my eyes

wileto pe ittosursi.

noet key perkupar takken an soke.   120

noet perkuoye, itti yarki pinsasur takkenta.

noet yalapa kap pane pane kaptitiye.

noet anpa pippirmayti takkenta.

sappurpa taylekuti an naoe.

kammai oippos naoe.   125

ome waliy nai, ome an okopo pankutoe.

teki tayleku ipakwenki tayleku poni apinkuoe ittoleteye.

pinsasuli pankuto takken.

papti an taysapin takkenta.

poni apinkutappoye.   130

poni apinkus nonikkir tayleku, neyse nonikkoku tayleku, pe an nai poer takken

soke.

a yarki an pukkwamar takken soysunto.

ipakwen tayleku an pankutoe.

sappurpar kus sokele an mas suli an taytappi.

pap pulet anse kornonikkoe.   135

anki poni yolenonikko takken soke.

an miamaytako takken soke, emal amie.

kormaypali.

ponik kut pittosursin.

tule kwen taysulil an kirmar ipe mas suto tak, purpa icakkwa anki yoles takken

soke.   140

a napnekki an puymarye.

okopsik teki takken per teki unmakkecik per teki takkenta.

emi an sunmakkwis takkenta, an muttik tayleku nate kwake icakkwat taylekuti

papti purpa pulet anse oupos sokele.

pe an ittotako takken "emi muttik tayleku sayla sunmakkwis, unmayti oipocun"

takken soke.

It will be a shame don't you hear.

Bad conduct can have no end see I say. 120

In this world it cannot be thought, that bad conduct will end see.

Bad conduct sleeps beside us day after day it sleeps.

Bad conduct always circles around with us see.

When I go indeed to the jungle.

When I wake up from sleep I go. 125

My wife is close to me, my wife gives me my beverage and I depart.

Then indeed one day indeed we can encounter evil you hear.

We departed without thinking about it see.

But Father saw us already see.

If we are going to encounter evil there. 130

When you come back home you have encountered evil indeed, when you came back home indeed, you are gravely sick see it is said.

This is the world we are in see it is truly said.

One day indeed I depart.

If there in the jungle it is said I see my plantains are missing.

If the devil comes to call me. 135

If evil comes to enter into me see it is said.

I look all around see it is said, to find someone.

And I shout.

I become like an evil spirit don't you hear.

If I see no one I take the uncles' plantains see, a bad soul entered into me see it is said. 140

This is the world we are in.

All the coconuts then see and then molesting women then see.

Now I am standing talking see, if I left indeed one night and Father caused a bad heart indeed a strong soul to enter into me it is said.

You will hear[6] see "now last night indeed the chief was standing talking, but he awoke molesting a woman" see it is said.

---

6   people say

panetse anka soylenonikko, takkeki maleko pitto, an nosatpar takken soke.   145

a yarki tayleku kwici ittolesokkua.

pittikki tayleku ise tar purtiar ante kamaytisun takkenta.

itti pap ikarki arpaet.

nopet tummat takken an soke.

nopet pippisurta.   150

pela taylekuti mullukampa tayleku.

tule saylakan mamait, walakan mamait, tayleku pel ipya kwinnitik.

tula an taysi takken.

punmar per teki takken soke.

tuttu warkwen tayleku ney sicipa tayleku anpok appinni an nuy nikka anpoy

sunmakkwisir, pat anki arpis takken.   155

an icakkwakwat pat.

an okkakkansa takken soke.

kwenatye taylekuti a ikarse emite anna nakkwis an nasokkarmala.

ase pe ani noni takken.

pittikki tayleku emite an teun karmaytimoka.   160

na san purpa kwake purkwarsurye an soy takkenye.

an kwake tula naye.

we yala tayleku papa tayleku yala pap tummat yala tar mettet kwake purkwarsuli

we yalaki taylekuti.

papti an epesnatmar takken.

ipi kakka sulimalat tayle ipi tar kwapin sulimalat pelatar kwaketi tula nanana

takken soke.   165

Next day they will come to talk to me, they will punish me with stinging nettles[7]

do you hear, for my bad conduct see it is said.   145

Since I am standing[8] indeed in this world.

I hope indeed that I go about with my breath held well[9] see.

This is working on Father's path.

There is big jealousy see I say.

There is enormous jealousy.   150

All indeed the round places[10] are like that indeed.

The chiefs who are lying here in hammocks, the poles who are lying here, indeed

all have their eyes alert.

The inhabitants are sitting looking at me see.

All the sisters then see it is said.

If they see me with a flower[11] indeed me a person with a name indeed talking one

dark night the two of us together, already they suspect me of bad behavior see.   155

This is already my bad behavior.

They tell lies about me see it is said.

Brother indeed this is the path now we have now climbed and we are about to go

along together.

You have arrived to the same place as me see.

I hope indeed now that I also go about well.   160

My body's soul has a heart that is not dead I say see.

My heart is alive.

This world Father indeed the great Father indeed left us this world he left us this

world and there are hearts that have not died in this world indeed.

And Father gave us this as he departed see.

Animals that do not have mouths[12] see animals that do not have tongues[13] all go

about with live hearts see it is said.   165

---

7   traditional Kuna punishment
8   governing
9   without giving in to temptation
10 islands
11 woman
12 cannot speak
13 cannot speak

sicir purwikana pe takke taylekuti kwake kwen nai kwen taylesur takkena.
nuskanapi pukkitar takkenta.
pap yar mettenat pittosursin.
yar pentaymalat kar takken soke.
tior per teki takken.   170
immar nunkumai, pe takke tayleku, suar icakkwasaar tayleku nunkumai.
pe yokasaar tayleku arkanki pe eputele.
e ipet ma takken soke e arsoket.
tior yappa mai takkenna.
pe apinsao takke siok, kace pe palacao, e nekka na sama takken.   175
anmar pule pitto tule mamatar tayleku, pukkwat.
per ipet nikkatsunnapi an puymar takken.
we yarkin pe ittosursin.
pe takke tayleku immar tayleku tey natet.
sikkwi purwikana nasaku tayleku pela tayleku pansus tulakan nasa tule pippi pe
takke kwakepi tula takken soke.   180
anmar pule sunye.
pap soysa tayle "itti yalaki macikwaye an pe urpemalat.
kwake tula a maci an pe nasikke.
yar nasokeka tiwal akkweka.
palu matta akkweka.   185
wetar akkweka, yauy tulakan ampikkusat, a akkweka.
kiar macikwa weki akkweti pe anka sao.
korpietpa na pese kolo nipa pe nakkwito.
pe itu neka nuet an sitappali.
arkanki arpaet perkuto."   190
papti tayleku anka ikar mettenatmalat.
e nappaki an kwicimar takken soke.
a napnekki tunkutani pittosursin.
teysokku "itti nappa nek siit, mer na saoye," kwen soylesur takken.
an tula peka soy pittosursin.   195
sappi walakwen tayleku tiylesokkalit nukki, an peka soy takken.
punmar ittopuymo takken soke.

Baby ants you see indeed whose hearts cannot be seen see.

Many tiny little animals see.

Father left the world as he departed don't you hear.

We are the ones who protect the world for him see it is said.

All the scorpions then see.　　　　　　　　　　　　170

You see, something is rotting indeed, a bad pole indeed is rotting.

From the moment indeed you touch it with your hand.

Its owner is there see it is said its defender.

The scorpion is there inside see.

It bites you back see, and you won't bother it again, for it is his house see.　　175

We humans you hear are even more like this indeed, we are.

We all have only one owner see.

In this world don't you hear.

You see indeed animals indeed well are this way.

All small birds indeed all indeed the hummingbird people you see them like

small persons but they have live hearts see it is said.　　　180

We are even more truly so.

Father said indeed "children I leave you in this world.

I hang a live heart on you children.

In order to multiply the world in order to care for the rivers.

In order to care for the sea.　　　　　　　　　　185

In order to care for collared peccaries, in order to care for the sea turtle people,

who remained.

For a short while children you will be caretakers here for me.

When I want to call you I will call you and you will go up.

I made a good house for you there also.

There it is no longer necessary to work with our hands."　　　190

And Father indeed left us this path as he departed.

We are standing on his earth see it is said.

We are growing up in this world don't you hear.

Therefore "we cannot reject, this world so well in place," it is said see.

I tell you in person don't you hear.　　　　　　195

In the name of the tree indeed about to be planted, I tell you see.

The sisters are listening too see it is said.

Mulatup tule an puymalat we yarki tayleku pippikwa an tunkuali.

anpa kek an nanae.

nappaki kep sikwiar nan yel an takke.   200

an aylatpaloe nan tayleku anka nappa nukkumayte.

mel aylaekala, kwae an oturtayye, soy pe ittosursin.

ayop tayleku an kwenatte unalesisun takken soke.

appakkar nappa uryapa sikwisaki, apkayala aylatikutakerye.

an itu mol aipiriarparsun takken soke.   205

aylater mer wakar attarekarye.

nan an sapetpar takken soke.

nappaki tayleku an akkutoe.

an winnatpaloe.

an ekka tayleku an winatsokku an winsus imatakke kwen pinsale ekka wakarki

make make takken.   210

ney wicursi takken soke.

a napnekki taylek emi an tunkutanimalat, iki tekitte kir, niymarye napneyti an

mesar samarso? "an napney sulit," kek an soymarsun takken soke.

itti nan tummat mait taylekua.

ima kwen an taymasuli.

pela yar tula nai pe takke yar tula nai kupinne.   215

emi opa kwakwa anmal oupos.

mas oupos.

op patto pel aratik takkenta.

nan tula napnek mette pittosursin takken soke.

sikkwi tulakan per namayte tayleku yalinpapa sikkwi tulakan wikote.   220

pel ipet nikkatpi takkenna.

yo tayleku tule tayleku olo tule tani soker tayle sappurpa natap.

ney yakkirmakkal ittoker kuosuli pap takkekwapa.

sikkwi tulakan urpit takkenta.

kikka sitap pittosursin.   225

We are Mulatuppu people we grew up indeed from little ones in this world.

When I was still not able to walk.

When I began to sit up on the ground then my mother treated me well. 200

When I fell again my mother indeed made a place for me on the ground.

She taught me quickly, so that I wouldn't fall, it is said don't you hear.

In this same way indeed my brother sitting here being counseled see it is said.

So that once he is seated in the boat, he does not immediately fall.

She put cloth around my body see it is said. 205

So that when I fell I would not scratch my face.

Because of my mother's love for me see it is said.

When I defecated indeed on the ground.

When I urinated.

I myself indeed when I finished urinating I did not think that my urine was rotten

and I painted my face all over with it see. 210

I was not conscious of what I did see it is said.

In this world indeed that we are growing up in, well how Uncles, Nephews can

we reject this world? we cannot say, "this is not our world" see it is said.

The great Mother who is there indeed.

She does not treat us as rotten objects.

This whole world is alive you see the world exists alive. 215

Now we planted corn seeds.

We planted plantains.

The corn is already all green see.

Mother left this world alive don't you hear see it is said.

All the bird people sing indeed among the mountains the bird people whistle. 220

They all have only one owner[14] see.

Before indeed the Kuna people the golden Kuna people came it is said see so that

if you go to the jungle.

Father saw to it that the place would not sound quiet.

He left the bird people see.

He formed the messenger bird don't you hear. 225

[14]   God, called Father in this speech

siyli urpitap takken.
siylipi namayma takken.
sikkwipi wikoti takken.
sallipi aciyti takkenta.
pap ney mette takkenta.   230
yar tula soy takken.
aki tayleku emite an tanimala.
taylekuti suar warkwen taylekua.
anmar tikesokkarsun takken.
akkusa an tiysamartipata.   235
ollole simur sii, tayleku anmar tiysatipa soke.
pirkakwenki tayleku   usis tulakan taylee simuryapa namaynai pe ittoto
pittosursin.
akkwaser namaynai pe ittotappo.
iskwir namaynai pe ittotappo takken soke.
tior tayleku tior tatakwat namaynai.   240
e simuryapa pe ittotappo, takken soke.
punmar topkutako takken.
unke tayle tako pittosursin.
auna kirmar soy takken.
"suar wala nuet tayleku, tiyle swilitikkit simur kwen niysulit pina maralet kwen
niysulit.   245
tikoye.
auna apsomalat aparkine.
ina turkan aparkine, suurmakkakwale.
ise tar par takkakwale."
kirmarti taylekuna, suar war tiyte takken an soke.   250
emit aaki an puymar takken, ip nasokekar takken soke.
masmu nasokekarye.
sappi tulekan tayleku per tule isper wala per tule.
payla war tule.
ikwa walakan per tursi walakan per tula takken.   255
kwennakwa emarki opicat si takken soke.
isper wala kwiskunoni takken soke.

He placed the curassow see.

Only the curassows are singing see.

Only the birds go about whistling see.

Only the woodpeckers go about pecking see.

Father left the world see.   230

The world is alive it is said see.

We came indeed now to it.

Indeed one pole indeed.

We are about to plant see.

If we do not plant it well.   235

If we plant one, indeed that has hollow knot holes it is said.

Within one year indeed   you will hear the *usis* bug people see chanting within
the knot hole don't you hear.

You will hear the spider chanting there.

You will hear the cockroach chanting there see it is said.

The scorpion indeed Grandfather Scorpion will be chanting.   240

You will hear it there within the knot hole, see it is said.

The sisters will become afraid see.

It will become necessary see to remove it don't you hear.

For this reason the uncles say see.

"A good pole indeed, must be planted smooth without knot holes without splits.   245

Plant it.

For this reason among the mass curing specialists.

Among the medicine men, well cleaned.

Extremely carefully inspected."

That is how the uncles indeed, planted poles see I say.   250

Now we live here see, in order to multiply things see it is said.

In order to multiply plantain roots.

The trees are people indeed all the *isper* trees are people.

The *payla* tree is a person.

The *ikwa* trees are all alive all the trees are alive see.   255

One type wins out among all the equals see it is said.

It is the *isper* tree that stands out see it is said.

aka kwenatti kusokkar takken an soke.

an aka kwicimo takken.

an ai ai namo, pal an saylakan api takken.   260

arkal a simo takken.

pela tayleku isper tulakan sanamaytako yolaki sanamaytako per kortikkit tayle
sikokua.

sucu tulakan se pattemai tayle e nis kopemalat pirki oci kople takken.

we sayla teki takken soke.

tayle ukkur tulakan se upomai, tayleku koe tulakan se upomai.   265

ikwa kwicimo takken, ikwa we kwake istarat niy takken soke.

ikwa emarpi maskun takken, t-u-m-m-a-k-a-n-p-i.

aki kirmar tayleku, purpar soysun takken, "ap-pak-kar-pe-mar-tum-ma-kan-pi-
mas-ki-o-kun-ti-pe-ku-ta-ker-ye."

we ikwa tule tekiit takken.

em pe tay takkenta.   270

yannupi kun takkenta.

molipi kun takkenta.

ai kwinpi kuntimo takken.

koe kek kunne.

ukkur kek kunne.   275

suir kek kun takkenta.

satte.

e ukkapi wis mae, e ukka, pe wis ittotisun takken soke.

nalle pe ittosursinta.

tule pukkwa, saylaki tule karmaytiun, weyop tule nallekusat takken soke.   280

kirmal itu patte otukkutikusye.

isperti tekisur soke.

pela siyli tulakan ukkur tulakan taylekuti.

nupakkemar se upomai.

mimmi pulatik se upomai, e nis kopemalat.   285

we isper war kwici takken.

My brother is about to become this type see I say.

I too am this one see.

My friend in the hammock my friend, among our chiefs is also one see. 260

So is the chiefs' spokesman sitting there see.

All indeed the *isper* people when they produce fruit in the dry season when they produce fruit it is all ripe see.

The butterfly people land on it see they drink its juice and it tastes delicious and sweet see.

The chief is like that see it is said.

Indeed the *ukkur* bird people enter its place, indeed the deer people enter its place. 265

The *ikwa* is also standing see, the *ikwa* has a bad heart see it is said.

Only *ikwa's* equals eat see, o-n-l-y t-h-e i-m-p-o-r-t-a-n-t p-e-o-p-l-e.

For this reason the uncles indeed, say in secret see, "you-should-not-give-food-on-ly-to-the-im-por-tant-peo-ple-that-you-must-not-do."

This *ikwa* is that kind of a person see.

Now you look see. 270

Only the white-lipped peccary eats see.

Only the tapir eats see.

Only friend squirrel gets to eat too see.

The deer cannot eat.

The *ukkur* bird cannot eat. 275

The *suir* bird cannot eat see.

Nothing.

They can lick its bark only a little bit, they can go about tasting, its bark a little see it is said.

It is stingy don't you hear.

In the beginning when there were people, when people were going about for the first time, people were stingy like that see it is said. 280

They would hide plates from the uncles.

Isper is not this way it is said.

All the curassow people and the *ukkur* bird people indeed.

Every one of the *nupakke* birds enters its place.

All their children enter its place, they drink its juice. 285

That *isper* tree standing there see.

sokkwicun takkena, "to-a-an-po-kwa-pur-tay-le-ku-ti-tu-le-nu-et-ti-pa?" soke.

ikwa war sokkwis takken "ke-ke-tu-le-pai-an-sa" soke.

"keke tule an akkallo tule niyli an saecu e tulakwen e tulapo nai, anki nain, tule
kek anpa an ola" soke.

nappirakwa.   290

toa ikwa olatii?

pippi kwicil anpa pe po pe walattar nerkwa kep   pe parmetterkepe.

soy takkenta.

isper wartina sun warkwen olale takken soke.

pela immarka pinnit takkenna, wirwir karka pinnit takken.   295

niskaka pinnit takken.

orsarka pinnit takken soke.

pela immal ukakkase tayleku per pinyemai.

isper tummati aylat sokele moe kwakkwaki miletoe.

tarkwamarki tiyletoe.   300

wakupmarki tiyletoe.

maskunnet nuetka pinnoe ittole takkenye   na ikar tayleku tummakan ittonait,
tuleun kus takken soke.

en oyokwis takkenta isper.

ipi-yop-ma-le-ti-pa-ta.

m-i-m-m-i-k-a-n p-u-n-m-a-r-se p-a-k-k-a-r p-e-r m-a-e m-i-m-m-i-k-a-n p-a-t
p-i-p-p-i m-a-s-i t-a-k-k-e-n-t-a.   305

ikwa pe maroenye key pe maretteta.

aka tayleku sayla tayleku kwake naittir teyop taylekuti punmarye tayleku sayla
noni sokele.

namaytako teyop se pe upopukkwa.

napir ittole takken soke.

kwenti tayleku icakkwasaartae.   310

pe top takkenta.

Standing there it says see, "who-of-the-two-of-us-in-deed-might-be-a-bet-ter-per-son?" it says.

The *ikwa* tree stands there and says see "no-o-ther-per-son-can-out-do-me" it says.

"No person can alter me no person can make me budge up to 20 persons up to 40 persons, moving against me, still no one can knock me down" it says.

It is really true.   290

Who can knock down *ikwa*?

Even if it is small you still need two you need five or six people then   for you to push it over.

It is said see.

As for the *isper* tree it can be knocked down by a single person see it is said.

It is transformed into all things see, it is transformed into a mixing stick see.   295

It is transformed into a soup paddle see.

It is transformed into a pounding stick see it is said.

It is transformed indeed into all kinds of things.

When a big *isper* is felled it is said its place will be strewn with squash seeds.

It will be planted with taro.   300

It will be planted with yams.

It will transformed into good food you hear see   they[15] indeed used to listen to[16] traditions, they used to be like people see it is said.

Now *isper* see standing in place there.

What-a-good-taste!

A-l-l t-h-e c-h-i-l-d-r-e-n a-l-l t-h-e s-i-s-t-e-r-s c-a-n e-a-t i-t a-l-l l-i-t-t-l-e c-h-i-l-d-r-e-n e-a-t i-t s-e-e.   305

On the other hand if you want to split *ikwa* you are not able to split it.

For this reason indeed if the chief indeed has this kind of a heart indeed if Sisters indeed this kind of chief comes it is said.

If he chants like this and you enter his place.

It sounds good see it is said.

But indeed if he behaves badly.   310

You are afraid see.

---

[15] the trees
[16] compete with

"wete ipi sayla anka wis oparroe.

sayla notii."

sun soyle pittosursin.

auna tayleku soylesun takken saylakan taylekuti.   315

"pe nue nanae.

sayla insar nukuo, arkal insar nukuo, ina tulet insar nukuo.

sayla siskwa nukuoe.

sayla ome nukuoe."

soyle pe ittosursin takken soke.   320

sayla ome key nuku karmaytii.

kakkanpi wis karmaytii.

urwetpi wis kama nialet ulutpaloe.

sorta tayleku pe taytii.

"sayla siskwa kati urwemokat sayla e siskwati ipika kek kar soke?   325

sayla maci kati ome mimokat.

wekatti akku takke."

"nappira" pe soymarmoye.

auna tayleku nekki tayleku purwi purwi weki sunmaysitae nekki oipotako waitar

si soker.

aynepa sunmaytasur takken.   330

mimmimala warpo an nikka, maci warkwen an nikka.

macikwa siko an walik.

punamala siko warpo.

sunmayto okwicito takken na purwi purwi tayleku kirmal akkwepa "peka an nuy

wis nikkus maikus.

kirmal anse irmaytako, nue apin nok oyoti sao.   335

noy taylekuti.

'ollipi tayleku katepinne wesa kirmarka uyti kutaker weki suli.'

papa weki soysasuli.

"What will this chief interpret for us?

The chief breaks the rules."

Truly it is said don't you hear.

For this reason indeed it is truly said see the chiefs indeed [say].   315

"You must behave well.

The chief first must behave properly, the chief's spokesman first must behave properly, the medicine man first must behave properly.

The chief's daughter must behave properly.

The chief's wife must behave properly."

It is said don't you hear see it is said.   320

If the chief's wife does not behave properly.

If she only goes about lying.

If she only goes about angry and keeps arguing in bad language.

The townspeople indeed are observing you.

"The chief's daughter also gets angry a lot why doesn't the chief talk to his daughter?   325

The chief's son keeps abandoning his wife also.

He does not recognize his own."[17]

"It is true" you say also.

For this reason indeed I always speak indeed about these various topics in the house when I awake in the morning it is said.

I do not talk in any other way see.   330

I have two children, I have one boy.

The boy sits at my side.

The two girls sit together.

I speak see about various topics indeed about how to take care of the uncles "for you I had a name.

When the uncles come to my place, you must give them a cup.[18]   335

A cup indeed.

'You must not indeed carry the cups dirty to the uncles.'

Father did not say this.

[17] = his family's faults
[18] beverage

saylaki taylekuti Ipeorkun nonikku weki soysasuli 'tipur kalumar nue akko' soysa.

papa maci saylaki wey tule unas."   340

mimmikanka kakkwen soyti takken.

"akku pe an ittoet   noar takkenye.

papa peka sokkwis pappa immar sao ma takken."

soytisun takken soke.

aka tayleku emite tayleku suar wala tayleku wis tike soymarsokkua.   345

na yalapa nanatakoe.

emi tayleku waysik tayleku an nuk nikkusmoka.

an kwenat asik nuy nikkumokoe.

tuleye tayleku na yarpa nanatakoet appakkar taylekuti kwenatti tayleku pokwa

nopkuti pe kutakerye.

sur takkenta.   350

appakkar nekkwepur soytakerye, "amma ia e kwennatti alapa pir pir ti takke."

pe soytakerye sur takkenye, ikar maitpa pittosuliwaliye.

ikar mamana takkenta.

saylaki tayleku ip tulekan tayleku wetar tulekan taylekuti, yannu tulekan tayleku

weki sayla amiekine.

napki naki nopkupukkwa.   355

"an pul an saylaka kuoe."

sulu tulekan korpukkwa.

titikwa tulekan korpukkwa taylekuti moli tulakan korpukkwa.

an itu napney nasmar takken soke.

anmarti emi a a surye tule mamatar o l o t u l e t a k k e n t a a n m a r.   360

"o l o i k i k k i t u l e y e," soyle pe ittosursinta.

apa taylekuti emite tayleku punmarye tayleku pe ittopuymoka.

In the beginning indeed when Ipeorkun[19] came here he did not say this 'you must
take good care of the gourd place' he said.

Father's son counseled the people here in the beginning."   340

I always say these few words to my children see.

"If you do not pay attention to me   it is bad see.

Your father is talking to you and you must do things for your father see."

That is what [I] truly always say see it is said.

For this reason indeed now indeed since we are planting indeed a pole we say.   345

We will be working side by side.

Now indeed I was also given a name indeed for the Panamanians.[20]

My brother will also be given a name for this.

People indeed you should not be jealous indeed of two brothers indeed the two
of them working together.

No see.   350

The village should not say, "that very same older brother goes from one place to
another with his own brother see."

You should not say this see, it is by the paths[21] that are there don't you hear.

The paths are there see.

In the beginning indeed the animal people indeed the collared peccary people
indeed, the white-lipped peccary people indeed when it was time to pick a chief.

On the earth there was much jealousy among them.   355

"I will be a better chief."

The sloth people would shout.

The monkey people would shout indeed the tapir people would shout.

That is how the world was before us see it is said.

But we are not now like that we are true people g o l d e n p e o p l e s e e w e
a r e .   360

"P e o p l e o f t h e g o l d e n i k i k k i ,"[22] it is said don't you hear.

Sisters indeed you indeed are now indeed listening also.

---

[19] Kuna prophet and leader
[20] to represent Mulatuppu to the Panamanian government
[21] In this case *ikar*, which I have generally translated as "way" or "path," has the meaning "rules."
[22] a mythical place

"emi tayleku pe akku an takke.

^ we sayla pialit sunmakkwici we?

akku an tak," pe anki pinsasurmar takken.   365

an nuy pe wis pe ittosursin.

mimmikanse pakkar sappinkanase pakkar tayleku "we sayla pialitti we?"

pe anki pinsasurmar takkenta.

"we ikit sayla toysipali, e kwenatti, e urpati," pe pinsasurmar takken, pe

wisipuymar takkenta.

aki tayleku, pinsa tayleku wekitpa taylekua.   370

kakkakwen saale   anna peka soymarmo takken soke.

pule tayleku suar wala nuet ina kale war nuet isper wala nuet?

anna tiymalotipaye.

talikwen pinapale tayleku e waska upokwici.

olo napsapa taylekuti mes enirkwici taylekua.   375

ipe pillikanpa mes tokemama nate.

tiylesaarti   kanna kuo takken, pirkapa taylekuti   kwiskutappo takken soke.

nue tiyles, pe ittosursin takken soke.

em an kwismokat tayleku yola pirka pakkepak apar kunatap takkenta.

saylaka kusat akkar takken soke.   380

anti tayleku suar ipetka kuculi, arkarka kucurpali.

yok apka tummmarpa sulenoni takken soke.

kirmar an apeketpar nekkwepur an takkeparye.

teakkar mekis takkenta.

teakkar emite karmaytisun, iki an kunatappi, an kutiitti an akku ittoye.   385

an nak opitiitti, an akku itto takkenta.

iki an nak opinatappi, anna wicur pittosursin.

emite tayleku nek an ninatap pirka an ninatapmala, pirka natappi pirka natappipa

an kwaymamanapali.

napir pal ittolepar pittosursin takken soke.

namakkeka tayleku wek an puymala.   390

auna punmarye soyleke, "itti onmakket neka, mer pe ieye."

"Now indeed I do not recognize you.

^ This chief standing speaking where is he from?

I do not recognize him," you do not think this way about me see. 365

You know my name don't you hear.

All the children all the young men indeed "this chief where is he from?"

You do not think this way about me see.

"This chief sitting here who is entering, his brother, his younger brother," you do

not think this way see, you know us see.

For this reason indeed, you know indeed here indeed. 370

I myself   tell you a few words see it is said.

How good indeed is this pole how good is this *ina kale* tree how good is this

isper tree?

That we ourselves might plant.

If its roots enter straight down indeed an arm's length and a half.

Standing stuck fast indeed within the golden clay indeed. 375

Entering and entangling themselves among the rocks.

Having been well planted   it will be firm see, it will remain standing

indeed   for many years see it is said.

If it is well planted, don't you hear see it is said.

Now I have also been standing indeed reaching nine and a half years see.

When I became chief see it is said. 380

I indeed did not become owner of the stick, nor did I become chiefs' spokesman.

I was chosen directly by the immmportant people see it is said.

By the choice of the uncles by the affection of the village.

Up to this moment I have been in place see.

Up to this moment now I have been going about, how have I been doing, I

myself do not realize how I am doing. 385

I do not recognize, the steps I am taking see.

I myself do not know, how the steps I take are going don't you hear.

Now indeed my functions are carrying us along the years are carrying us along,

the years are going along and as the years go along we go changing also.

It is true listen again don't you hear see it is said.

We are here indeed in order to chant. 390

For this reason Sisters it is said, "do not forget, this gathering house."

nana takkenta wek an tunkumalat.

weki an simu tiylemalat.

weki taylekuti.

mukan tayleku anapin tayleku anka samor enuysamalat.   395

nan pica koakanaki annulesmala.

nan tunwet iskanaki anmal annules takkenta.

anmal aa puyye.

emiskwa tayleku mimmikan tunkumalat.

nappaki simalat pirkapoto pirkappaatomalat.   400

nan picaki pal annulemasur takken.

nan tunwet iskanaki pal annulemasur takken.

nan mol iskanaki pal annulemasur takken.

per PANYALE CUNNAPIKUS takken.

pela tayleku panti cunnapikus takken.   405

a-a e m-i-m-m-i p-i-p-p-i-k-w-a t-o-a-y-a-k-i p-e-r p-i-r p-i-r-r-r-r.

a-a p-o-l-p-o p-e-r w-a-w-a-t-i-k-k-u-s t-a-k-k-e-n.

pirka kwaymaitpa, napir natap an soy takken, napir natapye.

ikar maitpa natap takkenta.

saylaki nek ikarti an pal amimalo tayteye   pinsasurmar takken soke.   410

keke an pal amimar takken.

en toa puretsie tule puret kwen niysurkus punmar takken.

ikkor wala panetse pe sayyenaonye kaska pe opinyoenye, kwen anmal

imaculiletteye.

ikkor taylekuti kurkinka pe opinyoen.

anmar kurkinka wicul imaysalette.   415

karsonka wicul an imaysarta.

morka wicul an imaysaletteye.

Attend it see here we grow up.

Here we plant the navel.[23]

Here indeed.

The grandmothers indeed washed indeed my swaddling cloth for me. 395

Our mothers covered us with pieces of underwear.

Our mothers covered us with used headkerchiefs see.

We are like that.

Now indeed children who are growing up.

Those who sit on the ground those who are two years old three years old. 400

Their mothers do not cover them with pieces of underwear.

Their mothers do not cover them with used headkerchiefs either see.

Their mothers do not cover them with used cloth either see.

Everyone USES DIAPERS see.

Everyone indeed uses panties see. 405

A-a-h t-h-e l-i-t-t-l-e b-a-b-i-e-s a-r-e a-l-l w-r-a-p-p-e-d i-n t-o-w-e-l-s.

A-a-h t-h-e-y a-r-e a-l-l p-e-r-f-u-m-e-d w-i-t-h p-o-w-d-e-r s-e-e.

The years[24] are changing, it is true they are going along I say see, it is true they
are going along.

The ways[25] are going along see.

We might search again for the ways of the past see   but we do not remember

them see it is said. 410

We cannot find them again see.

Now who knows how to weave Sisters there are no weavers see.

If tomorrow you want to go to chop up the *ikkor* tree so that you could convert

it into a hammock, we would not be able to do it.

So that indeed you could convert *ikkor* into a hat.

We would not know how to make a hat. 415

We would not know how to make pants.

We would not know how to make shirts.

---

23 are born

24 times

25 Here, and in the next line, *ikar*, which in this case I have translated as paths, has the sense of
"traditions;" see line 302 and note 21.

saylakinti papkan tey sur takkenta.

ikkor kaciki mekisa.

ikkor mor yosa.   420

ikkor karson yosa.

ikkor kurkin sisa.

napsa tayleku napsa tayleku kwinmetteki tayleku palu sii.

papkanki ney tani pittosursinta.

an wis taysa takken an soy takken, anpa pe emis tunkumalat peti taysasurye.   425

kwinmetteki tayleku mas kuttakoe.

palu patteka kwinmette sii.

napsa sii.

anmar tunkus takken an, a-nap-nek-na-tak-ken-so-ke.

teki an tunkutani ittolemarsokku, tekitte iki we Mulatup nekkwepurte anna mecar

parsamarye?   430

kek an mesar samarsun takken soke.

emiskintinye.

tayleku napnokki taylekua, peka emiskinti, palu patte siynonikkir, "we ipika nok

iskana we?

a?

an emis patte paysasursi?" pe soysaletteta.   435

sulinye, anpa ip nuetin takken, papkat takken soke.

a ikal emite par ikar sikkis an pal amiosurmala.

unnila namaypupusun takken, napir taeparye.

mer kakkansaetpar takken soke.

emite tayleku tese ukakka.   440

wis kakkakwen saale.

an peka sunmaymalat pukkitar puy pittosursin.

tese tayleku wis an pey soymarto, pe ittokua.

But in the beginning our fathers were not this way see.
They slept in an *ikkor* hammock.
They wore *ikkor* shirts.   420
They wore *ikkor* pants.
They put on *ikkor* hats.
They placed salt indeed in earthen bowls indeed in earthen bowls indeed in gourds.
The traditions of our fathers have passed don't you hear.
I saw a little of this see I say see, but you who are still growing up now you did not see this.   425
They would eat indeed in gourds.
They placed a gourd for a salt plate.
They placed an earthen bowl.
We grew up see, in-this-world-tru-ly-see-it-is-said.
Well since we grew up this way you you hear, well then how could we reject this village of Mulatuppu?   430
We cannot reject it see it is said.
And now.
Indeed if they indeed, placed for you now, an earthen cup as a salt plate, [you would say] "why this dirty plate?
ah?
Did I not now buy a plate?" you would say.   435
But no, it[26] is still a good thing see, it belongs to God[27] see it is said.
This way now is a way we will no longer encounter.
We can only chant about it see, so that we behave properly.
So that we do not lie see it is said.
Now indeed up to here.   440
I have given you a few words.
We are many more speakers don't you hear.
Up to here indeed I have told you a little, you have heard.

[26] the earthen cup
[27] is free

5. THE REPORT OF A CURING SPECIALIST: THE POETICS AND RHETORIC OF AN ORAL PERFORMANCE

In 1970, the village of Mulatuppu in eastern San Blas awarded a scholarship to Olowitinappi, one of its foremost curing specialists, to study snakebite medicine with a teacher in the Bayano region of Kuna territory who was well known for such medicine. In awarding this scholarship, the village paid tribute to the ability of Olowitinappi and at the same time contributed to the medical protection of their community and the continuity of Kuna tradition. On the evening of June 16, 1970, several days after his return from the Bayano, Olowitinappi delivered a speech reporting on his experience in the Mulatuppu gathering house.

As an ethnographic document, Olowitinappi's speech is most informative. It conveys a great deal about Kuna medicine and curing as the Kuna themselves view it, and it illustrates the ways in which medicines and associated forms of discourse are learned. It is also an excellent example of Kuna speechmaking and the sorts of rhetorical and poetic devices used by effective speakers.

For both Olowitinappi and his audience, this report is very significant. In this essentially nonliterate community, it is through oral discourse that knowledge and information is conceived, perceived, learned, taught, and transmitted. Olowitinappi's speech is the official, public actualization of his experiences.

For Olowitinappi, his report is a way of informing his community about what he has learned, providing testimony about his achievements. Olowitinappi explains that he has learned the medicines and curing practices appropriate to several types of illness – not only for snakebites, but also for various complications that sometimes follow snakebites. In addition, he announces that he has learned some medicine and curing practices concerned with childbirth, including chants and verbal secret charms. The speech itself, then, brings Olowitinappi prestige because in it he is able to show that he has added to his already formidable knowledge of Kuna medicine and curing.

For the audience, Olowitinappi's report is equally significant. The community learns from the report that its money has not been wasted because Olowitinappi has learned cures previously unknown in Mulatuppu. It also finds out in advance how he will go about his work and how much he will charge, and since Olowitinappi not only discusses medicine, but also reports in a colorful way on his experiences and observations while traveling, he provides them with information and entertainment.

Olowitinappi's report is a polished and sophisticated example of Kuna speechmaking, including, as is characteristic of both Kuna oratory and Kuna chanting, attention to narrative detail, mixing humor with seriousness, metaphor and other allusive devices, counsel, considerable metacommunication, and extensive quotation and quotation within quotation.

This report then both exemplifies one variety of Kuna formal speechmaking and illustrates the learning of Kuna medicine and curing. It also shows how personal and private pursuits like the learning of medicine and curing are related to the public and political system centered in the gathering house.

Social and Cultural Context and Assumptions

Olowitinappi's speech is one of many forms of discourse performed in Kuna gatherings. There are two major types of Kuna gathering. One, attended by men and women together, is the setting for the public and ritual chanting of Kuna chiefs. This gathering occurs approximately every other evening and at times in the morning. The other type of gathering is exclusively for men and occurs on evenings when chiefs do not chant. A variety of matters are dealt with at these men's gatherings, including legal, political, and economic affairs and disputes of all kinds. Humorous discussions and storytelling also occur here. And this is the setting for public reports, of unusual personal experiences, trips, and learning sessions of the type Olowitinappi was involved in.

Reporting one's experience is a significant verbal activity among the Kuna. It is the only way that individuals can let others know of their experiences and it is expected and required of everyone. Chiefs who have travelled to other villages in order to attend inter-island ritual meetings report on their trips in the form of a gathering-house chant. Anyone who has travelled, for politics, work, pleasure, or education (traditional or modern) reports, both privately and publicly, after their return. Olowitinappi no doubt reported on his trip many times – privately to friends and family in many settings and in many ways. His speech in the evening gathering is the public, official version of his experience.

The purpose of Olowitinappi's trip to the Bayano region was to learn medicinal and curing practices, with a focus on snakebites. It is useful to place this trip and the report of it within the total configuration of Kuna curing practices. Kuna curing involves a combination of herbal medicines and verbal discourse, the latter being communication between humans and spirits in a special, esoteric language, that of the spirit world. When an individual is sick, members of her/his family call on a diagnostician to determine the cause of the disease and the needed cure. This diagnostician is either a *nele* (seer) or medicinal specialist. The cure itself involves the use of herbal medicines gathered by the medicinal specialist who also verbally counsels the medicine (its spirit) in a short chant in order to activate it. In addition, the appropriate curing chant is also performed by a chant specialist. The relatively long curing chants are addressed to spirits and direct the actions of helpful spirits in their struggle against the hostile spirits that cause disease. A verbal secret charm with highly focused magical power might also be used.

Medicinal specialists and chant knowers learn their practice by apprenticing themselves to well-known specialists, precisely as Olowitinappi describes so nicely in his speech. Traditional Kuna teaching consists largely of a series of wide-ranging conversations between teacher and student. While students and teachers are sometimes from the same village, it is much more common for students to seek out renowned specialists from other, at times distant villages, as teachers. This provides them with more prestige and avoids conflicts between teachers and students. Students work together with their teachers, helping them especially with agricultural work, which is an important form of repayment while at the same time being a context in which student and teacher can observe local plants of medicinal value and converse about them. As is discussed in Olowitinappi's speech, teachers also charge actual money for what they teach. When a student has successfully learned either a chant or medicinal practice, the teacher acknowledges that his student is now also a specialist. This is done in various ways. If student and teacher are from the same village, the teacher makes a public speech in the gathering house. If the student has traveled to study with the teacher, the teacher writes a letter (or more frequently in this mainly nonliterate society, has a letter written) which is then read in the student's gathering house on his return. In these cases, the student also makes a public speech reporting in detail on his experiences.

Snakes and snakebite medicine occupy a special and most significant place among Kuna curing practices. In this tropical environment in which people walk, hunt, farm, wash clothes, and fetch water daily, actual physical snakes are a real and most dangerous reality. At the same time, snake spirits are among the most dangerous of spirits and can cause serious disease, even if the individual attacked never comes into contact with an actual, physical snake. No wonder then that the Kuna are so preoccupied with snakes and that there exists a complex of herbal medicines, chants, and secret charms, all focused on snakebite cure and prevention and cure and prevention of illnesses caused by snake spirits. In addition, there exists a chant whose purpose is to control the spirit of a snake and thereby enable its performer to raise an actual snake into the air. (See chapter eight.)

Because it is performed publicly in the gathering house, Olowitinappi's speech represents an intersection of the curing and gathering traditions. It makes private, esoteric matters public. And it relates Olowitinappi's abilities and prestige as a curing specialist to his role as an active political leader in the community.

An explanation of certain Kuna practices and beliefs is necessary for an understanding of aspects of this text, in particular, some of its allusions. The inter-island meeting Olowitinappi refers to at the opening of his speech is a frequent event involving representatives of several Kuna villages. Both ritual chanting by chiefs and political discussions occur at such meetings. In his speech in the Tigre gathering Olowitinappi uses the history of Inapakinya, a renowned chief of the village of Mulatuppu and leader of the eastern portion of San Blas, who died in 1938, to represent current Kuna concerns. At the time of Olowitinappi's speech, the Kuna were worried about outside incursions into their territory, by Panamanian settlers as well as mineral prospectors supported by the Panamanian government. In the 1930s, Inapakinya was a supporter of close relations with neighboring Colombia, rather than with Panama. His response to the offer of a new young woman in place of his older wife symbolized his views. The old woman is Colombia; the young woman is Panama. This discussion reflects Kuna concerns about outside encroachments. (Compare with the speech represented in chapter four, which also expresses concerns about the dangers of pressures, as well as changes, coming from outside the Kuna community.) The food and drink which Olowitinappi receives in the Ipeti gathering house on his arrival (line 123ff) is an instance of the Kuna custom of bringing beverages and food to the gathering house for distinguished visitors, such as chiefs or medicinal specialists.

The full set of Kuna curing practices is reported on by Olowitinappi. Victims of snakebite live in the house of a curer during their treatment. Olowitinappi is taught not only how to cure but how to prevent disease. Kuna midwives can tell at birth what disease or misfortune is likely to befall a newborn baby (line 258). Preventive medicine is then employed. This involves painting individuals' bodies black with the native dye Genipa Americana (line 259ff). It also involves planting medicine in the ground at the time fields are burned and before planting crops (the Kuna practice slash and burn agriculture), a time when snakes are likely to be observed, in order to keep them from harming people working there. Olowitinappi refers to snakes as *tupa* (rope or vine), a common Kuna euphemism. By means of his constant conversations with his teacher, at home, while walking, and while working in the jungle, Olowitinappi acquired the total gamut of snakebite curing practices – actual medicines and their names, associated verbal secret charms (called "secret," "soul," and "boat" in the text), and appropriate curing chants. The teacher speaks secretly (line 146), that is, he uses esoteric language. The word *ikar* is used to refer to chant, general way or practice, and portion, including line, of chant. In lines 305-312 Olowitinappi directly quotes a few lines of his teacher's recitation of a curing chant. The "clothes line" in the chant which Olowitinappi quotes his teacher reciting (lines 310, 312) is the rope used in the spirit world to catch evil spirits. *Apsoket ikar (The way of the mass curer)* (line 311) is a chant used in the prevention and cure of diseases and problems of epidemic proportions. Drawings are made with colored pencils in notebooks as mnemonic devices for both medicines and chants (lines 153-154, 175, 285).

Charging practices (for both future patients and future students) are part of the teaching process. Olowitinappi pays considerable attention to financial details in his report, particularly important since it is his village which supplied him with the money for the trip and for the needed notebooks, pencils, and cloth (line 201). The cloth is a gift to the teacher, to be used by his wife in making molas (blouses).

The *nelekana* (prophets) (line 316ff.) were the first great leaders of the Kuna. (See chapter three.) Ipelele (line 318) was one of the foremost of them. The Choco (line 315ff.), neighbors of the Kuna, are traditional enemies, but also, as certain traditions have it, sources of knowledge of medicinal and curing practices. Olowitinappi's teacher knows the chants of the elders (line 363ff.) because in addition to being a curing specialist, he is also a chief. It is rather common for Kuna traditional leaders to have roles in, that is to be specialists in, distinct domains, for example, both gathering tradition and curing tradition. Olowitinappi himself is both a curing specialist (having knowledge of herbal medicine as well as various chants) and a chiefs' spokesman. The letter discussed in line 440ff. is the proof that Olowitinappi has actually studied; it is his diploma. He showed it in the gathering house. In line 452, Olowitinappi refers to the fact that he has been sick for one year and was not able to work.

Given that the Kuna are essentially a nonliterate society and that Olowitinappi's report is an excellent illustration of Kuna oral discourse, it is interesting to note the significance of writing in relation to Kuna curing practices, as expressed in the speech. Mnemonic drawings are used to aid in the memorization of medicines and chants. The Choco is taught in the spirit world on the basis of a letter he brings with him. And Olowitinappi himself carries a written letter validating his experience. While statistically marginal, writing is clearly highly valued and at times crucial and is put to important use by such nonliterate individuals as Olowitinappi and his teacher.

Structures and Strategies

Olowitinappi's speech is organized into a series of narrative episodes, interspersed with counsel, from the teacher to Olowitinappi, on how to behave. The narrative episodes are the trip to Panama (participating in a meeting on the San Blas island of Tigre, speaking with the inhabitants of Wicupwala, another San Blas island, and purchasing eyeglasses in Panama City); the trip to the Bayano village of Ipeti (passing by both Panamanian and Kuna villages, not being able to get the boat repaired, and being appropriately received in Ipeti); the teaching process (difficulties in learning, success at last, learning names for herbal medicines, attention to financial matters, description of how to treat victims as well as prevent snakebites); and an invitation to return to study childbirth medicine (highlighted by the story of the origin of the learning of the chant used to grab the devil, including the report of the Choco's learning of this chant, a nicely microscopic parallel of Olowitinappi's report into which it is embedded, and ending with the tracing of the line of the specialists in the chant to its present knower and teacher). The speech terminates with a focus on counsel – reminding Olowitinappi to get a student/assistant, how to treat him, and how much to charge him and explaining to Olowitinappi how to behave in the face of the criticism he is sure to receive from other medicinal specialists in his village. This latter counsel is illustrated by a lovely miniature narrative about a sick person the teacher-specialist cured after other specialists had decided he could not be saved from death. (The speech represented in chapter four also discusses competition, rivalry, and jealousies among ritual leaders.) The final portion of the speech describes the writing of the diploma-letter. Then there is a coda, Olowitinappi telling his own village of Mulatuppu what he will do for them.

The speech makes use of a number of poetic processes and rhetorical strategies which, while all characteristically Kuna, also reflect Olowitinappi's individual style, because of his particular way of employing them. First, dramatization of the voice. I have in mind here loudness and softness, fast and slow speech, modulations of pitch, pause patterns, and two especially characteristic Kuna expressive devices, stretching out the voice and vibrating the voice. Such dramatizations of the voice constitute an aspect of oral performance particularly challenging for transcription, translation, and representation on the printed page.

With regard to rhetorical strategies, there is first of all the use of narratives. As is expected of Kuna report narratives, Olowitinappi includes considerable phenomenological detail, concerning people he met, places he saw, and things he did. Examples are his speech in the Tigre meeting, his description of the villages along the Bayano river, and, of course, his meticulous reproductions of his conversations with his teacher. He thus demonstrates his experience, his knowledge, and his acknowledged prestige. There is also understatement, irony, and humor. Thus Olowitinappi expresses his shame at being like a little kid in not being able to learn quickly. But of course his learning problems are overcome and he acquires knowledge quite impressively. Olowitinappi quotes his teacher saying that the medicinal specialists were going to *iploe* (literally smash to death) (line 433) a man whom they could not cure. But of course the Kuna would never kill a sick person. Quite the contrary. They try by every means possible to keep patients alive. This is a quite ironic and humorous way for Olowitinappi to say that his teacher is better than other specialists; he can cure patients when others fail. The statement is all the more humorous in that it is expressed through the quoted words of the teacher. There is a certain amount of parallelism and allusive speech, two important characteristics of Kuna verbal art, especially common in ritual speaking and chanting.

The most striking rhetorical strategy employed in Olowitinappi's speech is the use of quoted speech, a most characteristic Kuna verbal device and one which is also widespread in lowland South America (Sherzer 1983: 201-207). Much of this speech is not to be understood as being in the words of Olowitinappi on that evening in 1970 when he delivered it, but rather as quotes of other, previous times and places, of other speakers and voices, including his own, or of future times, places, and voices. In particular, the learning of the snakebite cure is presented through a series of quotations of Olowitinappi's teacher and conversations between the teacher and Olowitinappi.

Reported, quoted speech is a formal property of the text, which is literally punctuated with *soke* (say) and *takken soke* (see he says). The repetition of these forms, at the ends of lines, typical of the Kuna formal speech-making style, contributes to the cohesion and the rhythm of Olowitinappi's oral performance.

The strategic use of reported, quoted speech is striking for its omnipresence. Olowitinappi himself seems to be saying nothing. Such important matters as the prices he will charge patients and his own student/assistant are not presented in his own words, but in those of his teacher, and are to be followed as strictly as the curing practices he describes, also always in the words of his teacher. Notice that by quoting his teacher, Olowitinappi is able to anticipate particular issues and problems he will face in Mulatuppu – diseases, financial concerns, and personal criticisms.

Quoting is also a most effective way to demonstrate that knowledge has indeed been acquired. Thus when talking about having heard his teacher perform the chant for grabbing the devil and learned some of it, Olowitinappi quotes his teacher reciting this memorized text (lines 305-312).

Reported speech, multiple tellings, and tellings within tellings acquire baroque proportions in the story of the origin of the chant for grabbing the devil, which constitutes the climax of Olowitinappi's speech (lines 314-351). The extreme point of quotation within quotation is reached toward the end of this passage, when Olowitinappi is quoting his teacher, who is quoting Ipelele, who is quoting a Choco Indian, who is quoting a chief of the spirit world, who is quoting God.

It is important to point out two significant features of embedding quotations within quotations, the first having to do with the structure of the telling of narrative, the second having to do with the grammatical marking of embedded tellings. With regard to the telling of narratives, there is a single story line. What is embedded are not different stories but different tellers. This is what I have tried to represent by making use of the clearly insufficient western writing device of single and double quotation marks. With regard to the grammatical marking of embedded tellings, while Kuna grammar provides a rich potential in metacommunicative words, phrases, and affixes, there is not a necessary and unique formal, overt marking for every embedding. Nor do intonational changes mark more than a single level of embedding, and often they do not go even this shallow distance. Thus in spite of a general rule that the last character introduced into a narrative is most likely to be the next speaker quoted, it becomes very difficult at each moment of the narration (for analysts as well as for native members of the community) to decode exactly who is speaking. Competent listening and understanding involve following the story line, recognizing the process of the embedding of direct quotation, and following this to a certain degree. While I have disambiguated possible ambiguities in just who is speaking at particular moments by my use of quotation marks in the written representation of the text, such ambiguities do exist for the audience and perhaps even for the speaker as well.

Olowitinappi's speech is a superb illustration of the verbal artistry of Kuna speechmaking at its best. A modest man and a quiet speaker, Olowitinappi nevertheless draws on the full gamut of Kuna poetic and rhetorical devices in this most engaging report, a travel narrative in which the speaker's experiences are made relevant to the concerns of the audience. Here we have dramatic narration, understatement, irony, humor, allusion, metaphor, parallelism, broad generalization, minute detail, grammar, and the human voice, all working together in one performance. And this gathering-house event, which brings together in a single moment so many basic and crucial aspects of Kuna life – politics, economics, curing and medicine, learning and teaching, and personal relations – is focused within a text in which Olowitinappi's personal verbal artistry is expressed to the fullest degree.

The Text

In my transcription of Olowitinappi's speech, lines are determined by pauses coupled with falling intonation. Long pauses without falling intonation are transcribed as blank spaces between words within lines. Olowitinappi makes extensive use of the rich set of Kuna line-framing words, phrases, and affixes (*teki, takkarku, emi, teysokku, emite, inso, soke, takken soke, pittosursoke, -ye, sunto,* etc.) These tend to intersect with pause and pitch patterning, thus reinforcing the intonationally determined line structure. At times they occur line medially and, like the line-medial pauses, confer a certain contrapuntal rhythm to the poetics of performance. Beyond the line, I find no clearly marked poetic structure, such as verse and stanza, although these units do occur in other Kuna verbal genres. At a more macro level, the text is organized into episodes. Other conventional Kuna expressive devices which are found in this text are lengthening of vowels and consonants (indicated by doubling the letter which represents the sound in question), loud speech (indicated by capital letters), stretched-out speech (indicated by dashes between syllables), vibrating voice (indicated by dashes between letters), and decreasing volume (indicated by > before the stretch of speech affected). Rising pitch is indicated by ´ placed before the stretch of speech affected; falling pitch by ` placed before the stretch of speech affected.

With regard to reported, quoted speech, a very important structural and rhetorical feature of Olowitinappi's performance, in my transcription and representation, I have used quotation marks (single and double) whenever a speaker quotes another or himself, resulting at times in considerable quotes within quotes.

My relatively literal translation aims at providing a sense of the rhythm and style of Olowitinappi's speech. In particular, the translation preserves the extensive use of line-framing and metacommunicative words and phrases, as well as the continual use of direct quotation and quotation within quotation, features which are characteristic of the actual performance I recorded. Certain allusions are explained within brackets and in notes.

In conclusion I have opted for a transcription and representation which highlights expressive oral devices but in which grammatical and semantic devices emerge as well and a translation which is as close to the Kuna as possible while still being understandable and accessible to English readers.

teki emite wey peki pankusmarmoye.

takkaliku   Tikirse ante, kapitap.

aimal ikal ittoeti an tayle.

emi, pemar konkreso imaysat kiarsunto.

tek aimar per sunmaysaku, kakkwen an kar soymosunto.   5

"we Inapakinya soysa" takken an kar soke.

" 'emi ome seret an kwen iptaypisurye.

we ome nucukkwa anka uylenaitti tayleku an wiokoye.'

soysa" takken an kar soke.

"emite a ikar pemar opparsiitti.   10

we waymal ol amimalatti.

wekin malatsurye.

yotte Alemania kunai Italia kunai.

teysokkuti inso.

tayleku Europa waymala.   15

teyop   tatkan wiosmoye.

emite a ipakan anse tanimarmo" takken an kar soke.

"emite Kolompia an kwen iptaypinana" pe tay soke an kar soke.

" 'Panama aisal am papye' soymaitti.

unni e sakuyaka mani   unni 'ani pe attursamama' " takken an kar soke.   20

"ol amimalatkine iki mani mani kama pe insa?" an kar soke.

"mani tummat kama" takken an kar soke "unni arkatiit   unni aminasulit unar"

takken an kar soke.

"arpalealirte nekapar ekatparye.

anmarti satte" takken an kar soke.

"teysokku wis pe, teki appinmakke wilupmalan" takkenye an kar soymosunto.   25

"inso" soke soke "napir" soke.

"iy tayle takotipa" soke.

emit ati ittocurmosunnat.

Well now I left you.

And   at Tigre, there I slept.

The friends were listening to speeches I saw.

Now, for the congress that you had.

Well when the friends had finished speaking, I truly said a word to them also.   5

"Inapakinya once said" see I say to them.

" 'Now I don't want to leave an old woman.

This young woman you are giving me indeed I cannot care for.'

He said" see I say to them.

"Now this matter you are conversing about.   10

These foreigners searching for gold.

They are not from here.

They are from various places some Germans some Italians.

Therefore thus.

Indeed the Europeans.   15

In this way   they also mistreated our ancestors.

Now these days are coming to us too" see I say to them.

"Now Colombia does not want to leave us" you see it is said I say to them.

" 'Although Panama is our fatherland' it is said.

Only for its own bag is the money   only   'We [The Panamanians] are robbing

you' " see I say to them.   20

"These people looking for gold how much money how much money are they

taking from them do you think?" I say to them.

"They are taking a lot of money" see I say to them "they are only

prospecting   they are not even yet taking it away" see I say to them.

"When the work begins half is for them.

But for us nothing" see I say to them.

"Therefore you, well, must push back a bit" see I truly said to them also.   25

"Thus" they say they say "it is true" they say.

"Let us see what will happen" they say.

Now I did not hear[1] at that one[2] also.

---

[1]   was not present
[2]   the later meeting

teki aimarka kaypo wis soysa natmosunto panki.

tek osetotpali, wicupwalase.   30

tek kapitpali.

"aimal apsosmar" soka.

api wis kakkwen anka soymarpa.

"ai Mendez apsosmar" soke "sappurpa" soke.

a wiskus an natparsunto.   35

tek nakate panto.

Kolonse waci irpakke.

teki aki kapitpa uryaki.

teki   tat apal an kep pankutpali, Panamase.

Panama moskua   pankose mani wis otosipa aki, mani wis onoappa.   40

tulappaa an onospa.

ante ispe wis yopiparye.

"tulapo kakkanpe, kakka kwensak, kakka mannerkwa" soka.

teki anka onospa.

"pe, ipappase suo" soke.   45

ai Adriano anka sokku   "pe ittoleket" soke "pe napier nao" takken soke.

"pe sorpa an sunao" soke.

kartati kwaple, an ka uysa   kwaple an pennuysa.

teki mani, suitampekit an kal uysa natsunto, "wese nonikkir kinkwa, paynonikko"

an kar soke.

"napir" soke.   50

teeki aimarte okus tayle waci ilapakkeki.

tek anka apparmaysikuste.

taytisursokkutii   ittakkayop pinsale sunnawa.

tek inso apparmaysii, Kolon emar pankua.

Panamaki pe aipinet.   55

Well I said some words to the friends and left the next day.

Well we passed the whole day again, toward Wicupwala.   30

Well there we slept again.

"The friends were conversing" I say.

And they spoke some words to me also.

"We conversed with friend Méndez"[3] they say "in the mountain"[4] they say.

Having learned this I left again.   35

Well I moved on the next day.

We arrived at Colon at 4 o'clock.

Well there I slept again in the boat.

Well   when the sun was half way up in the sky I then left again, for Panama.

When I arrived in Panama   I went to the bank where I have been putting a little
money and there, I took out some money.   40

I took out thirty dollars.

I want to wear some glasses too.

"Twenty-six dollars and thirty cents" they say.

Well they took it out for me.

"You, in three days come and get them" they say.   45

Friend Adriano[5] said to me   "it's your choice" he says "if you want to go go" see
he says.

"After you leave I will go and get them for you" he says.

I gave him, all the papers   I paid everything.

Well five, dollars I gave him and I left, "when I come back here I'll buy, bullets"
I say to him.

"Alright" he says.   50

Well the friends were ready it seems at 4 o'clock.

Well they came running for me.

Since I had never seen this place   I believed it was close.

Well thus the trip, is as far as Colon.

From Panama you go.   55

---

3 a renowned chief from the village of Ustuppu
4 jungle mainland
5 an inhabitant of Mulatuppu and a relative of Olowitinappi

suittonkwen manattarmoka.

tek an pennus.

tek aimarte ur suap takke.

aaii sokkomala, kar mottor akkwesiit.

tek per otesku anmarkine, ´ muttikuarpinne.   60

tek anka wis selet takke.

muis seles wek opakkaleki anso.

tek selesku kep nakkwitepali, tiwarpa.

e walase nakkwitesunto.

kwenti anapa anmar seletet.   65

ney taysursunnawa ney muttikkucunnat.

kwallupi kapupuk an takke opakkal opakkar.

ney pukkwa na-te-ku taylene ekisnatapsunto.

"way pukkwatte" soke.

mottor urmaysiparsokku, ney nuk ekicursunnaya.   70

teeki, "Yanose kammalo" soke.

waci irampeki an anso.

aase an oarmasmarto.

tek anmar kammasunna ulacuyaki.

ti pelap wicurmo ney yolamo takke.   75

o-wa-wanmaymai, iy pe parsaosunna?

kwi surmosunnat.

tek anmal oipos natparsunto.

Maenayse.

tek peece an kalesmarpala.   80

ulacu aisar onakkoeyop pinsae   aimarte ulacu mattumaypie.

wayteka kar mattumaymoka.

"anka urko amisulitte" soke.

pinsa kamainai, tat yorukku nait.

sapan mata.   85

It costs 75 cents also.
Well I paid.
Well the friends went to get the boat see.
Some Choco friends, were taking care of the motor for them.
Well when we had loaded everything, ´ night had begun to fall.   60
Well we floated along a little see.
We floated a bit the distance from here to cross over there[6] I think.
Well having floated then we went up, along the river.
We went up the main branch.
Then we floated up a smaller branch.   65
The villages could not be seen it had become night.
Only the lights I saw flickering along the coasts.
I asked about the villages we saw as-we-went-a-long.
"They are Panamanians" they say.
Since the motor was making a lot of noise, I was not truly able to ask the names
of the villages.   70
Well "we will sleep in Llano" they say.
It was ten o'clock I think.
When we arrived there.
Well we slept in the pirogue.
There was not any rain the weather was good see.   75
We were shiv-ver-ing, what could we do?
But there were not any mosquitos.
Well when we woke up we left again.
Toward the village of Majé.
Well it was there we stayed a while.   80
Hoping to be able to raise up the pirogue   the friends wanted to repair the pirogue.
And have the Panamanians repair it for them.
"But why didn't you bring us wood?" they say.
For no reason we were walking along, it was noon.
Stomachs empty.   85

6   from the island of Mulatuppu to the mainland

kopet satte.
teekin natmarparsunto, kannar ulacu ´ ekwatte, ´ pinsa kalittos.
kep epippitesunto.
kep Maese opetapsunto.
"weki an ettinsunno" soke.   90
aate aimarte aki pukkwat.
e kwenatse opecunto.
"e ia" soyye.
tek opes natemarpali, mas   wis ittosmar an tayye.
"pia an kapitammarpalotipa?" soke.   95
"kapitappi Tapartinak" soka.
"wek Taparti ney nuy" soka.
tiwar tummat yomokat.
tey paneki nakkwitemarpali.
"yorukku neyse.   100
Ipeti" soke.
"wesik pe naoet" takken soke, "tiwar nakkwitet."
tat nakkwesik kwenti tat arkwanesik natmokat.
teeki, Ipetise yorukku.
tek kammama, osetotparsunto.   105
"tey waitarte, kinemarpar"·soka.
ati "aitiar nasunno" soke.
"iy tat momalo?" an kar soke.
"anmar tat nate mo" soke.
tikka an ittosurwa.   110
ante ipapo kusat.
t-e-y n-a-t-e-m-a-r-p-a-l-i.
iinso oarmakkarsun "weki pe peoet" takken soke.
takkarku nek kwanerkwa wis sii.
teeki, aite   teun sensote mamoye.   115

Nothing to drink.

Well we continued on again, once again ´ we lowered the pirogue, ´ for no reason
we had made the effort.

Then we had to pull it.

Then we left it there in Majé.

"Here we must tie it" they say.   90

There are many friends there.

We left it with a relative.

"His older brother" he says.

Well having left it we took off again, we   ate a little I see.

"Wherever will we sleep?" they say.   95

"We slept at the mouth of Taparti river" I say.

"The name of this place is Taparti" they say.

It is also a large river.

Well the next day we went up[7] again.

"At noon we'll get home.   100

To Ipeti" they say.

"Here is your route" see they say, "where the river goes up."

This one[8] leads to where the sun rises and the other to where the sun sets.

Weell, we got to Ipeti at noon.

Well we rested there, in fact we spent the whole day there.   105

"Well the next day then, we continued on again" I say.

"We must go by paddling" they say.

"Where will the sun be when we get there?" I say to them.

"We will get there when the sun sets" they say.

I felt that that I was far.   110

In fact two days had passed.

W-e-l-l w-e c-o-n-t-i-n-u-e-d o-n a-g-a-i-n.

Thuus we arrived "here is where you will stay" see they say.

So there were just six houses.

Well, our friend   the census taker was there too.   115

---

[7] the river
[8] river

senso etarpema.

tense kottamma.

"peki aimar tani" kar soke.

"pialit?" soke.

takkarku, "tata nakkwepalit" soka.   120

"napir" soka.

"tay" soke.

teki kopet irmakkal ´ an takke.

teki, "yannu masi" soka.

"mer naoye" soy tayle.   125

aimarte nasokkalit.

"mer nao" kar soke.

"teek, ampa pe naoku   pe immar satapposulitteye."

"tat pukeoe an" soke.

tey waci irpokin an insa.   130

napir mone.

tek ´ kapitmarsunna.

tek aite anka nasitepinne ´ an takke.

"sekretto ittokwelo" soke.

"a insa an pe oturtakkwelo" takken soke.   135

"tulakwen kakkanpeki"   an ukko takken soke.

"napir" an kar soke.

tek an pennus.

teeki, takkarku ´ an kwen ittosula.

kwen kaet an ittosurwa.   140

yeti a.

wiste iy saerkepe.

an oakkua.

(Laughter, unintelligible comments from gathered audience.)

maka an kwen ittosuli yeti.

(Laughter, unintelligible comments from gathered audience.)

Taking the census.

They called out.[9]

"Friends have come to you" they say to him.

"From where?" he says.

So, "from where the sun rises" they say.   120

"Good" he says.

"Come" he says.

Well beverages were passed around ´ I see.

Well, "there is a meal of wild boar" he says.

"Don't go yet" he says[10] see.   125

The friends were about to leave.

"Don't go" he says to them.

"Well, if you go   you won't be able to do anything when you get there."

"We'll get there with the setting sun" they say.

Well it was 2 o'clock I think.   130

Surely.

Well ´ then we slept.

Well the friend began to teach me ´ I see.

"First we will study the secret" he says.

"That is what I will teach you first" see he says.   135

"Fifteen dollars"   I will have to pay see he says.

"Good" I say to him.

Well I paid.

Weell, so ´ I didn't understand.

I couldn't catch it.   140

No ah.

I didn't know what to do.

I couldn't do it.

(Laughter, unintelligible comments from gathered audience.)

I didn't understand even a single thing.

(Laughter, unintelligible comments from gathered audience.)

[9]   to Olowitinappi's teacher
[10]   to the others

teki   > "nai nai nai" soyye.   145

arpakke ´ wis soysisunna.

(Laughter.)

pinket aparki.

(Comments from gathered audience: purwikan kusiyopi.)

eye   purwikan nue kusii.

immar per wicur pilekeyop natsunto.

(Comments from gathered audience: purwikan pinkerpa.)

teeki   paneki paloiposto.   150

"pankuosur"soka.

"ilakwen si osetotmalo" soka.

e maci kep anka narmakkarsunto.

tipuho imacunto.

" 'weki weki weki' soko takken, 'wea wea kwis' " takken soka.   155

"sokampe, kakkattar.

pait sokampe kakka paapak.

teki   nia okwayet" soka.

"teki a, per wisi."

tale tale wis katanikustole.   160

tek osetotku   wis kasakwakina, ampa kannal iettapali.

teki   tek an mettenattaparsunto, "an sorpa pe kannar kannar soysio" soke.

´ "soy-si-sun-na-ya."

(Laughter.)

ipapoki an kalecurpa.

wis talemas tayle.   165

"na yerpa" soka.

"kwen kwen puleke taette" soke a.

"napir" an kar soke.

kep parkwaisapar naipesik.

"naipe sekretto sunno" soke.   170

na-si-te-pa-li.

teyoppaliwa.

"napirmo" ankar soka.

Well   > "continue continue continue" he says.   145
Secretly ´ he was speaking a little.
(Laughter.)
Surrounded by shame.
(Comments from gathered audience: Like little kids.)
Yes   just like little kids.
As if I didn't know how to pronounce things.
(Comments from gathered audience: Little kids full of shame.)
Weell   next day we woke up again.   150
"You won't go out" he says.
"All day long we'll stay at home" he says.
His son then wrote for me.
He made the drawings.
" 'This this this' you will say see, 'like that like that' " see he says.   155
"It has, fifteen lines.
The other one has eighteen lines.
Well   it is to frighten the devil" he says.
"Well, you know it all."
Little by little I was catching on.   160
Well when the day ended   I had caught on a bit, and then I would forget again.
Well´   well he left me alone again, "after I leave you will sit saying the words
over and over" he says.
´ "You-will-sit-say-ing."
(Laughter.)
I needed two days to learn this.
I felt I had learned something it seems.   165
"It is good" he says.
"There are some who are worse" he says ah.
"It is true" I say to him.
Then we changed over to snakes.
"This is truly the secret for snakes" he says.   170
I-be-gan-a-gain.
It is just as difficult.
"It is good also" he says to me.

tey pel an, ilemaysapar tayle.
teki   kep ina anka narmakkarparsunto.   175
"we epuleko takken sailanaka" takken soke.
" 'toitar tayleku, ippiypa an arpatisuli' an soke.
ippo ippaa ippakke unni arpa" takken soke.
"impakkwa   impakwena   tiwar pannat nonitaette" soke a.
"potto ipapokusatti   ati sun ipapaapak an arpa" soke.   180
"potto ati potto poni   ainakkwistaette" soke.
"kwenti emiskwattina sur" soke "ati pursur an imay" soka.
"sekretto an pentakkette" soke.
inso sokene.
ina ittoarkua inso potto, we an pe soysamalata, wis an   eppenne ittosye.   185
ampa a epumoka.
a epumosokku iki pal an akku ittosunna.
pinsa impakwen wis akkar pimosunnata.
"aki wisi   an walik SURYE" an korsisunnaya.
"weti an walik sur" takkenye.   190
sappurpa anse oyoarku ´ takkarsunna.
al a ekka pimoka.
teysokku pursur anka natsunto.
tek inso arpanakucunto.
teki ipakwen   mas emitimarpali   aaki   sunmaynatappali "e purpakat
suitnerkwa" soka.   195
kal uytepali.
"pait e ulukat" soke.
kal uytepali.
pelap tulapo oarmattole.
natette anka, immar an wis paysa an natpalit.   200

Well I, got everything in order it seems.

Well   then he began to write down the medicine for me again.   175

"For this you must touch see the origin" see he says.

" 'Never indeed, have I worked many days' I say.

Only two three or four days I work" see he says.

"Sometimes   at times   people come from other rivers" he says ah.

"People who were bitten already two days ago   those I can work on[11] in eight

days" he says.   180

"Already in these already the evil spirits   have risen everywhere" he says.

"A person bitten the very same day is easy" he says "this one I handle very easily"

he says.

"The secret really helps me" he says.

Thus he says.

The medicine I studied there thus already, as I told you, a little I   had studied a

long time ago.   185

And I had also used it.

Since I had also used it how could I not learn it again.

But for no reason at times it has a slightly different name.

"This one   we DON'T have at our place" I would shout to him.

"That one we don't have at our place" see.   190

But when he showed it to me in the jungle ´ I saw.

That we have it too.

Therefore it went easy for me.

Well thus we were working.

Well one day   as we were clearing his plantain plantation again   there   we

were talking as we were walking along "the soul costs three dollars" he says.   195

I paid him again.

"The other is the boat" he says.

I paid him again.

Everything had now reached twenty dollars.

When I left, I bought some things as I went.   200

[11] cure

mor kinnit.

lapismala.

kwaternomala.

teymalat paylepalit.

kwaple   kwaple purwi purwi oeletet.   205

mottor   pennuspalit suitnerkwa.

teymalatse kwaple, tulakwen oarmaspalit.

pelap tulappakustole.

"aka tanikkitte" an kar soke "ipika an parsapokone."

teki.   210

teki inso, ipakante, ´kwen sanarkusula.

´yoisku ipampe pina.

an sapomasurmoka.

tey perkwaple anka ilemaysa tayle.

pinsa tayleku   emi, kalanukkisik kumaloet   pelakwaple narmas.   215

takkarku pilakansik   kwen kwen pilakan nikkat   "pilakanse kottoette" soke.

anka ilemaysapar tayle.

´pel anka ikal ukkenasa.

"nue salak" takken soke.

"tayleku pe sorpa emi   pepa akkaetti pe amitappo" takken soke.   220

"apakkar pe   amisurkutaerye.

pe amisulile, warkwen unnisur" takken soke.

anka   soymosunto.

"teki   teukki nainukanki   ina tiket" takken soke.

"nainu, tayleku pulalet pe niymartipa" soke.   225

"pinsa pe tiko" takken soke.

"manisur" soke.

´"nekkwepurkatitte" ` soke.

Red cloth.

Pencils.

Notebooks.

These purchases.

All   all small small expenses.   205

For the use of the motor   I also paid three dollars.

All these things, came to ten dollars.

The total of everything was thirty dollars.

"But that is what I came for" I say to him "Why should I save the money."

Well.   210

Well thus, the days, ´ were passing by rapidly.

´ Already ten days had quickly gone by.

He didn't keep anything from me either.

Well he put everything in order for me see.

For no reason indeed   now, some people get rheumatism[12]   he wrote it all.   215

So enemies' disease[13]   some have enemies' disease   "they are called[14] by

enemies' disease" he says.

He put everything in order again for me it seems.

´ He taught me all these rules.

"Carry on well" see he says.

"Indeed after you leave now   you must get an assistant" see he says.   220

"If by chance you   don't get one.

If you don't get one, one person alone can't do this" see he says.

He truly said   to me also.

"Well   with regard to the fields   planting medicine" see he says.

"If you, indeed have a communal farm" he says.   225

"You must plant for nothing" see he says.

"No money" he says.

´ "For it belongs to the village" ` he says.

---

[12] because of the snakebite
[13] gonorrhea
[14] get

"tayleku, aimala   peka soytao" takken soke, " 'ayleku nue   ainis' " takken
soke.

" ' pali walapo walappaa iplo' " takken soke.   230

"teysokku pe soko takkenye 'pek ina tikkoloye.'

ina tiysal ipapaapakka pe, tiempo nasikko" takken soke.

" 'mer se parnanao' " takken soke.

"teki pe tiysatki kep, ipapaapakkine   kep arpatpalo" takken soke.

"nekulup saalir" soysunto a.   235

"nekulup pe saartipa" soke.

"kepe   akkwio ittolesunto kwis kwise.

teysokku, pe kannar emuroku   kummaytoku kwen ´ akkarsulitte" soke.

"tey sale" takken soke.

"tanapakke pe tiko" soke "nainu tummat" soke.   240

"tey sale" takken soke.

"nainu warkwenat" soke a.

"ai kwensak warkwen   tiypimotipa" soke.

"ati suittompo" soke.

"ati nekkwepursulitte" soke.   245

"ati warkwen   ekat" pittosursoke.

anka soysunto.

"tuppu paitkinet tipa" soke.

"ati tayleku, suitpakke" takken soke.

"tuppu pait, sunna   tekit apepimotipa" soke.   250

"sun tey pe sao" takken soke.

"inso" soke "napirmo" an kar soke.

"teukkin" parsoke "tule nailikkustipa" soke a.

"ina   perkwaple pe, nutas" soke.

"takkarku, pane tayleku onoko" soke.   255

"Indeed, the friends   will say to you" see he says, " 'indeed many [snakes]
came out' " see he says.
" 'It is possible to kill two even three' " see he says.   230
"Therefore you will say see 'I will go and plant medicine for you.'
After having planted the medicine for eight days you, will regulate the time"[15] see
he says.
" 'Don't go there' " see he says.
"Well there where you planted it then, after eight days   then they can work again"
see he says.
"Within the earth do it then" he truly said ah.   235
"Within the earth you will do it then" he says.
"Then   you must dig did you hear shoveling shoveling.
Therefore, when you have covered it over again   when they come to burn it [the
field] ´ nothing will happen" he says.
"That is how it is done" see he says.
"You must plant in four places" he says "if the field is big" he says.   240
"That is how it is done" see he says.
"When the field belongs to one person" he says ah.
"If a single friend   wants to plant too" he says.
"You charge him one dollar" he says.
"This one does not belong to the village" he says.   245
"Rather a single person   is the owner" don't you hear he says.
He truly said to me.
"If there are persons from other islands" he says.
"These indeed, you will charge two dollars" see he says.
"Another island, truly   if they want it too" he says.   250
"Truly you will do it this way" see he says.
"Thus" he says "It is good too" I say to him.
"Well furthermore" he also says "if a person is bitten" he says ah.
"With medicine   you will cure, everything" he says.
"In fact, the next day indeed you will send him out" he says.   255

[15] stop people from going there

"onosokkalile pe nek, weki onmakkennekki pe soko" takken soke "'emi an
onosokkarye.

pan emi an onokoye.'

teysokku mimmi, koe kisikana   mukan soysa" takken soke " 'emi tayle ani
tup   mu nai' " takken soke.

"teyso pese maynonimalo" takken soke a.

"mukana   e nankana   pese maynonikko" takken soke.   260

"e nan maymoko" takken soke "e pap maymokoye.

e mimmi maymoko kwaple ati sicii kwenti yokkorpa mako" soke "e nan   e
pap   tey sale" takken soke.

"ippakke   kar wis tiempo uymoko" soke.

"aynep nanaetti pasur" soke "'kwenti paket' oparsunnat ippakke.

ina allietse" soysunto.   265

"tey sale" takken soke.

"weki an sortapukkwat anti anpe kakkappaa nikkatti   pel ina makarpi" takken
soke.

"teysokku anmala   toitar parkwayetisur" soke.

"ar takketi" tay soke.

"kusku tule, nek ipettimokatte" soke.   270

"ukak unnila   kin   walik kwici takkartamar" takken soke.

"melle tayleku   pese warmakkekarye" soy takken soke.

"tayleku   pasur pe takkekarye aka ina mayle" takken soke.

"peti nekkwepur tummat sokkuti   iki kwaplemakkar pe mako?" soke.

"kwen kwen sikki na ittomalatti pe oko" takken soke.   275

"ati ipapaapak pe oko" takken soke "ati, nue sikkit" takken soke.

"tayleku   inso kwen kwena, sappin seret tipa, punakwa seret tipa   ome seret
tipa   ati pese oko" soke "suitpakke" soke.

"When you are about to send him out of your house, you will announce in the gathering house" see he says "'now I am about to send him out.

Tomorrow I will send him out.'

Therefore with regard to babies, to newly born infants   the midwives said" see he says " 'now it seems this one belongs to the vine   has this potential' " see he says.

"Therefore people will come to you to be painted" see he says ah.

"Grandmothers   and their mothers   will come to you to be painted" see he says.   260

"The mother will be painted also" see he says "and the father will be painted too.

Their baby itself will be completely painted black but the others will be painted only up to the knee" he says "the mother   the father   will be done this way" see he says.

"Four days   you will give them to rest" he says.

"It doesn't make any difference if they walk about" he says "but 'they must wait' you will affirm the four days.

Until the medicine goes away" he truly said.   265

"That is how it is done" see he says.

"Here I have thirteen of my people   all are painted with medicine" see he says.

"Therefore we   are not at all afraid" he says.

"They [snakes] are always seen" see he says.

"Because they also are owners of,[16] our land" he says.   270

"So that they are only around   close by   are seen nearby" see he says.

"So that indeed   they don't approach you" he says see he says.

"Indeed   so that they don't bother you that is why the medicine is painted" see he says.

"Since your village is really big   how can you paint everyone?" he says.

"You will bathe those who are affected by this disease"[17] see he says.   275

"You will bathe those for eight days" see he says "those are very affected" see he says.

"Indeed   thus sometimes, a young man, sometimes a young girl   sometimes an older woman   will come to you to bathe" he says "it costs two dollars" he says.

---

[16] belong to
[17] have potential to be bitten by snakes

"mani pippipar" takken soke.

"suitpakke oyle" takken soke.

tese ukak aite, anka ikal ukkesunto.   280

"tayle wese, an arpama" takken soke.

"pe ikar pait apepalirtina   pe turtaypar" takken soke "punmarkat an kanipar"
takken soke.

"ampa ayop ilemakkal an kanipar" takken soke.

"mu sokattulakwen kakka pakke an nikka" takken soke.

"teysokku kwaple narmakkar nait e kartakine, anse kwaple oyosat," pe takken
soke.   285

"we a mu a mu a mu kwikwis" takken soke.

ai Manisiytinappi a ittonamoka, ipampe kapiapmo anse.

anyalaparsunto.

teki   teysokku ati, nekapar nasis tayle, "suitnerkwa an wis seti" soka.

"turkwen e mani" soka.   290

"ati punmarkat."

inso sokene.

"nuekampi" an kar soke.

"nia kaet an wispar" takken soke.

"teysokku   pe namaypipartipa" soke.   295

"turtaytapar" takken soke.

"nia kaet takkarku ´ kiakkwapal a.

tule, tupki warmastipa" soke.

"niase kottetaette" soke.

"kal an namay" takken soke.   300

"kal an sunmayye.

tek an sama" takken soke.

"muki, tayleku kwenkwen mukin ailatta" takken soke, "nia impakwen nakustaet.

"It's cheap" see he says.

"Two dollars for bathing" see he says.

Up to this the friend, truly counseled me. 280

"It seems up to here, is my work" see he says.

"If you want to learn another chant   if you want to study again" see he says "I also know the one having to do with women"[18] see he says.

"And like the other one I again have it ordered" see he says.

"I have twenty-four parts about childbirth" see he says.

"Indeed it was all written in his notebook, he showed it all to me" you see I say. 285

"These are for this birth these are for this birth these are for this birth" see he says.

Friend Manisiytinappi[19] was also studying it, he also stayed ten days at our place.

At my side.

Well   indeed as for him, he only finished half it seems, "I only brought three dollars" he says.

"It costs ten dollars" he says. 290

"The one having to do with women."

Thus he said.

"It is good" I say to him.

"I also know the one to grab the devil" see he says.

"Therefore   if you want to chant again" he says. 295

"Come study another time" see he says.

"The one to grab the devil so ´ is short also ah.

If a person, encounters a vine"[20] he says.

"It might happen that he calls the devil"[21] he says.

"I chant for him" see he says. 300

"I speak for him.

Well that is what I do" see he says.

"In childbirth, indeed at times, in childbirth they [women] faint" see he says, "the devil sometimes attacks them.

18 childbirth
19 another Kuna medicinal specialist, from another village
20 is bitten by a snake
21 becomes crazy

kal an sunmay" takken soke.

" 'emi we, neka an imas' " takken soke.   305

" 'ipa, ipanerkwa an imaysamar' " takken soke.

" 'emi ina an tiysa' " takken anka soke.

"kwaplen kal an namaysa" takken soke.

" 'emi we sappi, na kwikwicit, kwipa tummakan ailasat a.

kwaple anka mortup, ney pilli pakkese an oupos' " takken soke.   310

´ apsoetyop ittolesunna.

" 'kaopikine, an, mortup ote' " takken soke.

"teysokkuti   aiye, teki an ikar kanima" takken soke.

"teysokku we   kwenna kwenna soy" takken soke " 'pi-la-kat-ye.'

pilakatsur" soke.   315

"eppenne tayleku nerkan aitearkua.

nerkan tummakan aiteskua.

tayle ipeler warkwena   sanale kaluyapa, 'kalumattuye' ney nukatyapa toysa"

takken soke.

"emi aki karta   sappurpa oyokwici taylear" takken soke.

" 'teki karta anniy susmar' soke.   320

'teki karta apsolearku' "   soy takken soke " ' "ina   anse turtaytamaloye.

tominkoki pe takoye."

teki, aimala   karta amisat yappa naetkine.

ai pila   yapa toysa' takken soke.

'pila ipa   ipampe kakka attar yokkuap' takken soke.   325

'nekurpa.

tey pilase ekislearsun' takken soke.

' "emi an wey toytekua.

emi tayleku, an toyteku nek sicit" takken soke.

"ipya kasa yopye.   330

tek an toysaku taisik, ne-ka-nu-et" takken soke.

I speak for them" see he says.
" 'Now I prepared the farm' " see he says.   305
" 'For six, six days we prepared it' " see he says.
" 'Now I planted the medicine' " see he says to me.
"All this I chanted for them" see he says.
" 'Now these trees, standing there, the big *kwipa* trees, fell down ah.
I sent the entire clothes line, down to the fourth level under the ground' " see he
says.   310
´ It truly sounds like *The way of the mass curer*.
" 'Within the *kaopi* tree, I, lowered the clothes line' " see he says.
"Well   friend, indeed I have this chant" see he says.
"Well   there are those who say" see he says "'it-be-longs-to-the-Cho-cos.'
But it does not belong to the Chocos" he says.   315
"A long time ago indeed when the seers started to come down.
When the great seers came down.
It seems Ipelele   corporally entered a stronghold, a place called "Kalumattuye'"
see he says.
"Now there in the jungle   he showed a letter it seems" see he says.
" 'Well they took the letter away from me' he says.   320
'Well when they read the letter' "   he says see he says " ' "come   to my place
to learn medicine.[22]
You should come on Sunday."
Well, the friends   who found the letter did not want to go.
Friend Choco   entered inside' see he says.
'The Choco stayed there fifteen   fifteen days' see he says.   325
'Under the ground.
Well the Choco was asked'[23] see he says.
' "Now when I entered this place.
Now indeed, when I entered the place was dark" see he says.
"As if my eyes were held shut.   330
Well when I entered some more, it-was-clear" see he says.

---

[22] the letter says
[23] when he returned, to report on his experience

"we naptule pukkwayop" takken soke.

"tule sanakwarpuy" takken soke.

"naipe   suaripet" takken soke.

"tekine akkwaser   a arkar" takken soke.   335

"aase   akkwaser kep anka, macikwa amis" takken soke.

" 'saylase an perpeap' soke.

tey saylase an perpeapku, sayla anka soy" takken soke " 'ipi pe saye?'

an soy" takken soke " 'an   an we karta setani takkenye.'

a soketpa kartate parmitsokkutina   yok an oturtakkar" takken soke.   340

"nuet" takken soysunto.

" 'pap weki anka nek uysamo' takken soke.

' "yoo tayleku mimmikan   olo tule wek anpakuoet   mer ponikan

toitar   appinkaekala   weki   ina uymai pe saoye"   anka tios soysa takkenye'

soy takken soke.

teysokku an mosku uatuk kwirri an ku" takken soke.

"uysir pukkitar" takken soke.   345

"teysokku anka ina imaysa" soke "kannal uatuk an nukus takken.

teysokku emi an kannar noarparku, teyop an kuspar" takken soke.

"ina an turtacokku   kannal an nutasparye.

asu noyse pakkar kwirri an kus takkenye.

eysokkuti emite perkwaple pe an takken" soke "nuet takkenye." '   350

nue nappira tayleye pinsaarmosun" takken soke.

"aa kep emi tayle an sayla ´e sakkamo anso.

a turtaysamo" takken soke.

"kep a an sayla   kep e sakkase turtasmo" takken soke.

"a ikal emite an   kanimo" takken soke.   355

"teysokku an   an peece pankuarpimosokku   teyop pani pankutanimo" takken
soke.

"teysokku ipika tayleku   icakkwa an pek ukko" soke.

"Like the people on this earth" see he says.

"Are those people corporally" see he says.

"The snake   is policeman" see he says.

"Well and the spider   he is spokesman" see he says.   335

"When   I got there the spider then got me, a boy" see he says.

" 'To take me to the chief' he says.

Well when he took me to the chief, the chief says to me" see he says " 'What have you come to do?'

I say" see he says " 'I   I brought this letter see.'

By order of this letter because it was sent   immediately they taught me" see he says.   340

"It was good" see he truly said.

" 'God gave me this place' see he [the chief] says.

' "Before indeed the children   the golden people[24] lived here   so that they don't encounter   evil spirits   here   you will administer medicine"   God said to me see' he says see he says.

Well when I arrived there I had my ears all bitten up" see he says.

"There were many bats" see he says.   345

"Well he administered medicine to me" he says "he cured my ears again see.

Well now when I left once again, the same thing happened to me" see he says.

"Since I had learned this medicine   I cured myself once again.

I was all bitten up to my nostrils see.

Therefore now you see me" he says "completely well see." '   350

This seems to be true and I also believe it" see he says.

"It then now seems my teacher's ´ father-in-law I think.

He learned too"[25] see he says.

"Then my teacher   then he also learned with his father-in-law" see he says.

"I also now   have this chant" see he says.   355

"Therefore I   since I also had to travel far   similarly you also have traveled to me from far away" see he says.

"Therefore why indeed   would I give you bad counsel" he says.

---

[24] the Kuna
[25] with the Choco

"tayle an nuk nopi an apekette" soke.

"ipika kirmar namay" takken soke.

" 'kattik immar turtaymarye.   360

kattik immar tiymarye.

pap neyse ikar nuetye.'

kirmar namakket an wismar" takken soke.

"anpalla an namaytimo" takken soke.

"teysokku ipika aiye an pey nailekuo" takken soke.   365

"teysokku teyop pe tayleku sappinkan nikkusar pe oturtaymokoye."

anka soysunto.

"pe sappinkwen amioeti   unnila pe pentakko" takken soke.

"immar wis yaipa pe saalir" takken soke.

"mas emiartipa" soke.   370

"okkop tipa" soke.

"ipi peka wis sapitipa" soke.

"pelakwa" takken soke.

"tuppu pait tipa" soke.

"pe mani oesacun   ati pe oeko, pese mani   uymoko" takken soke.   375

"teysokku aiye mer toitar onaypalo" takken soke.

"kwenna kwenna mani tayleku karkesaila   uyteta" takken soke.

"sayla teki eka soysayop takkenye" aite anka ikar ukkarsunto.

"teysokku emi tayleku pe mekoeti   kirmarki aypinekarsurye.

unni kirmar pentakkekarye.   380

pe meko" takken soke.

"tayleku nappanek okannoekar" takken soke.

"tuppu peka   napir   pe takkekar" pittosursokeye.

"kwenti tayleku, inso 'kirmarki aypineka immar turtaysaye'   pe pitamalar"

takken soke.

"Indeed I want my name to be known many places" he says.

"That is why the elders chant" see he says.

" 'Learn many things. 360

Plant many things.

The road to Father's[26] house is good.'

I know the chants of the elders' see he says.

"I have also chanted the same ones" see he says.

"Therefore why friend would I trip you up" see he says. 365

"Therefore when you have your student indeed you will teach him the same way."

He truly said it to me.

"The student you will get   he will help you only"[27] see he says.

"When you have some little things to do" see he says.

"When you clear plantain plantations" he says. 370

"Or coconut plantations" he says.

"Whatever thing you want to do" he says.

"Everything" see he says.

"As for people from other islands" he says.

"The money you spent   that money which, you will spend   they will give you

too" see he says. 375

"Therefore friend don't raise the price" see he says.

"There are those indeed who put the price   very high" see he says.

"As if their chief[28] told them to do so see" the friend truly counseled me.

"Well now indeed you must   not turn around[29] the elders.

But only help the elders. 380

You must" see he says.

"Indeed in order to strengthen the earth"[30] see he says.

"So that your island   truly   recognizes you" don't you hear he says.

"In fact indeed, thus some people will say about you   'you studied things in

order to turn around the elders' " see he says.

[26] God's
[27] will not pay you
[28] teacher
[29] hurt
[30] your village

"pe okakkansatamalarye."   385

anka soysunto.

"ikal iskana mama" takken soke.

"ati an pentakketsurmar" takken soke.

"ikal iskanati tayleku   'tios an takkoteye'   kwen soylesur" takkenye.

"ati pinsa turtayle" pittosursoke soke.   390

"kin nekkwen kannoetsur" takkenye.

aite anka soysunto.

"teysokku aimar mesar pe sapier, kwen akkarsurye.

pe kwen payokosurye.

teysokku   aiye mer keker ittokoye.   395

iki tipa pe nappanekkine   inaturkan serkan mamapartipaye.

tupa ikar wismalat mamatipaye.

mamasurpartipaye."

soysunto.

"teysokkuti kirmar itu, pe itu mamaitti   inso, peece an penkus" takken soke.   400

" 'pia wekit ina partanikkoye?

sailakkar wekit ina an kwen taytisurye.'

anki ululear" takken soke.

"a-ni-e-ka-so-ke-yo-pi   'an pur kanna ina wisi'   e-ka-so-ke-yo-pi   aimal

anki pinsas" takken soke.

´ "ani ekar soysulitte" soke.   405

"wepa tayleku ai   immar turtaysatpali   an turtasmo" pittosursoke soke.

"emi tayleku itu ikar wismalat   perkwaple milema" takken soke.

"pel ankatpikus" anka soysunto.

"pela Ipeti ankat pukkwa   tayle Ikkanti pukkwa   tayleku Narkanti mai   emi

Acutup anse arpipa" takken soke.

"iki taetmotipa?" soke.   410

"They will be telling lies about you." 385

He truly said to me.

"There are evil ways" see he says.

"These are not helpful to us" see he says.

"It is not said   of these evil ways indeed   'they will lead us to see God' " see.

"These are taught for free" don't you hear it is said he says. 390

"They do not serve to strengthen" see.

The friend truly said to me.

"Therefore if friends criticize you, it is nothing.

You should not pay attention.

Therefore   friend do not be bothered. 395

Perhaps in your village   there are elderly medicine men.

There are perhaps those who know the way of the vine.

And again perhaps there are not."

He truly said.

"Well the elders, who were before you   thus, they competed against me" see he

says. 400

" 'Where could this medicine have come from?

Before we didn't have this medicine.'

They criticized me" see he says.

"As-if-I-was-say-ing-to-them   'I know medicine better than you'   as-if-I-was-

say-ing-that-to-them   the friends didn't have confidence in me" see he says.

´ "But I did not say that to them" he says. 405

"The friend[31] indeed   had learned things   and I learned them also" don't you

hear it is said he says.

"Now indeed those who before used to know chants   all of them are disappearing"

see he says.

"All are mine"[32] he truly said to me.

"All those in Ipeti are mine   indeed in Ikanti there are many   indeed in Narkana

there are some   now someone also came to me from Acutuppu" see he says.

"And how might he behave?" he says. 410

---

[31] my teacher

[32] my students

"wese arpiku   napir tae tayleke" takken soke.

"e tuppu mosku iki taettipa?" soke.

"an nuk isoettipa?" soke.

"ani eka immal icakkwa soysayopi   ai nanaettipaye" anka soke, ´ "wicurmosun
pitto pinsan" soy takkenye.

"teysokkuti ai akkal akkal an kwen kumasuli.   415

ilakwen an   tayleku weki taniku" takken soke.

"unni tayleku, kirmar sorpali   untar an pentayma" takken soke.

"kwen kwen pirkakwento   nailikkusmalat   an pentayti" takken soke.

"inso tayleku kwen kwen kar noe.

kwensak emi   an ipe   tua tetterkwa ti" takken soke.   420

"an pentas" takken soke.

"emi tayleku, e inatulet sokkar" takken soke " 'pe tiynamarsunye.

par nukuosulitteye.'

nunusaila appanma" takken soke.

"teki anse noni" takken soke.   425

"niwalappakus ottartani   kep anse ninoni" takken soke.

"emi wis pentas" ´ pe pittosursoke ` soke.

"emi karmayti ampa" takkenye.

"al an taysat Panamaki.

suarki nanasunnata."   430

"ampalla aswe enay" takken soke.

"ampalla tayleku ua makke ampalla ua soe   sappurpa yannu makke, yannu
maysar opestae   kep e pap suaptas" takken soke.

"an ipe tekitte ´ iplopimalanatte" soke.

"teysokkute emite   teki anti wis pentaymain" takkenye anka soysunto.

"teysokkute emit a ikar pe amitanisokku, ikar nuet" takken soke.   435

"tayleku napir peka   nekkwepurti pinsas" pittosursoke soke.

"teysokku nue salak" takkenye anka soysunto.

"teysokkuti inso tayleku nekkwepurka   nue pe soytappo takkenye.

emi teysokku, mer pe penkuekala.

"When he came here   he behaved well it seems" see he says.

"When he got back to his island how did he behave?" he says.

"Did he slander my name?" he says.

"As if I had said bad things to him   how will the friend go about" he says to me,

´ "I do not know really I think" he says see.

"Therefore friend I do not behave just any way.   415

I am always   indeed this way" see he says.

"I am only indeed, helping   the elders a lot" see he says.

"Some sick people   for one year   I have been helping" see he says.

"Thus indeed some have fractured bones.

One now   I have   with a torn thigh muscle" see he says.   420

"I helped him" see he says.

"Now indeed, his medicine man said to him" see he says " 'they are surely going

to bury you.

You will never get better again.'

He smelled very bad" see he says.

"Well he came to my place" see he says.   425

"For three months he had been suffering   then they brought him to my place" see

he says.

"Now I helped him a little" ´ don't you hear it is said ` he says.

"Now he is still walking about" see.

[Olowitinappi says to teacher] "I saw him in Panama.

He was going about with a stick."   430

[The teacher responds] "He still climbs up after avocados" see he says.

"He still indeed spears fish he still catches fish   in the jungle he kills wild boar,

the wild boar that he killed he leaves   then his father goes to get it" see he says.

"And this one [patient] of mine well ´ they wanted to smash him to death" he says.

"So now   well I was helping him a little" see he truly said to me.

"Well now this chant that you came to gather [study], it is a good chant" see he

says.   435

"Indeed your village   thought well of you" don't you hear it is said he says.

"Therefore do well" see he truly said to me.

"Therefore thus indeed you will say well there   to your village see.

Now therefore, so that they don't contest you.

emite kartate an peka parmitmo" takken soke.   440

"emit peti karta wiculi.

tukkin narmas anso.

pekin pinsatamalarye."

anka soysunto.

emi, Maenakki narmaynonikkit Maenakki ate karta tulet maita.   445

e maci, kar soysat   "pe ase narmaytappoye."

aki anmar narmaynonisunto.

teysokkut a, emite   na teki arpitte emite kannar an pes nonimarpali.

wiskat ittolekena.

toitar akkal akkar   kus kwen ittolesuli.   450

teysokku inso an arpaetti   iy tayletakotipa.

"inso tiosti   pule ponikante   anse oyosurmalar   ar pirkakwen anpa an
arpasur" pe ittosursokeye.

"inso tayleku   ponikan ittakka tayle arpalirti   emis, arpaleket   pinsa pese
oyotmalo" pittosursokeye an soysunto.

"teysokku tiospi wicun" pittosursokeye.

PITTOKUA, tese ukaysunto.   455

Now I will send a letter for you" see he says.　　　　　　440

"Now you don't know letters.

That you yourself wrote it I think.

They can't think."

He truly said to me.

Now, when we arrived in Maenak we wrote it in Maenak there is a man who

knows how to write.　　　　　　445

He told, his son　　"you will write it there."

It is there that we wrote it.

So ah, now　　well this is how my trip was and now again I have returned to you.

A little has been learned.

Nothing out of the ordinary　　happened.　　　　　　450

Well thus my work　　I don't know how it will be.

"Thus if God　　does not send　　evil spirits to me　　so that again for one year I

am not able to work" don't you hear it is said.

"Thus indeed　　if evil spirits come near it seems　　now, what I worked[33]　　for

free I will show to you" don't you hear it is said I have truly said.

"Well only God knows well" don't you hear it is said.

YOU HAVE HEARD, up to here.

[33] learned

6. *THE HOT PEPPER STORY*: STRATEGIES IN TEXT AND CONTEXT

Kaa kwento (*The hot pepper story*) is one of many stories told among the Kuna. Some of these stories are humorous, but while *The hot pepper story* contains elements of humor, it deals with quite serious matters. My analysis of *The hot pepper story* begins with one telling, or performance of the story. This telling is discussed in some detail and compared with other performances. Both the story and the events of which the telling of the story is the central part are analyzed in order to demonstrate the interplay between the significance of *The hot pepper story* and the contexts in which it is performed. An important feature of the structure of *The hot pepper story* is that it lends itself to multiple interpretations; this feature can be understood as functional in Kuna social and cultural life when situated in the actual contexts in which it is exploited, and when viewed in terms of a blending of tradition and modernization which is characteristically Kuna.

The version of *The hot pepper story* that is presented here was recorded on February 18, 1971, in the Mulatuppu gathering house. It is told by Mastayans, one of the chiefs of Mulatuppu, to a group of men. More particularly, it is told to an elderly, well-known chief from the village of Achutuppu, who at the time was visiting Mulatuppu for several days in order to chant Kuna tradition in the gathering house. Mastayans, together with a group of Mulatuppu men, is keeping the visiting chief company and entertaining him in the gathering house on this morning, as is required by Kuna custom. Were there no visitor, the gathering house would be locked closed and most of the men of the village, including the chiefs, would be off working in the jungle mainland or fishing. Mastayans announces that he will tell *The hot pepper story* if the visiting chief will serve as his responder. The visiting chief agrees and does so, participating in the performance by ratifying each line with an affirmative grunt, a *teki* (so it is), a repeated word or phrase, a comment or laugh, or a question. The structure of the telling of *The hot pepper story* is thus Mastayans as teller, the visiting chief as addressee-responder, and the group of men in the gathering house as audience. This communicative structure (sender–receiver-responder–audience) is a very common Kuna one, characteristic of events ranging from the most ritual and ceremonial to the most informal and everyday. (See Sherzer 1983: 196-200.)

Possible Contexts for Performance of *The hot pepper story*

It is necessary to begin this exploration and explanation of *The hot pepper story* by contrasting the performance reported on here with other possible performances and by viewing the ethnography of this event in relation to a more total Kuna ethnography of speaking.

The hot pepper story, like other Kuna stories, can be performed in two different ways in two different contexts for two different purposes: A story can be spoken by chiefs or other knowers of stories, typically in the gathering house but also in one's own home, for example, to young children. In such performances, there is a focus on entertainment, amusement, play, and humor.

A story can also be chanted by chiefs in the gathering house, usually in the evening, to an audience of men and women. The chanting of stories is practiced in the eastern portion of San Blas, which includes Mulatuppu. Inhabitants of the western portion of San Blas do not feel that it is appropriate to chant stories and criticize those who do so. While a chanted story may be pleasing, amusing, or humorous to the listeners, the ultimate purpose of all chanting is to illustrate proper and improper modes of behavior and to call on the community to follow the former.

Further examination of these two ways of performing stories is essential for an understanding of the problem posed in this chapter. Stories, when performed in spoken form for amusement in the gathering house, are told on days when people do not work in the jungle or fish (holidays, or days when there is an interdiction on work because of an eclipse, and so forth); when there is a chief visiting from another village and men sit around the gathering house with him; or just before the evening chanting of chiefs. The stories are a diversion for the pleasure and amusement of those present – a small group of men during the daytime or the gradually gathering group of men and women at night. Stories are told in colloquial Kuna, in the style appropriate for gathering-house narration. They are easily understood by all Kuna. The focus is on the play and humor of narration. The narrator alternates fast and slow, loud and soft speech, imitates voices and sounds, and tries to make his audience laugh. The audience, especially a single person in it at whom the story is directed, asks questions and makes humorous comments. There is much laughter. (See chapter seven for the presentation and discussion of the telling of a very popular story.)

Stories are one of a number of genres, topics, or themes that can be chanted in the gathering house by chiefs. Others are tribal myths, legends, and history; reports of personal experiences, including dreams; and counsel to particular individuals, groups of individuals, or the community at large. (See chapters three and four.) There are regional and individual differences in practice and attitude in San Blas with regard to what topics are appropriate for chiefs' chanting. Inhabitants of the western portion of San Blas criticize those of the east for chanting biblical themes, non-Kuna history, for example about Christopher Columbus and Simon Bolivar, and personal dreams, as well as stories.

Chanting is a most serious affair. The subject matter is drawn on by the chief for the purpose of his moral instruction to the audience. The performance is in the form of a ritual dialogue between two chiefs in which one chants verse by verse, with the other responding *teki* after each verse. The linguistic variety is phonologically, syntactically, and semantically distinct from colloquial Kuna. In this style, metaphors abound. It is the mark of a good chief not only to use conventional, traditional metaphors, but to elaborate and develop them in personal and appropriate ways. The chief states and stresses his moral as he chants. After the chant, there is an interpretation in colloquial Kuna by a chief's spokesman. This interpretation explains the message of the chant. The interpretation of the chant, by both chief and spokesman, is thus part of the structure and strategy of its performance. (See chapter three.)

The performance of *The hot pepper story* presented here is an interesting case with regard to these two Kuna ways of performing stories. *The hot pepper story* is spoken and told primarily for amusement, on the occasion of a visit of a well-known chief from another village. But the visiting chief takes on the role of responder, as he might in a chanted version of the story. While there is no spokesman's interpretation, Mastayans does provide a short moral using a metaphor, or at least an allusive term, as part of the end of the story. The special properties of this particular performance of *The hot pepper story* are important to the analysis of its strategic structure and are discussed below.

It is useful to place the distinction between two ways of performing stories (spoken and chanted) within the larger system of Kuna discourse. The three principal Kuna ritual discourse types are the chanting of chiefs, the chants of curing and magical control, and the shouting of puberty festivals, each in a particular linguistic variety and style quite distinct from colloquial Kuna and, especially in the case of the latter two, not intelligible to nonspecialists. The addressees of curing and magical and puberty festival discourse are spirits, which are believed to understand the linguistic variety involved.

The efficacy of these texts resides in convincing the object to perform an act or acts, either after having heard the text or simultaneous to the hearing of the text. There is no interpretation and none is necessary since the spirit-addressees understand the language of the text. (See chapter eight.)

The chanting of chiefs is addressed to humans – the audience that is present and expected to listen to the performance. The spokesman's interpretation is for them and is needed, both because of the metaphorical language of the chants and because of the belief that reformulation and repetition are needed in order to drive home the message. Spoken stories, like reports and personal narratives recounted in the gathering house, are in colloquial Kuna. There is no formal interpretation as part of the performance. None is needed since the message is clear and easily understood by all those present and no allusive message is involved.

The Story and Interpretations

The hot pepper story, as told by Mastayans, has a deceptively simple narrative structure. It is about an old woman, a grandmother, who asks a young boy to watch over her plum tree and who buries him alive in the ground when he seems not to do so properly. The boy is later discovered by his sister while she is picking hot pepper from a plant growing above him. He is dug out of the ground by his parents and punishes the grandmother. The telling consists of six parts, with subparts within them.

1. The opening, which consists of metacommunicative commentary about the story-telling event itself (lines 1-9).
2. The grandmother's problem with her plum tree and the actions she takes concerning it (10-89). These include asking the boy to guard the tree (23-28); the boy's first-night's failure to catch a culprit (44-55); and the grandmother's burying the boy in the ground as a punishment (56-72). This part ends with the boy's parents looking for him and mourning his death (73-89).
3. The growing of the pepper plant and the discovery and saving of the boy (90-147). This part includes the pepper plant growing at the grandmother's house (90-101); the boy's sister going to pick pepper at the grandmother's house (102-108); the boy speaking to his sister and mother (109-127); the boy being dug out of the ground (128-138); and the boy reporting on his experience (139-147). As discussed below, with regard to my translation of the text, there is some temporal jumping and discontinuity

involved here, especially when the text is approached from the perspective of western European cultural logic.

4. The punishment of the grandmother (148-166).
5. The moral (167-170).
6. The coda, which like the opening, is metacommunicative (170-171).

The textuality of Mastayans' performance of *The hot pepper story* involves a series of repeated and permuted thematic elements and words, all of which contribute to its denseness and complexity. Repeated thematic elements include the boy dying and the grandmother dying; the growing of a plum tree and the growing of a pepper plant; the boy twice sitting and watching but not discovering a culprit; the girl and then her mother hearing the calling of the boy; and the girl going several times to gather hot pepper at the grandmother's house.

Repeated and permuted words are grouped within certain semantic fields crucial to the narrative. These include the semantic field of watching, *nakkuleke* (take care of), *etarpe* (guard), *arkae* (watch), *takke* (see, look), and *akkwe* (care for); of rising and growing up, *ainie* (grow), *nakkwe* (rise), *tunkue* (get big), and *serkue* (grow up); of throwing and falling down, *arkwane* (fall), *ekwane* (throw), and *patte* (fall down); of dying, *purkwe* (die), *perkue* (finish off), and *opeloe* (put an end to); of digging and burying, *tike* (plant, dig, bury), *kwie* (dig), and *akkwie* (dig); of producing and getting ripe, *turpamakke* (produce fruit), *nakue* (get ripe), and *okkinnoe* (get red, ripe); and of burning, *kunamakke* (burn) and *kwapunye* (flame).

There are also repetitions in form created by the repeated use of the same or similar sounding words. Examples are *pinna pinna* (slowly); *purkwe* (die)/*perkue* (finish off)/*opeloe* (put an end to); *kwane* (gather)/*arkwane* (fall)/*ekwane* (throw); and *kwie* (dig)/*akkwie* (dig).

The constant shifting of point of view (caused by temporal disjunctions and moving in and out of quotations), coupled with the repetition and permutation of a small number of thematic elements and words, characterize *The hot pepper story*'s textuality. While these textual processes are reflections of an underlying Kuna cultural logic, it is only by investigating actual discourse, actual verbal performances, that we can uncover this logic and see it in action. It is interesting that similar textual patterns are characteristic of certain works within the French new and new new novel, a most avant garde and self-consciously experimental contemporary enterprise. (See D. Sherzer

1986.) Of course a quite different cultural logic is involved in the French works, in which texts are considered experimental and breaking with tradition. In the Kuna case they are quite in keeping with tradition.

The hot pepper story shares features with other stories and myths found in South America as well as all over the world. It contains good deeds and evil deeds, punishments and rewards, deaths and a rebirth, and a moral. In terms of diffusion, the probable source is the singing bone or speaking hair motif of European folktales, now widespread in Latin America.[1] At the same time the story has similarities with the stories of Zipacna, Blood Woman, and the attempted resurrection of Seven Hunahpu in the Quiché Mayan *Popol Vuh*, which was written shortly after the Conquest and follows a hieroglyphic prototype. (See Tedlock 1985: 94-971, 114-115, and 159.) Whatever its origins, which perhaps involve a combination of Central American, South American, and European elements, it is most interesting that this motif has reached a tropical forest Amerindian society and become well integrated into its social, cultural, and verbal life. As rich as *The hot pepper story* is with regard to narrative development and symbolic oppositions, features that no doubt add to its role as a story told for amusement and entertainment, it does not provide an internal interpretation of the narrative development or symbolic oppositions, thus making it most useful for Kuna chiefs, in that they can develop an interpretation of their own choosing as part of the structure of the telling.

When chanted in the Kuna gathering house, *The hot pepper story* can be given various interpretations by the chief and the spokesman. These interpretations can be both general and particular and they can be opposed or in contradiction to one another. At the most general level the text can have to do with proper behavior and ways of treating other people. At a more particular level, it can have to do with the raising and care of young children. At a still more particular level, it can have to do with the care of babies, especially at birth, by midwives. And at the most particular level, it can have to do with what to do with babies who are born socially inappropriate – twins, albinos, those with birth defects, or the products of an illegitimate relationship. Contradictory interpretations result from differing points of view taken with regard to the issues involved in the care and treatment of babies, children, or people in general.

---

[1] I am grateful to Roger Abrahams for pointing this out to me. See Mackensen (1923) and Thompson (1961): Type 780 *The Singing Bone* and Type 780B *The Speaking Hair*.

A clue to the possible interpretations of *The hot pepper story* and its place in a Kuna ethnography of speaking is provided by the moral offered by Mastayans at the end of his narration on this particular morning in 1971 (lines 167-170).

> For this reason the ancestors said see it is said "If on this earth the
> grandmothers bury birds they are thrown there see.
> The grandmothers will be carried to a place called *pursipu* [white ash] the
> place of the chiefs of ashes where then there are many flaming
> trees all standing everywhere the grandmothers are punished there.
> Those who do not know how to take care of birds those who bury birds in
> this world.
> They are thrown there" the ancestors chant this see.

The word *sikkwi* (bird) had not appeared in the story, and what the grandmother had buried was a boy. But *sikkwi* is a euphemism for baby, and when babies die they are buried in their house in the village, by the midwives if the death is at birth. Adults are buried in the cemetery outside the village.

This useful hint enables us to examine *The hot pepper story* in greater detail, starting with the ways in which the text is open to multiple interpretations. First there is the question of whether there is a need or purpose for interpretation at all, and what the nature of interpretation might be. Put another way, can the story be taken point by point for what it is with no meanings other than the actual characters and actions described, or are these to be viewed as somehow symbolic of or representative of something else?

Among the possible interpretations there are the most general, such as, what are the reasons for or the meanings of the punishments and rewards, of both the grandmother and the boy? That is, what is the significance of the story, taken as a whole? Then there are particular, local interpretations, details in the narrative whose significance is not overtly explained in the text itself. These may also be viewed as features of the text where there is a choice such that the overall general structure of the text (not its interpretation) would not change if another choice had been made. Examples are: Why the title *The hot pepper story* and not the plum tree story or the grandmother story? Why does the grandmother have a plum tree and not a coconut tree, banana tree, or *ikwa* (wild fruit) tree? Why does a pepper plant grow up where the boy is buried and not a coconut, banana, orange, or plum tree? Why does the tree belong to a grandmother and not a father, mother, or grandfather? And why a boy and not a girl?

Understanding of some aspects and details of the story depends on explaining certain Kuna linguistic, social, and cultural presuppositions, which are not stated explicitly and overtly in the text but are essential to it. Discussion of these presuppositions shows the necessity of placing the text in the context of the language, society, and culture of which it forms a part. At the most general level of the plot, there are the punishments and rewards. The boy is punished for not properly caring for the plum tree, but later comes back to life. The grandmother is punished for having buried the boy. The boy is punished in this world, and the grandmother is punished in the afterworld. The Kuna believe that individuals are rewarded and punished in the afterworld for their good deeds and misdeeds in this world. The rewards and punishments are often appropriate to the individual's role in society.

It is interesting to consider just what the boy is punished for. He was asked by the grandmother to watch over the plum tree. It is common Kuna practice to hire someone to take care of a possession. However, a plum tree is very unimportant in the Kuna tree-plant ranking system; it is owned, but its fruit is free for anyone to take, in any quantity, at any time. (See Howe and Sherzer 1975). So the grandmother had no right to try and protect her fruit. Furthermore, it is never made clear what happens to the fruit, if the tree is merely old and no longer productive, if someone actually comes and takes the fruit, or if the boy is somehow responsible. Nor is it clear exactly who the boy is and what his relationship is to the old woman, the *muu*.

The word *muu* has three meanings in Kuna and all are potentially relevant to an understanding of the story – grandmother, old woman, midwife. I have somewhat arbitrarily chosen grandmother in my translation. The grandmother kills the boy by burying him. Although it is appropriate to bury dead infants on the spot, the boy in question was neither dead nor an infant; so burying him was a misdeed. The grandmother and the boy do not have individual, proper names. Rather they are general types, as are the boy's parents and his sister. The grandmother and the boy furthermore constitute a pair of antagonists in many ways similar to the paired antagonists of Kuna trickster tales. (See chapter seven.)

The pepper plant that grows up on the spot where the boy was buried gives the story its title. The pepper is hot and is used as a condiment in food. According to the Kuna system of ranking plants and trees, pepper is owned, but the owner must give an asker permission to pick some if needed for a meal. This is why the boy's sister asks for and obtains permission from the grandmother. It is important to note that in this case the grandmother is behaving perfectly appropriately. She *akkwe* (takes care of, line 100) the pepper plant and makes it available for others to use, a moral act for which individuals are positively rewarded in the afterworld. Yet this is precisely what does her in. The plate and golden hook used by the boy are part of a complex of objects believed by the Kuna to exist in the afterworld for their use. The grandmother's eternal place of punishment, Sodom, is clearly borrowed from Christian tradition, but it is given a Kuna name as well, *sappi pirkwen* or *pursipu*, and it is full of trees from the Kuna environment.

The complexity and richness of the text are further elucidated by examining it in terms of the symbolic oppositions found by Claude Lévi-Strauss (1964-1971) to be pervasive in lowland tropical forest South American mythology. Thus the drama between the grandmother and young boy running through the story opposes age to youth and female to male. The two plants in the story, the plum tree and the hot pepper, oppose unproductive and unripe to productive and ripe; and sticky and sweet to hot and spicy. It might be argued that grandmother is to boy as plum is to pepper; that is, old, unproductive, weak, and falling on the one hand and young, productive, powerful, and rising on the other. Furthermore, according to the Kuna tree-plant ranking system described above, plum/pepper opposes relatively wild (nature) to relatively owned (culture). Since the plum is not eaten as part of a Kuna meal and the pepper is, and since pepper is used almost exclusively with cooked food, plum/pepper also opposes raw to cooked.

The narrative development relates these various oppositions and introduces others, which it also relates to them. The story is essentially about misbehavior and punishment for misbehavior, and life and death. In brief, because the plum tree lacks life, the grandmother asks the boy to find out who is causing the problem (misbehaving toward it). Because the boy does not properly protect the plum tree (misbehaves), he is punished with death. The grandmother dies on this earth but comes back to life in heaven. The boy comes back to life on this earth and goes up to heaven to punish the grandmother for her own misbehavior. In the course of this narrative development, the opposition up-above/down-below is introduced. The fruit of the plum tree falls down, the boy is buried underground. The pepper grows up out of the ground, the boy comes out because of it and after it, and the boy goes up to heaven to punish the grandmother.

These textual explanations and explorations enable us to understand the plot of *The hot pepper story* in general and in detail, including some of its potential symbolism in Kuna life. They do not, however, reduce the text to a single, unambiguous interpretation; rather, they make the various possibilities for interpretation more interesting and intriguing, denser and richer. Thus we know why the grandmother is punished in the text – for killing the boy. But what does this symbolize? Was the boy not wrong at all, or not seriously wrong, or was he guilty of something? Are there circumstances under which the grandmother would have been justified in killing the boy? More particularly, following the clue provided by Mastayan's offered moral, was the grandmother punished for killing a baby born with some kind of defect? (That is, should a birth defect be taken as lightly as failure to care for a plum tree?) Or was the grandmother punished for failing to see that there really was no defect, or that it was minor? (That is, is failure to care for a tree that anyone is permitted to pick from not a defect?) The Kuna are a society of more than 30,000 individuals, living in more than 50 villages ranging from traditional and conservative to progressive and acculturation oriented. There are a variety of points of view on how to deal with birth defects just as there are on other subjects. The history of the Kuna, which involves considerable missionization[2] and acculturation, along with both reactions against and accommodations to both of these processes, is of relevance here. Flexible texts such as *The hot pepper story* enable leaders such as chiefs, symbolic moralists who are expected to take public positions in metaphorical language, to exploit a single plot in several ways. The same story can be used to justify and symbolize various and even contradictory points of view. This is an instance of the impact of history on Kuna speaking practices and Kuna verbal art.

Mastayans' Performance of *The hot pepper story*

Let us return to the actual performance of *The hot pepper story* which I recorded. The strategy and structure of this telling must be understood from several intersecting and interacting perspectives. First, there is a story, told for amusement. Mastayans' telling of the story entertained the assembled group and especially the guest of honor. Second, Mastayans' inclusion of a moral using allusive language and stating explicitly

---

2   Notice that *The Agouti story* (see chapter seven) was told on the occasion of the anniversary of the Baptist mission in Mulatuppu.

that "the ancestors chant this" (line 170) relates this entertaining telling to the more serious telling which might occur if this story were performed chanted.

The conversation between Mastayans and the visiting chief which follows the telling of *The hot pepper story* deals with precisely the fact that this same story can be chanted. Mastayans opens (lines 6, 7) and closes (line 170) his telling by giving credit to his teacher, Mantipaytikinya, a chief from the village of Mammimullu, with whom he has been studying. He points out that "he was teaching me **some**" (line 7) and "I have told you **a little**" (line 171). These are formulaic understatements used by ritual leaders which indicate that more is known, by Mastayans himself, by his teacher, Mantipaytikinya of Mammimullu, and by the ancestors. These statements not only give credit to his teacher but also serve to remind the audience that Mastayans himself is a knowledgeable and diligent chief; one who gains prestige for himself and his village by travelling to other villages to study with venerable traditional specialists. Mastayans, by combining elements of an entertaining telling (first perspective) with an allusive moral indicating potential for serious chanting and framing devices characteristic of ritual discourse (second perspective), leads us to a third perspective with regard to structure, strategy, and, ultimately, interpretation.

The immediate message of Mastayans in performing this story on this day is to announce to a well-known visiting chief and to his own village that "I Mastayans am a knowledgeable chief, one who studies with others to learn the traditions of our ancestors and performs them for my own village by chanting in the gathering house." Mastayans utilizes the rich and intricate potential of *The hot pepper story* to the fullest. He tells it well and it is well appreciated by the audience. Although he provides a moral, he never, any more than the text itself, takes a stand on the crucial issues raised in the story. Grandmothers should treat babies well, but what does this mean? What does treating well or not treating well entail? His moral is just as open to multiple interpretations as the story which led to it. Mastayans is indeed a knowledgeable chief, a clever political leader.

Further Considerations

Understanding of the structure and significance of *The hot pepper story* depends on placing it in its Kuna context in two senses: an explanation of the linguistic, cultural, and social presuppositions necessary for an appreciation of the laconicity of the narrative and of the potential for alternative interpretations inherent in it; a focus on the performance of the story, in actual settings, in which various analyses and interpretations are offered by the performers themselves as part of the strategy and structure of the performance.

It is interesting to note in passing that careful examination of the text in relation to Kuna language, culture, and society suggests still other analyses and interpretations. One interesting one, which has not been discussed because it is not offered by the Kuna as part of their performance of the story, has to do with Kuna social organization and residence rules. The Kuna are matrilocal; a man after marriage goes to live in the house of his wife. The grandmother in *The hot pepper story* does not live in the same house as the boy; that is, she might be the mother of the father of the boy, but not of the mother. It might be argued that she is punishing her son, lost according to Kuna residence rules, by killing his son. According to such an interpretation, the grandmother would be reacting against the rules of Kuna social organization; the story would be a reminder not to do so.

From the point of view of Kuna ethnography of speaking, it is possible to view the performance of the story in terms of a particular constellation of components of speech (Hymes 1974). Thus:

Setting: gathering house; morning, afternoon, or evening
Participants: chief, chief's spokesmen, audience of gathered men or men and women
Ends: amusement, social control, demonstration of personal knowledge
Act sequence: story, responses, interpretation
Key: playfully, humorously, seriously
Instrumentalities: spoken colloquial Kuna, chanted gathering-house Kuna
Norm of Interaction: verse or line and then response, audience comments and laughter
Genre: story

This constellation of components is a set of resources that are exploited by Kuna individuals as part of the dynamic, emergent structures and strategies of everyday communicative life. Thus, in the performance focused on here, Mastayans utilizes this particular constellation of components of speech in a unique way for his own personal reasons of the moment. The dynamic structure of the event relates the backdrop and ground rules of Kuna speaking practices to the details of interactional life on that particular day. In a sense, Mastayans' clever exploitation of *The hot pepper story* can be compared to such small, strategic bits of verbal behavior in our own society as namedropping (for example, "You'll never guess who I saw at the club today?"), in which social interactional moves are achieved by reference to a prestigious person or place. But the Kuna way to be clever with language, to gain prestige and acquire recognition, is typically through long verbal performances, whether these are memorized texts or verbal structures developed during performance.

The approach I have taken to *The hot pepper story* is structuralist in that it is concerned with the structural properties of the story. But these structural properties are not viewed as static organizational features or underlying abstract logic. Rather, the dynamic structure of the text is focused on by analyzing the story in relation to the contexts in which it is performed, in terms of the potential for openness of interpretation, and in terms of the ways in which this potential is exploited during performance. This approach is consistent with trends in poststructuralism, which are concerned with dynamic, rhetorical aspects of texts and text-context interrelationships.

Lévi-Strauss, as we have seen, in his extensive study of lowland South American mythology, has investigated myths that share such features with *The hot pepper story* as relations between young and old and men and women, the interplay between life and death, and the origin of plants. But this story, as recorded here, has a narrative development and especially a moral that is completely different from the interpretations given by Lévi-Strauss. The story has to do essentially not with the raw and the cooked and nature and culture, but rather with how to treat people, especially babies, at birth. No doubt at a more abstract level, the occurrence in the story of such basic oppositions as male/female, young/old, productive/unproductive, and life/death is related to the significance and interpretation the Kuna themselves provide. These are the elements which set the stage and weave the intrigue which lead to the moral. They contribute to the potential of the text for openness and multiplicity of interpretation.

Since his primary interest is in abstract, logical structures of myths, independent of particular cultures or societies, Lévi-Strauss's method is to look at similar myths in many societies; the increasing breadth of comparison and contrast leading to the positing of more and more abstract structures. There is no doubt about the validity of searching for underlying or abstract structures of myths or stories. This is in part what analysis is all about. At the same time, however, it is important to insist on ways of relating posited underlying constructs to actually performed events. We are in a privileged position with regard to the Kuna, in that they themselves posit underlying structures or meanings in the form of interpretations of the symbolism of the text and its message. Most important, they do so as part of its very performance for an audience to hear, learn from, and criticize. This is not to say that an outside analyst should simply record and repeat Kuna-performed interpretations; but further and deeper analysis should relate in principled ways to Kuna performers who themselves are involved in the analytical process.

Many of the myths which Lévi-Strauss studies are etiological, their significance or point being reported as an explanation of the origin of fire, cooking, plants, or death. *The hot pepper story*, as I recorded it and as interpreted by the Kuna in their performance of it, is not etiological, but either entertaining, rhetorical, or both. Lévi-Strauss's etiological myths look to the past in order to explain the origin of and reason for the present. *The hot pepper story* looks to the past – not mythical in the Kuna sense – in order to call for a particular mode of behavior in the future. Thus, in spite of its possible etiological origin (in diffusional terms), the Kuna *hot pepper story* is now at its core thoroughly rhetorical and political. As has been shown here, in the particular performance I recorded, the teller, Mastayans, uses the story for two rhetorical-political aims: to argue for a particular mode of behavior, by means of an entertaining telling; to convince his immediate audience, especially the visiting chief, that he, Mastayans, is a good chief, that is, a knower and performer of Kuna tradition.

Since *The hot pepper story* was recorded and analyzed in the context of performance, it is difficult if not impossible to compare it with the myths which form the basis of Lévi-Strauss's study, or with similar myths reported by other collectors or analysts of South American Indian mythology. The latter are reported essentially as summaries of referential content, outside their performance context, and rhetorical purpose is rarely mentioned. However, comparison with similar stories in other American Indian societies does support the notion, already pointed out by T. T. Waterman in a careful study of many North American Indian folktales (1914), that referential content is independent of the point or explanation provided by particular societies, groups, or occasions. Although Waterman did not study actual performances of tales, his insistence on the separability of content and explanatory element or moral points to a potential for the use of tales in the rhetoric of performance, in which morals are developed and stressed independently of particular referential contents. The concept of potential for rhetorical use, inherent in a text, is similar to Kenneth Burke's notion of "literature as equipment for living" (1957). Thus the same or similar story can have quite different interpretations or purposes in different societies. Even within a single society it is possible for the same story to be structured differently by different groups. The Hopi are a well-documented American Indian case of this. Fred Eggan reports that "it soon became apparent that the origin legends of the same clan from different villages showed major contradictions and that even within the same village the stories of associate clans did not always correspond" (1950: 79). As Nancy Parrott Hickerson has reviewed the Hopi situation:

> There is, in fact, no body of Hopi tribal mythology – there is simply the mythology of the several Hopi clans. These clan traditions are related to one another – there is a common geographical setting, and a basic similarity as major events of creation and important supernatural figures recur. However, the mythology tells, especially, of events and places which bear on the properties, prerogatives, ceremonial responsibilities, and political claims of the individual clans (1978: 39).

Lévi-Strauss has the Hopi case among others in mind when he writes, "La même population, ou des populations voisines par le territoire, la langue ou la culture, élaborent parfois des mythes qui s'attaquent systématiquement à tel ou tel problème en envisageant, variante après variante, plusieurs manières concevables de la résoudre" (1964: 338).[3] Notice, however, that *The hot pepper story* resolves its problems in various ways within the same text; rather, it leaves open to interpretation possible solutions to the problem, and, ultimately, leaves open just what the problem is.

With regard to *The hot pepper story*, no studies of this singing bones motif exist that provide contextual information about societal interpretation, function, and purpose as I do here. We can speculate, however, in the Waterman and Burkean sense, on the basis of the way similar stories are reported and classified in collections of Amerindian folktales. Relatively similar stories are found among the Umotina of the northern Mato Grosso and among the Zuni of the North American Southwest. The Umotina have a myth in which a couple buries a boy and afterward from his corpse grow various crops, including pepper (Oberg, 1953: 108-109). In a Zuni myth, two brothers bury

---

3   The Hopi case is discussed on p. 339.

their grandmother, and on the spot where they bury her, a hot pepper plant grows up (Cushing, 1901). Both of these stories are reported as if explaining the origin of hot pepper. It is quite the contrary, of course, in the Kuna story, in spite of its title,[4] which is perhaps evidence of diffusion from groups in which it is used etiologically.

That the same story or myth can be open to various interpretations as a strategic, structured part of its performance is a natural feature of a nonliterate, American Indian society, in which discourse is central to social and political life. The openness of structure of *The hot pepper story* is particularly well suited to the Kuna gathering in which individuals, especially chiefs and other political leaders, gain prestige, jockey for position, and convince others on the basis of creative, adaptive, strategic use of speech.

It seems useful, by way of summary, to place this study within a paradigm of possible ways of going about the analysis of literature in nonliterate societies (it is furthermore interesting to compare these with the ways of studying humor discussed in chapter seven):

> (1) Literature is studied in and for itself, abstracted from its use or sociocultural context, perhaps becoming grist for various textual mills – linguistic, structuralist, and so forth.
> (2) Literature is seen as a reflection of some other aspect of the life of the people who produce and perform it, an aspect claimed to be more basic – social organizational, economic, psychological, and so forth.
> (3) Literature is viewed in relationship to contexts provided by the society and culture in which it is found, and attention is paid to the functions and situations of performance.

While the approach developed here falls most clearly within the third way, it moves along a continuum that ranges from structuralist to ethnomethodological. The former approach is oriented toward abstract structures and tends not to be interested in concrete contexts. For the latter, context is the focus of analysis and the text is secondary. Careful attention to both text and context, their intersection and interaction, is crucial to an understanding of the Kuna *hot pepper story*.

---

[4] For the significance of titles, see Hymes (1959).

The Text

In my representation, *The hot pepper story* consists of 171 lines. Lines are determined by pauses coupled with falling pitch. This line structure is reinforced by the constant ratifying responses and comments by the visiting chief. These are labeled VC and placed within parentheses, as are audience comments. Part of the poetics of performance is created by the interplay of relatively longer and relatively shorter lines. Rhythm is also created by means of long pauses, without falling pitch, within lines (transcribed as blank spaces between words) and by the extensive use of certain words and phrases, such as *teki, kepe, takkarku, emite,* and *takken soke*. These words and phrases, which serve as line-framing elements, typically occur line initially and line finally. At times they occur in the middle of lines, however, playing off contrapuntally against the pause patterning. Kuna oral expressive devices which are found in the text are lengthened sounds (indicated by double letters), loud speech (indicated by capital letters), stretched-out speech (indicated by dashes between syllables), vibrating voice (indicated by dashes between letters), and changes in pitch level. Rising pitch is indicated by ´ placed before the stretch of speech affected.

The translation mirrors the original Kuna with regard to line structure. As in the Kuna version, pauses within lines are represented by long spaces. The line-framing words are translated with a set of equivalent English expressions – well, then, thus, indeed, now, see, say, it is said, and so on. Readers are thus provided with a sense of their functioning in the poetics of performance.

The translation is relatively literal. Again, this is in order to capture as much as possible the Kuna poetics of performance, which I feel would become lost in freer translations. This is particularly important in that this text repeats and permutes a small number of words and thematic elements.

The Kuna tense-aspect system, especially as it is used in the performance of narratives, such as *The hot pepper story*, is strikingly different from that of western European languages, notably English. This, of course, poses problems for translation. Given my aim of being as literal as possible in my translation, while still having it be accessible to English readers, I have retained the aspectual details (such as specifying whether an action is beginning or in progress, or where it occurs) and the seeming temporal disjunctions which are characteristic of Kuna cultural logic. In lines 92 to 111, the narrator jumps back and forth from past to present, from the boy alive with his family to buried underground and presumed dead. In line 148 the boy who has just come out of the ground is already a man and the grandmother has already died. These quite consistent temporal disjunctions in Kuna narration, like the moving in and out of quotes, may prove difficult for English readers. They are there in Kuna, however, and are characteristic of Kuna cultural logic and especially the verbal art of narration; thus I have not tampered with them in my translation.[5]

---

5   English (and other European) language oral narrators also make tense-aspect jumps; for example, present tense may be used in narrating fast and vivid action. Thus some aspects of what I am talking about here may be characteristic of oral discourse more generally and not specifically Kuna.

ka kwentoki peka an sunmaymarsunno tekir.

peka sunmaynayop samosunnoet.

peee, weti an apinsuoetit.

peka sunmaynayop sasunno.

(VC: aaa.)

peka sunmaynayop sasunnoettene.   5

(VC: eye.)

(Unintelligible comments from gathered audience and brief conversation with

Mastayans.)

takkarku   we kwento sunna   we Mammimullukine saila Mantipaytikinya.

(Unintelligible comments from gathered audience.)

(Laughter.)

a wis anka irkwen, wis an oturtaynaikusto we, ka kwento kin.

wis napir salasik.

tey "napir" soke.

(Unintelligible comments from gathered audience.)

"teee, takkarkute, mu warkwen mai" soysunto.   10

muu.

"mute takkarku sirwel ipet mu ma" takken soke, mu sirwel ipet.

mu sirwel ipette mai takkarku ipakwena   sirwer, turpamaytakokua   yer kepeunti

sirwer turpamaytakoku kwane.

silekwa pakkekwace kwantii.

teki silekwa pakke kwantii, ipakwenki sirwer iskuarto ipe.   15

"sirwer takkarku, e turpa patterpakuar" takken soke.

sirwer turpa taynae e ipet taynaoku, sirwer turpa pattemai   perkwaple.

"key sirwer nue kwankusa."

I will tell you *The hot pepper story* indeed.

I will do so as if speaking to you directly.

You, will be my responder.

I will do so as if speaking to you directly.

(VC: aaah.)

I will really do so as if speaking to you directly.   5

(VC: Yes.)

(Unintelligible comments from gathered audience and brief conversation with Mastayans.)

So   this story indeed   that Mammimullu chief Mantipaytikinya.

(Unintelligible comments from gathered audience.)

(Laughter.)

He was once, teaching me some, some of this *hot pepper story*.

It seems to have some truth.

Well "it is true" it is said.

(Unintelligible comments from gathered audience.)

"Well, in fact, there was once a grandmother"[6] it is said.   10

A grandmother.

"This grandmother in fact was the owner of a plum tree there was a grandmother"
see it is said, the grandmother was the owner of a plum tree.

There was a grandmother who was owner of a plum tree in fact once   the plum
tree, when it produced fruit   before when the plum tree produced fruit well it used
to be possible to gather a lot.

It was possible to gather up to four baskets.

Well one day this plum tree, from which it used to be possible to gather four baskets
went bad.   15

"The fruit in fact, of the plum tree began falling down" it is said.

The owner went to see the fruit of the plum tree and when she went to see, the plum
fruit had fallen   all of it.

"It is impossible to gather plums."

---

6   As I have discussed, the Kuna word *muu* has three meanings – grandmother, old woman, and
midwife. I have chosen grandmother in the translation. Even though the ambiguity present in Kuna is
thus lost, I feel that grandmother is the most basic of the three meanings.

aki mu sokkar takken soke weteka   "ipikala   an sirwer iskustipa?" soke.

"e turpa   key nue anka nakukusa.   20

tekisokku turpati key nue anka nakukucokku   toa an ipe   sirwer turpa eputipaye?"

mu pinsatisunto.

(VC: etto.)

"tek ipakwenkine   emite muteka   kep macikwa   amis" takken soke.

sirwerki nakkulekeka.

(VC: e.)

mu sokku macikwaka sokku   "maciwakwaye pe anka sirwerki nakkuleko" kar

soysun.   25

"pe anka sirwer etarpoye.

wekine   pe anka sirwer etarpetakokua   pitti, ani sirwer turpa epu pe taytako"

sokeye.

(VC: etto so.)

maciwakwa sokku "napir" soke.

tek inso   sikwicunna, sirwer, tukkuki.

(VC: e.)

´ taysikucunna.

(VC: e.

     Unintelligible comments

       arkasikwicunna.)

arkasikwicunna sirwer turpa taysikwicunto.   30

(VC: aa.)

mute kar soysat.

(VC: ipi e turpa eputipaye?)

eye ipi e turpa eputipaye?

tey wepali   inso ipa oipoarkua   mu taynatsunto.

(VC: ee.)

"That is what the grandmother said" see she says   "why ever   did my plum tree
go bad?" she says.
"Its fruit   does not get ripe for me.   20
Therefore since the fruit does not get ripe for me   who might it be   that is
touching my plum fruit?"
The grandmother was thinking.
(VC: That is it.)
"Well one day   now this grandmother   then got   a boy" see it is said.
To take care of the plum tree.
(VC: Yes.)
The grandmother said to the boy she said   "grandson[7] you will take care of my
plum tree for me" she said to him.   25
"You will guard my plum tree for me.
Here   you will come guard my plum tree for me   you, will come see who is
touching my plum fruit" she says.
(VC: That is it then.)
The grandson said "alright" he says.
Well thus   he sat, on top, of the plum tree
(VC: Yes.)
´ he sat looking.
(VC: Yes.
        Unintelligible comments.
        He sat watching.)
He sat watching the plum fruit he sat looking.   30
(VC: aah.)
As the grandmother had told him.
(VC: What might be touching her fruit?)
Yes what might be touching her fruit?
Well when she   thus awoke   the grandmother went there to see.
(VC: Yes.)

---

7   The boy is sometimes referred to and addressed as "boy," sometimes as "grandson." Since Kuna
kin terms are frequently used to address nonkin, usage of these terms in the text should not be
understood as necessarily implying kin relationships.

wepa mu taytapkua   takkampa sirwer pattepukkwa, e turpa.

(VC: ampa pattepa.)

wepa mute sokku, wakwaka sokku, weteka   "pe taysa" sokeye "an sirwer turpa

tule opattisat pe taysa" sokeye.   35

(VC: ee.)

wepa sokku, "sur" soke "an taysasur takken tule an kwen tacur" soke.

(VC: Unintelligible comments.)

"an kwen taysasur" takken soke.

"napir" soke.

teysokku "napir" takken soke.

"tekirtina   emi pe anka seto nakkulepalo" kar soysunto a.   40

(VC: etto.)

"seto pe anka nakkulepaloye.

(VC: Unintelligible comments.)

nuekwa pe anka taysunnoye a.

toa nue sirwer turpa ani eputitipaye."

(VC: macikwa.)

macikwa macikwa macikwa kar   sikwicunto.

(VC: etto.)

muti nattasunnat neyse.   45

(VC: neyse.)

eye sirwer ipetti nekki kammatasunto.

(VC: ee.)

"kepe   pane oipospar" takken soke.

ekisnapali.

"ekiciarparkuaa   par takkarkuu   sul ampa sirwer turpa na   key pattispar"

soke.

(VC: ampa sula.)

tey ekispali wakwase   "pe taysa" sokeye a   "an sirwer turpa   toa epus pe

taysaye?"   50

"sur" soke "an kwen tacur" soke.

(VC: etto.)

"inso" soke.

When the grandmother got there to see   she saw again that her plum fruit, had
fallen all over.

(VC: It had still fallen again.)

And this grandmother said, she said to the grandchild, here then   "did you see"
she says "did you see the person who caused my plum fruit to fall" she says.   35

(VC: Yes.)

And he said, "no" he says "I didn't see anyone" he says.

(VC: Unintelligible comments.)

"I didn't see anyone" see he says.

"Alright" she says.

Therefore "alright" see she says.

"Well   now tonight you will take care of it for me again" she said to him ah.   40

(VC: That is it.)

"Tonight you will take care of it again.

(VC: Unintelligible comments.)

You will look very carefully for me ah.

Who might well be touching my plum fruit."

(VC: The boy.)

The boy the boy the boy remained seated   for her.

And the grandmother went back home.   45

(VC: Home.)

Yes the owner of the plum tree is sleeping soundly in her house.

(VC: Yes.)

"Then   next day she awoke again" see it is said.

She goes to ask again.

"When she asked again   when again she saw   the plum fruit had fallen again"
it is said.

(VC: Again.)

Well she asked the grandson again   "did you see" she says ah   "did you see
who touched   my plum fruit?"   50

"No" he says "I didn't see anyone" he says.

(VC: That is it.)

"Thus" it is said.

mu istar mu sanpakusku, "eka nue nakkulesuli," takkarkua   mu, urwe a.

(VC: urwe.

    "pe arkatisuli."

"eye arkatisur an pe tayye" kar soysunto a.

(VC: Unintelligible comment.)

napir.   55

kep mu pinsaarsunto "macikwa ilakwen opelokoye uaya   akku an itto" sokku,

"ilakwen   opelokoye a."

kep mu nappa kwicarsunto.

(VC: nappa.)

nappa kwicatti   talipakke wirkue wilup nappa tiysasunto.

nappa kwicasunto muu.

(VC: Unintelligible comments.)

kepe muteka   kep arkan yoet ekwacasunto nappa yapa.   60

(VC: Unintelligible comments.)

tey wakwaka sokku "an arkan yoet arkwas takkenye a.

(VC: aa.)

pe anka sunaye."

(VC: aa.)

aa   teki wepa   maci kep arsan kal okwicicunto, nappa yapa.

    (VC: mm.)

kep maciwakwa aitecunto nek urpa.

(VC: mm.)

kep aiteskua, olarkan amiarkua   arsan ikkir susa.   65

(VC: aa.)

arsan onakkwicunna.

(VC: key parnakkwe.)

key parnakkue iy pe parnakkosunna?

(Unintelligible comments from gathered audience.)

The grandmother got very furious at this point, "he doesn't take good care of it for me," so in fact   the grandmother gets angry ah.

(VC: Angry.

"You were not watching.")

"Yes I see that you were not watching" she said to him ah.

(VC: Unintelligible comment.)

It is true.   55

Then the grandmother thought "I will put an end to[8] the boy right away he doesn't pay   attention to me" she said, "right away   I will put an end to him ah."

Then the grandmother dug the ground.

(VC: The ground.)

She dug the ground   four arm lengths deep in the ground she dug.

She dug the ground the grandmother did.

(VC: Unintelligible comments.)

Then this grandmother   then she threw a ring inside the ground.   60

(VC: Unintelligible comments.)

Well she said to the grandchild "my ring fell, see ah.

(VC: aah.)

You will go get it for me."

(VC: aah.)

Aah   well this   boy then stood a ladder up for her, inside the ground.

(VC: mm.)

Then the grandson went down under the earth.

(VC: mm.)

Then when he had gone down, when he began to look for the ring   she grabbed the ladder away.   65

(VC: aah.)

She raises up the ladder.

(VC: Impossible to climb up again.)

Impossible to climb up again how can you climb up again?

(Unintelligible comments from gathered audience.)

---

8   This translates the Kuna verb *opeloe*, literally, "to cause to end."

were.

kep a emurucunto emur emur emur nappa taska.

(VC: wakwa wios.)

wakwa purkwis.   70

(VC: purkwis.)

purkwicunna.

yapa meretisunna.

tey wepa mai   kepe wakwate nan nikkat a, pap nikkapalit.

kep amiarsunto.

"pia an maci nattipa?" soke.   75

(VC: aaa.)

nan imaytikucunna "pia ani wakwa nattipa? macikwa pia ani nattipaye?"

(VC: Unintelligible comment.)

tek imaytisuli muse ekiciarsunto, "pe an macikwa pe taysa?" sokeye.

"sul an pe ipe kwen tacur" kar soysunto, "an taysasurye.

napir" soke.

tey nanpa potisunto mimmipa.   80

pap potisunna mimmipa.

tey pinna pinna pinna iet   iete a.

(VC: iete.)

tikkasurkucunnat iearsunto.

(VC: mu ietsun?)

e nan ietsunna.

(Unintelligible comments from gathered audience.)

muti wisi na nappa tiysat.   85

(VC: ati wisi.)

atina wisi.

(Unintelligible comments from gathered audience.)

e nan potisunnat mimmipa.

(VC: etto.)

tek a potii   sanpakus pinna pinna iealir pini ieter pini.

It's steep.

Then she covered over the ground cover cover cover closed.

(VC: Poor grandchild.)

The grandchild died. 70

(VC: Died.)

He truly dies.

He was there inside.

Well he was there   then this grandchild has a mother ah, he also has a father.

Then they looked for him.

"Where might my boy have gone" they say. 75

(VC: aaah.)

The mother was searching "where might my grandchild have gone? my son where might he have gone?"

(VC: Unintelligible comment.)

Well he would not appear and she went to the grandmother's place to ask, "did you see my son?" she asks.

"No I did not see yours" she said to her, "I did not see him.

It's true" she says.

Well the mother was crying for her baby. 80

The father was crying for his baby.

Well slowly slowly slowly they forgot   they forgot ah.

(VC: Forgot.)

After a lot of time had gone by they really forgot.

(VC: The grandmother forgot?)

His mother forgot.

(Unintelligible comments from gathered audience.)

But the grandmother of course knew since she had buried the ground. 85

(VC: But she of course knows.)

As for her she knows.

(Unintelligible comments from gathered audience.)

The mother was crying for her baby.

(VC: That is it.)

Well she was crying   after a while slowly slowly she came to forget again she forgot again.

(VC: ee.)

pasur ittokus.

(VC: ee.)

"tek ipakwen kaarmaytii, punolo nikkapar" soke a.   90

(VC: ee.)

kwenti susukwa ipe purkwisatteta.

tek ipakwen maskuttasunnoe.

"maskunnar" sokele   punorka sokkartasunto sus kepe "muuu   ney tikkarpa kep
ainiarsun" soke a.

(VC: etto so.)

"ainiarto tiylesat nappa askin   ainiarto immar mattutikki ainiar" soke.

(VC: ee.)

tey tunkutanisun mu taytisunna i-pi-wa.   95

(VC: ipi ainiali?)

eye.

tey pinna nakkwe ainitani ainitani ainitani tey turpamakkarsunto.

(VC: ee.)

tey turpamakkarku e san nakuar takkarku kaa.

(VC: kaa.)

mm, "ka" takken soke.

(VC: ee.)

tey muuu   ka, akkwemasunna mukatka kusparsunto kate a.   100

(VC: aa.)

ka ai o-k-k-i-n-n-o-t-e ka kuarku.

weparte e macikwa purkwisatteka, maskunnalile, sokkartasunto mimmi punorka.

(VC: ee.)

"punorye we mu maitse pe anka ka wis ekisna takkenye kapa maskunpiye a."

(VC: ee.)

kal ekisnattasunto.

(VC: ee.)

(VC: Yes.)

She did not feel anything anymore.

(VC: Yes.)

"Well one day as it happens, she has a daughter also" it is said.   90

(VC: Yes.)

In fact it was her brother who died.

Well one day always as they were going to eat.

"While they were beginning to eat" it is said   the boy always said to his sister

"near the graaandmother's   house then there is something growing" he says ah.

(VC: That is it then.)

"It was growing on top of the ground   something very small was growing" he says.

(VC: Yes.)

Well the grandmother saw that it was getting bigger what-was-it?   95

(VC: What was growing?)

Yes.

Well slowly it rises it keeps growing up keeps growing up keeps growing up indeed
it produced fruit.

(VC: Yes.)

Well when it produced fruit its flesh got ripe in fact it was pepper.

(VC: Pepper.)

Mm, "pepper," see it is said.

(VC: Yes.)

Well the grandmother   is taking care of, a pepper plant and the pepper plant
belonged to the grandmother ah.   100

(VC: aah.)

The pepper my friend g-o-t r-i-p-e that is what happened to the pepper.

And as for the boy who had died, while he was beginning to eat, he always said to
his baby sister.

(VC: Yes.)

"Sister go to that grandmother who is there and ask for some pepper for me see I
want to eat with pepper ah."

(VC: Yes.)

She would always go to ask her.

(VC: Yes.)

tey wepa muka soytapsunnoe   "pe ka wis apeye."   105
(VC: ee.)
mu "napir" soke mu kar ka kwanattasunna
(VC: ee.)
ka, kwane   tek mu kuti.
tek ipakwenkine, maskunnetkinpali, ekisnatparsunna.
(VC: ee.)
wep punoloka soysunna "ka pe kwanna takkenye."
(VC : Unintelligible comment.)
"teki ka kwannapsun" soke.
(VC: ee muse.
    Unintelligible comment.)
teki, muse kwannattasunto, mu ka ipetka kusparsunna.   110
tek e punoloka na kaa kwannai   tule sunmakkarsun nappa yapa.
(VC: aaa.)
aa, "'PU-NO-LO-PI-PI-YE'   soy" takken soke.
(VC: ee.)
" 'punolo pipiye' kaa sunmay" soke.
(VC: aa, nek urpa sunmak?)
"nek urpa tule sunmay" soke.
"pu-no-lo-pi-pi-ye" soke.   115
wepa "punolo pipiye," sokkua, ittocunna a
(VC: aa.)
tule ese kole.
kwakkiali kaki mellet nanse natparsunto.
nanka sokku "ka kwannai tule anse korar takkenye.
ka urpa anse korar takken   'PU-NO-LO-PI-PI-YE' anka soyye a.
an kwakkit" takken soke.   120
(VC: kwakkite.)
e nan ittosuli a.

Well she went there and said to the grandmother   "I want some of your pepper."   105
(VC: Yes.)
The grandmother says "alright" and the grandmother would always go to gather
pepper for her
(VC: Yes.)
pepper, gather   well the grandmother was there.
Well one day, while eating again, she went to ask again.
(VC: Yes.)
And she [the grandmother] says to the girl "you go and gather the pepper see."
(VC: Unintelligible comment.)
"Well she went to gather the pepper" it is said.
(VC: Yes to the grandmother's place.
       Unintelligible comment.)
Well, she always went to the grandmother's place to gather it, the grandmother is
the owner of the pepper plant.   110
Well a person began to speak from inside the ground   to the girl who was
gathering pepper.
(VC: aaah.)
Aah, " 'LIT-TLE-GIRL'   it says" see it is said.
(VC: Yes.)
"'Little girl,' the pepper speaks" it is said.
(VC: Aah, from under the earth it speaks?)
"From under the earth a person speaks" it is said.
"Lit-tle-girl" it says.   115
She heard, that it said, "little girl" ah
(VC: aah.)
a person is calling her.
She got frightened chased away by the pepper and she went back to her mother's
place.
She said to her mother "while I was gathering pepper a person called me see.
From under the pepper it called me see   'LIT-TLE-GIRL' it says to me ah.
I got frightened" see she says.   120
(VC: Frightened.)
Her mother did not believe it ah.

(VC: ittosuli.)

kar soysunna "pe   namar takkenye, pe ittonaoenye a."

kep e nan sunnat ittonatmosunto.

(VC: Unintelligible comment.)

"kep e nan inso punolo ka kwatteku inso korarpar" soke.

(VC: aa.)

" 'pu-no-lo-pi-pi-ye   pu-no-lo-pi-pi-ye'   korma" soke.   125

(VC: ukak tek korma.)

aa, tek korma.

pap yoy pinsaale nan yoy pinsaale "tena sus   tule an opurkwisat weki manap

ittokusye a."

(Unintelligible comments from gathered audience.)

kep a, eye, ka ipetka kucunto kep ati   kep kwicarsunto.

(VC: ee.)

takke nappa yapa ipi mai.

(VC: ee.)

tey yapa mai   wepa   korarsunna kep kwicarsunna eskorokine a

(VC: ee.)

mastiketki.   130

(VC: ee.)

"wepa korar" takken soke a   "wesikki an nono maiye."

(VC: "wesikki.")

"wesikki an naytukku maiye."

(VC : ee.)

itto tule sunmak.

(VC: ee.)

kep pinna pinna pinna pinna kep akwiar.

(VC: nan akkwinasun.)

nan akkwinasun macikwa.   135

(VC: etto.)

takkar inso takkarku macikwa mai, tule keppe   sirwerki nakkulemaikusat tule mu

tiysaku   a   turkucun kannar.

(VC: Did not believe it.)

She [the girl] says to her "you   and me let's go see, so that you can go hear ah."

Then her mother herself also went to hear.

(VC: Unintelligible comment.)

"Then with her mother thus when the girl gathered pepper thus it called again" it is said.

(VC: aah.)

" 'Lit-tle gir-l   lit-tle gir-l'   it is calling" it is said.   125

(VC: Only indeed calling.)

Aah, indeed calling.

The father at once thought the mother at once thought "it is our son   the one who the person killed who was heard here ah."

(Unintelligible comments from gathered audience.)

Then ah, yes, it was the owner of the pepper plant then that one   then they began to dig.

(VC: Yes.)

To see what was inside the ground.

(VC: Yes.)

Well from inside   he   called then they dug with a shovel ah

(VC: Yes.)

with a digging stick.   130

(VC: Yes.)

"And he called" see he says ah   "over here is my head."

(VC: "Over here.")

"Over here are my feet."

(VC: Yes.)

One could hear the person speaking.

(VC: Yes.)

Then slowly slowly slowly slowly then they dug.

(VC: The mother is digging.)

The mother is digging up her son.   135

(VC: That is it.)

So thus so the boy is there, the person who then   took care of the plum tree the person whom the grandmother buried   he   came back to life again.

(VC: aa.

    muu nue imas palamiletsunto.

mu kep amilearsunto.

(VC: Unintelligible comments.)

kep wepa   suste nononisunto a.

(VC: Unintelligible comment.

    muu parsoylekoe.)

kep ekiciarparsunto   "pia ipika, wey pe kusye?"

teki, sokkarsunto.   140

"sailaki muu, wek an kaarmaytii   mu sirwel akkweka an siarta" takken soke a.

(VC: ee.)

"teki mu eka sirwerki nue nakkulesur an takketpa, muu   an itu nappa kwicaye.

(VC: ee.)

aa mu an ekwaca takken nappa yaparye."

(VC: olarkan ekwacaye.)

a, olarkan ekwacaye.

"emite a muu   emite nappa yapa an tiysakua   emite anpa mai, we ka ainiar   an

pese koca" takken kar soysunto.   145

(VC: etto.)

AA.

"napir" soke.

tekirtin   macikwa   patto macikwatina   unni   serkukucokku   kep "mu annik"

soke "mu anse perkuo takkenye."

(VC: aa.)

kep macikwa nekkunatse natku kep macikwa nacunna   nipa nacunto.

(VC: ee.)

patteki nakkwis nipa nate.   150

(VC: aah.

 The grandmother really did well she was caught.)

The grandmother then got caught.

(VC: Comments.)

Then he the brother came out ah.

(VC: Unintelligible comment.

 The grandmother will be talked about.)

Then they asked him "where why, did this happen to you?"

Well, he told.   140

"There used to be a grandmother, I was going about here the grandmother
always placed me here in order to care for her plum tree" see he says ah.

(VC: Yes.)

"Well seeing that I did not take good care of her plum tree, the grandmother dug
the ground for me.

(VC: Yes.)

This grandmother threw me see inside the ground."

(VC: She threw the ring.)

Ah, she threw the ring.

"Now this grandmother now after she buried me inside the ground now while
I was still there, this pepper plant began to grow I called you" see he said to
them.   145

(VC: That is it.)

AAH.

"It is true" he says.

Well as for the boy already he was a young man since he had grown
up then "as for the grandmother" he says "I'll finish the grandmother off[9] see."

(VC: aah.)

Then this boy who had gone up to the surface of the earth then this boy left he
went up to heaven.

(VC: Yes.)

He rose up on a plate and he went up to heaven.   150

---

9 This translates the Kuna verb *perkue*, "to finish."

kep immar nue olo acuer suapsunto.

(VC: ee.)

papse suap ittolesunto.

(VC: mm.)

kep a noniku   kep muse natparsunna.

mu takkarku soke "wis-ku-sa-tte."

(VC: aa.)

mute sokaypa wawanmakkesi topkusikicunna.   155

(VC: etto.)

kep a acuer nukarki kep kacun mu imasku kep MOK.

kep selearparsunto.

(VC: ee.)

mu selearmosunto, tule acuer nukarki   kep aakar nakkwicun nakkaaate mmm.

(VC: ee.)

patte epippilet naa naaate.

sappi pirkwen sikki emi

(Comment from gathered audience: sotoma nek.)

sotoma sik.   160

(VC: ee.)

"sotoma sik ney pulet so sailakan ney" takken soke.

(VC: ee.)

ikwa walakan kunanamakkekwikwisnae.

(VC: ee.)

paila walakan kunamakkwikwisnae.

(VC: ee.)

tese kep mu takken so aparse.

(VC: ee.)

Then he surely took a golden hook there.

(VC: Yes.)

He took it from his father's place it seems.

(VC: mm.)

Then having returned here   then he went to the grandmother's place.

The grandmother indeed it is said "she-al-rea-dy-knew."

(VC: aah.)

The grandmother is sitting trembling with fear by the fireplace she is seated there
afraid.   155

(VC: That is it.)

Then he grabbed her then with the teeth of the hook he did it to the grandmother
then MOK.[10]

Then she was carried away again.

(VC: Yes.)

The grandmother was carried away also, with the teeth of the *tule*[11] hook   then
she rose off she went mmm.

(VC: Yes.)

She is pulled along in the plate she's going she's gone.

To *sappi pirkwen* now

(Comment from gathered audience: The place of Sodom.)

to Sodom.   160

(VC: Yes.)

"Sodom is a very dangerous place the place of the chiefs of fire[12] " see it is said.

(VC: Yes.)

There are many burning *ikwa* trees standing everywhere.

(VC: Yes.)

There are many burning *paila* trees standing everywhere.

(VC: Yes.)

There then is the grandmother see in the middle of the fire.

(VC: Yes.)

---

[10] *Mok* is an onomatopoetic particle, the sound of a hook entering flesh.

[11] Kuna

[12] there is much fire

mu per tippilet.   165
(VC: Unintelligible comment.)
aa.
aula we papkan soyte takken soke "yoo we napnekkine mukana   sikkwi
tiysamalatti   tese pattema takkenye.
(VC: ee.)
pursipu neysik pur saila kepe tar sappi walakan per kwapunyekwikwis   mukan
parmilema mukan ase oturtaylema.
(VC: mm.)
wey yarkine   wicur sikkwi akkwismalat sikkwi tiysimalat.
(VC: mm.)
tese pattemaye"   we papkan ki namay takkenye   anka soyto.   170
(VC: ee.)
ase peka wis kiar soke.
(VC: yer pe an imasa.)

The grandmother is all toasted.   165

(VC: Unintelligible comment.)

Aah.

For this reason the ancestors said see it is said "If on this earth the

grandmothers   bury birds   they are thrown there see.

(VC: Yes.)

The grandmothers will be carried to a place called pursipu[13]   the place of the

chiefs of ashes where then there are many flaming trees all standing everywhere

the grandmothers are punished there.

(VC: mm.)

Those who do not know how to take care of birds those who bury birds   in this

world.

(VC: mm.)

They are thrown there"   the ancestors chant this see   he said to me.   165   170

(VC: Yes.)

Up to here I have told you a little.

(VC: You did it well for me.)[14]

---

[13] white ash

[14] In the preparation of the translation I have benefited in various ways from correspondence with Brian Swann. While he was in the process of preparing his own translation of the story, based on an earlier version of mine (Swann and Krupat 1987: 172-180), I saw new possibilities for translations of words and phrases. I drew on some of these possibilities from his freer translation while at the same time maintaining a literal adherence to the actual Kuna performance. His version and his questions about mine also made me formulate more explicitly certain aspects of the nature of Kuna cultural logic which are present in this story and which I discuss here. It is a tribute to the richness of this Kuna story that it can be fruitfully translated in various ways.

Chief Mastayans seated in his hammock

7. *THE AGOUTI STORY*: ON PLAY, JOKING, HUMOR, AND TRICKING

Storytelling is one of the many verbal events that take place in the Kuna gathering house. While the gathering house is essentially a setting for regular nightly meetings, there are times when it is kept open during the day, because of the visit of a chief from another village, a holiday, or a momentous natural event, such as an earthquake or an eclipse. On such days it quickly fills with men who sit, talk, joke, and tell stories. Women of the village pass through with beverages of various kinds – coffee, chucula (a native sweet drink made of chocolate and bananas), oatmeal, and Koolaid – for the chiefs and others present. It was on such an occasion, the visit of a chief from another island, that *The hot pepper story* was told. (See chapter six.) It was on another such occasion, the anniversary of the Baptist mission on Mulatuppu, on April 21, 1970, that Chief Muristo Pérez of Mulatuppu told *us kwento* (*The Agouti story*).

The stories told in the gathering house are of various kinds. There are narratives of personal experience, including reports of individuals of trips they have made or of unusual experiences they have had. (See chapter five for a report of a trip to learn ritual medicine and curing.) Reports are long, involved, and often suspenseful and humorous. The narrators hold the attention of their listeners even though the facts may already be known in considerable detail. Other stories describe actual and usually recent events, as well as the exploits and foibles of others, both Kuna and foreigners. Again, humor is highlighted. Finally, there are fictional tales, which the Kuna call *kwento*, a name borrowed from the Spanish *cuento*. These are sometimes about humans, such as the young boy and the grandmother. (See chapter six.)

The most common fictional tales deal with animals. A very popular form of animal story is the trickster tale, in which animals trick and fool one another. Although various combinations of animals, including lobsters, chickens, turtles, and devilfish, appear in such tales, the paradigm story involves a pair of habitual antagonists. *The Agouti story*, which is a great favorite, consists of a cycle of episodes in which Agouti (Dasyprocta agouti), a Central American long-legged rodent, continually tricks large and dangerous Jaguar. The methods used in this tricking are both physical and verbal. The audience has heard this story many times before. But it loves every moment of it. Muristo is a wonderful story teller. As is the common Kuna storytelling pattern, Muristo tells this story to another person, in this case his spokesman, Armando.

Armando responds with short utterances or comments, while the audience listens, laughs, and occasionally comments as well. As in the telling of *The hot pepper story* (see chapter six), the comments of the responder punctuate the narration and contribute to its oral rhythm. Muristo alternates fast and slow, loud and soft, and high-pitched and low-pitched speech; dramatically and expressively interchanges short and long pauses; rapidly repeats certain words; imitates noises, actions, and voices; quotes conversations, including minute and circumstantial particulars of questions, answers, requests, and commands; and relates the narrative in passing to familiar humorous incidents that have occurred in the community.

While *The Agouti story*, like other humorous stories, is most often performed in spoken form, it can also be chanted, by chiefs, as part of gathering-house ritual.[1] When chanted, the purpose is as much to provide a moral as to amuse and this moral is interpreted for the audience by both chiefs as they chant and chief's spokesmen as they reformulate the chant into a spoken version more intelligible to the audience. (See chapter three.)

Humor

Humor is a salient and central feature of the Kuna world. In fact the intersection of speech play, verbal art, and humor permeates every aspect of Kuna social, cultural, and especially verbal life. In most general terms, speech play is the manipulation of linguistic elements of any kind and at any level, in relation to each other, in relation to other communicative modes, such as gesture and music, and in relation to the social interactional contexts in which people speak. This definition of speech play includes certain properties of discourse or text often considered to be artistic, such as phonological and morphological repetition, syntactic and semantic parallelism, and metaphor. It also includes the breaking of expectations, such as the sudden and surprising deletion of a word or phrase that has been repeated several times. Play involves both harmony and tension and is both verbal and social.

Verbally artistic language for the Kuna, in ritual and in everyday speech, involves an actualization of various potentials of speech play, with regard to both text and performance. The salient features of Kuna verbal art are the elaboration of line and

---

[1]   This is true in Mulatuppu. In most of San Blas, trickster tales like *The Agouti story* cannot be chanted however.

verse structures, parallelism and repetition, manipulation of elements of content, the use of esoteric and figurative language, and the dramatization of the voice. (See chapter two.)

Kuna humor, like verbal art, is intimately related to play. Joking and humor are notoriously difficult to translate from one language and culture to another. I hope here to provide some flavor of the Kuna variety. The Kuna do not have jokes of the type found in the European tradition, jokes that end in a clearly marked punch line, which actualizes a set up. Nor do they have interactional jokes in which the punch line consists of a victimizing of the receiver-respondent of the joke. At the same time Kuna life is punctuated by a great deal of verbal humor and joking. Laughter is omnipresent.

One common form of playful humor involves play or nicknames. Many animals have play names and they are usually based on physical characteristics of the animal. Examples are *sortukkin nakue* (hangs by tail = monkey), *kwapin arat* (blue-green tongue = tarpon), *naras asu* (orange nose = curassow), and *kapur ipya* (hot pepper eyes = crab). It is interesting to note the similarity here between play names and the metaphors which are used in quite serious and ritual contexts. Play names can be used by themselves, as a humorous focal point, in conversations whose sole purpose is recreation and amusement. They are also used in stories about animals, in order to talk about the characters in the story and embellish the humorous aspects of the performance. Play names are also used for humans. Typically these are based on animals, thus relating the human and animal worlds. Examples are *kelu* (jack), used for an albino business man who, like this Caribbean fish, is slippery, white, and fat, and *ia korki* (Uncle pelican), who looks and acts like a pelican and lives in a house built by the water on the rocks. Play names are also used for outsiders – Kuna from other villages, Panamanian officials, Peace Corps volunteers, and anthropologists. Among the Kuna themselves, with outsiders, and in animal stories, play names are part of the teasing, bantering, and riddling interactions of which the Kuna are forever fond. In *The Agouti story*, the pattern of using animal names for humans is reversed. Agouti and Jaguar use human kin terms with one another. Jaguar is Uncle and Agouti is Nephew.

Another area of verbal humor is imitation and mimicry. Everyday verbal imitations are usually very brief and draw on the stereotypical verbal features of a particular social role or genre. Thus a Kuna man, passing through the relatively empty gathering house during the daytime, might stop in front of the empty hammock of a village chief and for a few seconds imitate the chanting of chiefs, using the very characteristic melodic shape of this chanting and its unique lexical, phonological, morphological, and syntactic features, in particular the elements used to frame lines and verses. Or a man or woman might sit on a bench and mimic a couple of lines of a magical, curing chant, including the characteristic pose which involves a closed hand raised to the face. These imitations, which terminate in marked laughter on the part the performer and others present, are typically fleeting; longer imitations, for example those performed by drunks, are considered inappropriate and might be reprimanded. Foreigners are also the butt of fleeting imitations. Black Colombian sailors who trade with the Kuna at times speak some Kuna. The Kuna enjoy imitating their accent.[2] Imitation and mimicry are important features of *The Agouti story.*

A third area of everyday play, joking, and humor is the verbal put on or trick, called *yartakke* in Kuna. Verbal tricking within everyday interaction is extremely common among the Kuna. It often occurs between close friends and family members; it can also be used with outsiders. There are many possible topics for verbal put ons, common among them hunger, sickness, death, physical deformity, and sexual relations and adventures. Matters related to economic relations are also common. Here are a few examples:

> A woman tells a visitor, "My child is a dwarf. He can't grow."
> A woman returns a gourd to a friend which she had borrowed from her in order to carry some food. The lender says to the borrower, "I lent you a new gourd and that you returned an old one."
> A woman tells a friend, "Julio (a local man) gets angry at his wife and beats her."
> A man enters a friend's house to visit him; a member of the friend's family tells the man, "Your friend has died."
> A woman tells a friend, "Linda (a local woman) always pees in a cooking pot."
> A woman makes a lot of noise to imitate an animal, thus frightening a neighbor who lives right next door.

---

[2]   These brief foreigner imitations resemble the Apache portraits of "The Whiteman," analyzed by Basso (1979).

These verbal tricks are sometimes in response to questions, about a particular person or topic, sometimes mini-narratives embedded in conversations. They are typically followed by laughter and facial or hand pointing in the direction of the victim, thus clearly framing the narrative as non-literal and non-serious. Another interactional form of tricking is for one person to tell a second to go ask a third about a particular topic, tricking both the second and the third.

There is a fine line between verbal tricking, relatively brief and clearly marked by laughter, and some types of request behavior. Requests often take the form of statements of need which manipulate and stretch the truth without being lies. Thus:

> An old man tells a visitor that his son and provider of food is away and that he will therefore have no food all day. While the old man may partially be performing a verbal trick, he does not overtly mark it as such and would not refuse food if the visitor offered it.
>
> A renowned visiting chief tells a wealthy village store owner that he, the chief, was a good friend of the store owner's deceased father and that now he is poor and cannot afford a needed pair of pants. The store owner gives the pants to him from his store.

In both of these cases human individuals have been fooled in ways quite akin to the way animals are fooled by other animals in trickster tales. This type of request exploits the very strong, often expressed Kuna ethic of generosity to the needy, especially with regard to food. Kuna vocabulary is quite explicit in distinguishing joking and making fun (*totoe*), tricking (*yartakke*), and lying (*kakkan sae*). While the first two are quite acceptable and appreciated as humorous, lying is looked down upon in the extreme and in fact calling someone a liar is a most serious insult.[3]

Humor is not compartmentalized by the Kuna, restricted to particular specific or marginal occasions and places. Rather play and joking turn up everywhere, often side-by-side and even within the most serious forms of speech and action. From the most

---

[3] Kuna everyday verbal tricking is in some ways quite similar to the put ons described by Susan Philips (1975) for the Warm Springs Indian reservation and other North American Indian communities. See also Paredes (1977) who analyzes the role of play, humor, and put ons in native/outsider relations. Howe and Sherzer (1986) analyze the relationship between Kuna put ons and the narratives told about them, with a focus on Kuna/outside anthropologist interactions.

everyday and passing joke to the full-fledged performance of a trickster tale, humor is not just time out and time off from the serious stuff of life. Its close association with misfortune and   disaster, its actualization of, reflection of, exaggeration of, and commentary on social and cultural realities, and its playing around with ritual matters flirt with danger and no doubt heighten its appeal. In many ways play and humor are at the heart of what it means to be Kuna.

The Agouti story

Animal trickster tales incorporate all the forms of verbal play and humor I have described here, with a focus on interactional tricking. Tales such as *The Agouti story* are traditional narrative versions, with animal actors, of very common and everyday interactional behavior. While these tales can be recognized as Kuna shapings of stories which are widespread in native North and South America and beyond, they both reflect and speak directly to current Kuna realities. They represent the Kuna conception of their own conversational, especially conversational tricking behavior, verbally dramatized within narrative form.

There is another relationship between everyday tricking and trickster tales. While the Kuna tell traditional animal trickster stories like *The Agouti story*, with areal links throughout the Americas and beyond, new trickster tales are also invented and told, privately and publicly. These draw on everyday tricking interactions for their narrative content and are structured on the model of the traditional trickster tale, complete with nicknames and embedded dialogues.

Before presenting and examining *The Agouti story* it is most useful to provide an overview of the salient elements and themes of Kuna humor, which are reflected in it. First, there is the constant presence of tricksters and tricking in Kuna verbal life, from the everyday put on, to the narrative replay of the everyday put on, to the narration of traditional trickster tales, to the use of put ons and tricks by spirits in ritual and magical chants. Second and often quite related to the first, there is playing in various ways with the boundaries between the ritual and the everyday, the serious and the comical – in fleeting and flirting mimicry; in deadpan, unexpected humorous commentary about sex, disease, and death in serious, ritual contexts; in the narration of ordinary, banal events in the texts of ritual magical chants in ritual languages; in the telling of comical trickster tales and other humorous narratives as well as playful banter in the public, political, and ritual center, the gathering house. In all of this there is no blurring of genres, but rather an intersection, juxtaposition, interpenetrating, touching, and flirting with boundaries, including the creation of ambiguities, tensions, and even dangers. Finally there is the humor of actual performance, the dramatization and manipulation of the voice and the interaction with the audience.

Muristo Pérez's performance of *The Agouti story* is a superb illustration of the interplay of speech play, verbal art, and humor in Kuna discourse. In Muristo's telling, *The Agouti story* consists of seven episodes between Agouti and Jaguar and an interlude in which Jaguar is home with his wife. The structure of each episode is quite similar. Jaguar is pursuing Agouti in order to eat him, "in order to eat his head," he repeats often. Agouti prevents this from happening by offering Jaguar an alternative – something to eat or a short nap for example. Each time Jaguar accepts and is physically hurt because of it, usually resulting in his fainting. This enables Agouti to escape and Jaguar to realize he has been tricked.

Each episode is thus about trickery and the frustrations that follow from trickery. The characters come and go to and from scenes set before their arrival. Apart from the interlude, there are just two characters, who call each other "friend," and, most frequently, "Uncle" (Jaguar) and "Nephew" (Agouti). Agouti and Jaguar are both talked about and talk themselves, in a very colloquial and chatty style of Kuna. The narrative is thus moved along both monologically (Muristo's descriptions) and dialogically (Muristo's dramatized quotations of Agouti and Jaguar's face-to-face conversations). Lines tend to be short and in this sense laconically expressive.

Humor is achieved in the performance by means of an exaggeration of the contrasts between wily Agouti and bungling Jaguar, the direct quotations of the dialogues between them, minute descriptions of their behaviors, and the use of kin terms, rendering them human-like and animal-like at the same time; by means of the expressive imitations of noises (*TAK*, the sound of the *ikwa* fruit smashing against the animals' testicles, *KOT-TOK TAC-CAK*, the sound of the avocado entering the mouth of Jaguar) and of actions (stretching out of syllables as Jaguar jumps around, repetition of sounds as Agouti runs down the path); and by means of the interactions with Armando and other members of the audience, in particular by references and allusions to recent events in the village.

While the story is for the most part accessible to a non-Kuna readership, certain explanations heighten appreciation of the verbal artistry and humor of the performance. The two animals, Agouti and Jaguar, provide a comical contrast. Agoutis are small, intelligent, and highly-strung animals who flee in panic at the slightest alarm. They feed on fruits in the jungle mainland. The Central and South American jaguar is big and dangerous, but, apparently, somewhat clumsy. Jaguars eat agoutis when they can catch them. The Kuna also eat agoutis; they fear, but do not eat jaguars, who attack both animals and humans. Agouti is thus a little guy, while Jaguar is a big guy. The little guy constantly taunts and intimidates the big guy. It is because of the contrast between Agouti and Jaguar that it is so funny when Agouti is called "big boy" as he knocks out Jaguar (first episode: line 43). These animals' eating habits, as well as the Kuna's own constant concern about where the next meal will come from, render hilarious Agouti's repeated acknowledgment, almost invitation, to Jaguar to eat his [Agouti's] head in counterpoint response to Jaguar's threat and promise to do just this.

Muristo utilizes the Kuna verbal suffixes of body position to visualize in a quite realistic and yet comical way the natural positions of the animals. Agoutis, when eating, sit up straight. This is precisely how Muristo describes Agouti in line two of episode four and elsewhere. Jaguar, on the other hand, is always standing, sometimes quite comically, as in line 15 of episode four as he is standing waiting, mouth open, for Agouti to throw him the avocado.

The kin terms used between Agouti and Jaguar not only make them seem human, but are also humorous because of the particular relationship they connote. Agouti is *nika* (nephew) and Jaguar is *kilu* (uncle), in particular the uncle-in-law in whose house nephews are born according to Kuna matrilocal residence rules. Along with the affection of close kin, this relationship is also marked by the anxiety and tension of authority.[4]

Some of the episodes include details and allusions particular to Kuna life. The *ikwa* fruit of the first episode grows wild and is hard to open, like a nut with a hard shell. Line 40 relates this story to a recent event in the community. A chief's spokesman, who is albino and is known for his joking behavior, on seeing a Black Colombian sailor on the boat dock open his fly and take out his penis in order to urinate in the water, hit him in the genitals with a banana which he happened to be carrying. Kuna relations with Colombian Blacks, very special and omnipresent outsiders, are

---

[4]   While *nika* and *kilu* are kin terms and are used as such in everyday Kuna life, they are also extensively used as terms of address and reference with the sense "youth, junior man"/"elder, mature man." This renders their appearance in *The Agouti story* all the more humorous. I am grateful to James Howe for this observation.

ambiguous and ambivalent. The Kuna insist on maintaining strict social distance from the Colombians, who they treat as inferior and yet feel compassion and friendship toward. The Colombians, who are major trading partners of the Kuna, are obliged to sleep on the dock, or on their boats anchored out at sea. The Kuna buy such staples as sugar and coffee from the Colombians and in return sell them coconuts in large quantities. A most typical scene in a Kuna village is a dock crowded with Kuna carrying coconuts and Colombian sailors busy buying them up, against the background noise of the thud, thud, thud of coconuts hitting the deck of the visitors' boats as they are meticulously counted. The albino who was involved in this particular memorable incident was probably on the dock in some combination of buying, selling, curiosity, and sociability. Muristo's sudden bringing together of Agouti and Jaguar with the Kuna/Black sailor incident breaks up the audience, no doubt because of its surprising and laconic actualization of all of the tensions, ambiguities, and humor involved in both Agouti/Jaguar and Kuna/Black Colombian sailor relations as well as their intriguing similarities. Similarly Armando's comment in line 21 of episode three refers to the recent playful antics of some Kuna individuals.

The burning of a fallow field before planting in episode five is part of the Kuna practice of slash and burn agriculture. The sudden and incongruous incorporation of an explanation of origin (That's how Jaguar got his skin all stained [line 70 of episode five]), perhaps retained from the original diffusion of this story into the Kuna repertoire, but more likely inserted here just for humorous purposes, is quite incongruous in this story which otherwise does not focus on such matters; this incongruity provokes laughter.

The distinction between husband and man made by Jaguar's wife in the interlude in which he is at home with her depends on the Kuna words *maceret* and *sui*, the first of which can mean either man or husband but the second of which can mean only husband. There is much laughter as the wife makes this distinction. Armando's interjection (line 15 of the interlude) refers to the six horsepower motor the Kuna use in their dugout canoes.

In episode six, the tin houses that make so much noise when Agouti climbs on top of them are the kind of houses built by Panamanians. They contrast with native Kuna houses which are constructed out of bamboo and thatch. It seems as though Agouti and Jaguar are here in a Panamanian town. At the same time, since more and more Kuna villages have some houses with tin and composition roofs, this episode introduces a bit of tension between tradition and change, as the very native Agouti and Jaguar are playing around on very modern style constructions. Agouti's rump seems so large in episode seven in part because agoutis elongate their rumps when frightened.

Anthropologists have not paid particular attention to play and humor, treating them as either marginal or secondary to more basic, traditionally given concerns, such as social organization and kinship, or more recently, political economy and the world system. (See Apte 1985.) But playful and humorous discourse is not marginal to reality in such lowland South American societies as the Kuna. In fact, this discourse is a concrete actualization and recreation of, reflection and exaggeration of, as well as commentary on what happens in real Kuna life. Fact is fiction and fiction is fact. Trickster tales are an excellent example. Trickster tales are extremely common and popular around the world. This can be no accident. They are significant to the people who perform them and enjoy listening to them and they are revealing to others, like us, who want to understand these performers and listeners. Especially revealing is the particular stamp, the specific construction of reality that each society and and each performer create out of tales no doubt diffused from elsewhere and learned from others.

What do animals, like the trickster Agouti and his victim Jaguar, represent for the Kuna, in addition to the pure pleasure of listening to great storytellers such as Muristo recount their humorous antics? Why is it important to tell these trickster tales and to tell them publicly? According to Kuna belief, animals were once people. Because of their bad behavior, including especially their trickster behavior, they became animals. But they still retain some of their human characteristics. And animals, like humans, but also like plants and objects, have souls, and in the world of spirits, a very real and active world for the Kuna, and crucial in magical and curing ritual, they are quite like humans. They have social organization, including husbands and wives, chiefs, and spokesmen; they speak to one another; and they joke with and trick one another. They engage in such very Kuna daily activities as burning fields for planting and eating avocado, and they share such daily Kuna emotions and concerns as hunger, pain, disease, and death. More particularly, and in exaggerated form, *The Agouti story* is about competition, rivalry, and antagonism between friends and relatives. This is a very meaningful theme in this society which places so much emphasis on an egalitarian and cooperative ethic and yet pits individuals in competition with one another – chief with chief, curer with curer, chant knower with chant knower, and brother-in-law with brother-in-law. *The Agouti story* then, while overtly about animals, is quite clearly also about humans, in particular the Kuna, their social life, their exploits, their fears, their morality, and their humor. (Compare with Beidelman 1961.)

At the same time, *The Agouti story*, while being a fictional account of anthropomorphized animals, is also a fictional account of real animals, who the Kuna observe every day and appreciate as part of the unique natural world that is theirs and is most significant to them.

Trickster tales have remarkably wide distributions. They seem to diffuse relatively easily. The same story, with variations and adaptations to local ecologies and cultures, is at times found in Europe, Asia, Africa, and the Americas. The episodes of *The Agouti story* in particular have links well beyond the Kuna.

The first episode, with different animal actors and different fruit, is found in many American Indian groups, including the neighboring Choco, but also the more distant Kamsa to the South and the Tzeltal Mayans to the North. In the Tzeltal version, the trickster is Possum, the dupe is Puma, and the fruit is from the Grugru Palm tree.[5]

The second episode, of probably European or African origin, is found in Europe and Africa and among Spanish Americans and Indians of Mexico, including again the Tzeltal. In the European version, the trickster runs away with the victim's goods.[6]

The third episode is also probably of European or African origin. It is found in Europe, Africa, among Blacks in the West Indies, among French and Spanish Americans, and among American Indians as far north as the Navajo and as close to the Kuna as the Choco. In the European version, Wolf dives into the water for reflected cheese.[7]

The fourth episode is found among Spanish Americans in Puerto Rico, Chile, and Peru. The animal actors are Rabbit and Wolf and the fruit is a coconut.[8]

While stories similar to the fifth episode can be found elsewhere, this episode depends crucially on the nature of slash and burn agriculture and, at least in its Kuna form, probably has a local origin. The sixth episode, while not as intimately linked to Kuna ecology and culture as the fifth, seems to be local in its focus on tin-roofed

[5]   Personal communication from Stephanie Kane for the Choco, Alberto Sibundoi for the Kamsa, and Brian Stross for the Tzeltal.
[6]   See Thompson (1961): 437: tale type 1530.
[7]   See Thompson (1961): 27: tale type 34.
[8]   See Thompson (1961) : 39 : tale type 74C.

houses. The seventh episode is more general and like episodes one through four is probably widespread.

In spite of its areal and diffusional links, *The Agouti story* has been shaped into a quite Kuna form. With regard to content, the actors, Agouti, Jaguar, and Jaguar's wife, and their props, the *ikwa* fruit, the avocado, the burning field, and the tin roofs, are elements of Kuna ecology and culture. The narrative details are pages out of Kuna daily life. In particular, the conversations between Agouti and Jaguar and Jaguar and his wife are mirror images of Kuna verbal interactions. The verbal trickings are reframings of the playful duping of which real human Kuna are forever fond. Muristo dramatizes the adventures of Agouti and Jaguar in the most traditional of Kuna narrative styles, in a unique and personal way drawing on and creatively utilizing the broad range of Kuna elements of narrative poetics and rhetoric, play and humor. With regard to social and cultural context, this gathering-house telling, for fun and amusement, but related to the serious ritual and moral purpose of the same setting, including the possibility of this same story being ritually chanted, demonstrates the degree of integration of *The Agouti story* within Kuna life. Muristo's performance of *The Agouti story*, with regard to content, textual structure, dramatization of the voice, and social and cultural relevance and interpretation, is a manifestation of the essence of the interplay of Kuna speech play, verbal art, and humor, so basic to Kuna verbal life.

Explanations and interpretations of humor abound in the literature, anthropological and other. One classical anthropological approach follows the macro-sociological, functionalist line begun by Radcliffe-Brown (1940, 1949) and argues that humor is an obligatory reflection of certain social relationships. In this sense play and humor support the social order, perhaps as a necessary expression of it, thus keeping people in their places, perhaps as a letting off of steam. Another interpretation seems to be just the opposite. It argues that joking and humor are subversive, that they attack hierarchy in favor of equality. (See Douglas 1968.) Still others see humor as a way of coping with the serious and often tragic world around us, making us laugh instead of cry. Play and humor are also often considered to be pure entertainment, pleasurable moments separate and distinct from the serious and central concerns of life, an interpretation that perhaps best applies to and thus derives from western, urbanized societies. Freud views humor and joking in psychological terms, as a relief from latent tensions and an expression of subjects considered tabu in non-humorous discourse. (Freud 1905.) Freud, along with Bergson and many others, also see humor and laughter as being produced by surprising juxtapositions and incongruities involving, particularly in the case of Freud, an expression of latent, especially sexual repressions and aggressions.

None of these general and simple explanations neatly fit the Kuna. They probably all apply, at some level and at some moments. But in the ethnographic and discourse-centered approach I employ here, play and humor are studied as they are actualized in forms of discourse and approached in textual, contextual, and intertextual terms, and in terms of the thick, complex, and circumstantial realities of Kuna life. For my goal is to explore, explain, and illustrate what the Kuna consider funny and why, rather than force other models on them. Ultimately my approach leads us much closer to the delicate, subtle, and yet central ways play and humor figure into the Kuna world.

The text

In my representation of the Kuna version of *The Agouti story*, lines are determined by a combination of falling pitch and long pause. Long pauses without accompanying falling pitch are represented by a large space between words. Extra loud speech is indicated by means of capital letters. Decreasing volume is indicated by > placed before the stretch of speech affected. Dashes between syllables indicate stretched-out speech. Dashes between letters indicate that the voice is vibrating. Expressive lengthening of sounds is indicated by the doubling of letters. Faster speech is indicated by a dotted underline under the words which are spoken faster. Slow speech is indicated by stretching out the letters of the words affected. When part of a line is higher in pitch, this is indicated by raising the words. When a whole line is higher in pitch, this is indicated by ^ placed before the line. The translation is relatively literal, but accessible enough to readers of English to be able to appreciate the flavor and the humor of Kuna trickster tales. I use brackets to fill in anaphoric references not overtly expressed in the Kuna text but needed in English.

First episode

tek itto Armando.

takkarku anmar kwento wis ittoerkepe a.

kwento.

us kwento masunto.

takkarkua   usteka   acu epokwa   penkusokkarsunto.   5

acute   us epokwa usu   us yartakke a.

acu soetit.

taytapsunto a.

takkarku us kan-na-re-ke-siit.

kir takkarsunto acu.   10

palimaytesunto.

palimatku   wepa soysunna, napir soke.

takkarku usu maskunsi.

takkal "ikwa kunsi" soke.

ipepirki   sisunto.   15

ipepirki sii, maskunsiit, wepa kirka   us soysunna   kirka.

"emite   kunmoko" soke soke.

"palimaynatappit a, kunno" sokket "e nono kunnoye."

(Armando interjects: napir e nono kalekoko an epinsa.)

"sur" soke, "ipu pe kunsiye napir soke kunnosoke weye."

napir soke.   20

"pe iki maris?" soysunto a.

^ "iki pe marisye?"

"sur" soke "an aluki maris takken soke."

^ "aluki an maris takken ittos.

pe takko soke" a.   25

akkwa amicunto akkwa akkwa   amis.

us alu ekaaarsunto alu ekaa ipepir apin mesicunto.

TAK ikwa TAC AK

(Armando interjects: manna pureke.)

First episode

Well listen Armando.

So let's listen to a bit of a story now.

A story.

It's *The Agouti story*.

So and Agouti Jaguar the two of them they were about to compete with each other. 5

And Jaguar Agouti the two of them Agouti Agouti is a trickster ah.

Jaguar is a hunter.

He got there and saw him ah.

So Agouti is sit-ting-up-straight.

Uncle saw him Jaguar did. 10

He started chasing him.

When he started chasing him over there say, it's true it is said.

So Agouti is sitting eating.

So "I'm sitting eating *ikwa* fruit" he says.

On top of a hill seated. 15

Sitting on top of a hill, sitting eating, there to Uncle Agouti says to Uncle.

"Now you are going to eat too" he says it is said.

"He is going along chasing him ah, he is going to eat" he says "he is going to eat his head."

(Armando interjects: its true his head is going to be caught I think.)

"In point of fact" he says, "what are you sitting eating it's true I am going to eat some too" he says.

It's true it is said. 20

"How did you split it open ah?" he said.

^ "How were you able to split it open?"

"In point of fact" he says "I split it open with my balls" see it is said.

^ "With my balls I split it open.

You watch" he says ah. 25

He got a rock a rock a rock he got.

Agouti ooopened up his balls his balls he op he set them against the side of the hill.

TAK the *ikwa* fruit TAK AK.

(Armando interjects: Wow what pain!)

"pe takken soke" a.

napir soke.   30

a acu key takke a.

"wey pe samoko" kar soysunto.

tekka akkwa kal amismosunna.

ikwa eti alu pirki nue sicunnat a.

ittosa.   35

usti yamu yartaysat.

eti akkwa akkwa apin eti sarsosatwa aluki imaculit.

acuti aluki nue sioet.

kep immmaysat   TAK.

takkarku matunki sarsocunto.   40

(Audience laughs uproariously.)

(Armando interjects something unintelligible.)

napir soke.

(Armando interjects something unintelligible.)

teki   takkarku   immma aluper sokku.

us macitar oesto o-i-co-may-ti-sunto.

a.

acu tule wiles.   45

nekoette   oete.

us sateparto aparmatparto.

apparmaysi apparmaysi apparmaysi appar o-al-le-na-tap-pi ikarpal a.

Second episode

kir neywiskuarsunto acu.

acu neywiskuarparku   napir soke.

"pia tule nate?

anki toto" soke kep palimayteparsunna, ka-te-pa-li-par.

partaytapku   parkaletapparsunto.   5

takka ipe kwicis ipepir weki a.

ar-kwan-ta-ni-kwi-ci-sun-to.

napir soke.

"You see" it is said ah.

It's true it is said.   30

Ah Jaguar is astounded ah.

<u>"Here you're going to do it like that too"</u> he said to him.

Well he got a rock for him too.

But the other one placed the *ikwa* fruit right on top of his balls ah.

Did you hear?   35

This Agouti he tricked him for the fun of it.

This one he smashed against the stone the stone he didn't do it on his balls.

But Jaguar is going to place it right on his balls.

Then he diiid it   TAK.

So he smashed him in the banana.   40

(Audience laughs uproariously.)

(Armando interjects something unintelligible.)

It's true it is said.

(Armando interjects something unintelligible.)

Well   so   he diiid it he finished off his balls it is said.

That big boy Agouti knocked him out he-sure-made-him-jump-a-round.

Ah.

Poor Jaguar.   45

He passed out   he fainted.

And Agouti took off again started running again.

<u>Running running running run</u> laugh-ing a-long down the path ah.

Second episode

Uncle came to Jaguar did.

When Jaguar came to again   it's true it is said.

"Where did that guy go?

He's making fun of me" he says then he started chasing him again, catch-ing-him-a-gain.

When he got there he saw him again   he got there and reached him again.   5

So he was standing on a hill here on a hill ah.

It-was-fal-ling-straight-down.

It's true it is said.

wepase warmakkarku kar soysunna "ai iki pe kukwisye" ka sok "pentaytae kirye,"
soke.

"emi tayleku, purwatar tummat tani takkenye akkwa anki arkwantamalo teysokku

apinka   an p-e-n-t-a-y-y-e" kar soysunto a.   10

(Laughter from gathered audience.)

acu kinmoka   kep apin katapsunto weki a.

"apin pe weki   kao" kar soysunto "anti peka siynakweloye ittosa.

suarki anmal apinmakkoette" soysunto "tek an purkwemaloye."

acu al-laa-ma usti pinna pinna iptatmosunto aparmaytemosunto.

suli suar kwen arkusku sii   sunna arkwantakoe?   15

(Laughter from gathered audience.)

"tule pinsa pe yartaysat"

mm us sateparto.

ittosunto us o-al-le-na-tap-pi ittokwicunto "a al an yarta"   iptakkarsunto pinna

pinna   arsuntakoe? arkusku siit.

(Laughter from gathered audience.)

Third episode

parsateparto ukkin.

takkarku   tipirki sii taytappa, maskunsipinpa uste.

napir soke.

kepe   kar soysunna   "pe kunno soke" soke "matu" takken soke "yer kulleye.

matu nuet kulle" takken soke.   5

"pia pe amicun" soke.

takkarku ni taru a.

pe tay soke   matuyop ni mee, tiurpa natasursi a.

ni talet nait.

"we an suappitte" kar soysunna, "tiulak.   10

yer kullekette" soke.

"pe an takkoen" soke a.

kep us arkwattesunto, swillak.

When he got there he says to him "Friend how can you be standing there like that"
he [Jaguar] says to him "come help Uncle," he [Agouti] says.

"Now indeed, a big wind is coming see the rock is going to fall on us therefore help
me   a-g-a-i-n-s-t i-t" he said to him ah.   10

(Laughter from gathered audience.)

Jaguar is ready   then he went there and held against it ah.

"Against it here   you hold" he said to him "and I'll go and cut a stick for you did
you hear.

With the stick we'll hold it tight" he said "well if it's not done we would die."

Jaguar heeeld-on and Agouti slowly slowly left he ran on again.

But the stick was well in place   truly how was it going to fall?   15

(Laughter from gathered audience.)

"This guy tricked you for the fun of it."

Mm and Agouti took off again.

He heard Agouti go-ing-a-long-laugh-ing he stood listening "he tricked me"   he left
slowly slowly   how could it fall? it was in place.

(Laughter from gathered audience.)

Third episode

He continued on.

So   he got there and saw him sitting on the bank of the river, sitting eating Agouti
was.

It's true it is said.

Then   he says to him   "you're going to eat" he says "bread" see it is said "it
tastes good.

The bread tastes good" see it is said.   5

"Where did you get it" he says.

So the moon was full ah.

You see it is said   the moon shines like bread, reflecting under the water ah.

It was a full moon.

"I really got it" he says to him, "under the water.   10

It really tastes good" he says.

"You'll see" he says ah.

Then Agouti went down under the water, swish.

takkar inso senonikkiwa.

eti kuar kanina senonikkit.   15

kuar su, kuar kanina arkwattet, kwenti ni nait sun pe   se warmakko?

(Laughter from gathered audience.)

teki kep arkwatteparsunto.

takkar key toke a.

acu key toyto.

"tekirti akkwa tukkarki an pey ettinno" kar soke.   20

"kinpali," akkwa tukkar ettisa, kep arkwatto na-kat-te.

(Armando interjects: oros saku yapa an mesis an soke.

Muristo responds: yeku manturapet.

Laughter.)

napir soke.

man sikwitap ai   opilumaynasunto   tiulak   a-i   immmakke napirka tup ittiris

kannar nononisunto.

kekkusa (laughter) o-som-mai nappa pirki.

usti sateparto.   25

Fourth episode

untar neywiskuarpa kep parnatparsunto.

nai nai nai takkar asweki nipa sii

kun-si-pin-pali a.

aswe kunsipinpa.

(Armando interjects: kunsi.

Laughter.)

napir soke.   5

emite wete   "nue pe an yartaytiku emiski pe anse nono kulleko" kar soysunto.

kir "sur"soke.

"en tayleku yel aswe kulleke kunmoko soke" soke "pittoen" soke.

tekkar, "yeeer kulle."

"tekirti an pe kan nakkoloye" a.   10

So thus he brought it up.

This one really brought up what he had already. 15

Having gotten it already, having gone down for it already, how are you going

really   to reach the reflecting moon?

(Laughter from the gathered audience.)

Well then he [Jaguar] went down too.

So he is unable to enter ah.

Jaguar could not enter.

"Well I'll tie a stone around your neck" he says to him. 20

"OK ready," he tied the stone around his neck, then he went down down-he-went.

(Armando interjects: I put him in a rice bag I say.

Muristo responds: What a pity.

Laughter.)

It's true it is said.

He got there and sat down the friend   was bobbing splashing wildly   under the

water   t-h-e f-r-i-e-n-d   diiid it truly he broke the rope and came out again.

He couldn't last any more (laughter) he-lay-fal-len on the ground.

And Agouti continued on. 25

Fourth episode

After a while he came to again then he continued on.

On on on so there he is sitting up in an avocado tree.

Already sitting eating a.

Already sitting eating avocado.

(Armando interjects: sitting eating.

Laughter.)

It's true it is said. 5

Now this guy [Jaguar (said)]   "since you've been doing a good job of tricking me

now your head is going to be eaten" he said to him.

"In point of fact" Uncle says.

"Now indeed this avocado tastes good you're going to eat some too" he [Agouti]

says it is said "you'll taste some too" he says.

Well, "it tastes goood."

"Well I'll climb up for you" ah. 10

nakkwicunto.

nipa tukku.

"turut peka amis kwacat" a.

kep kirka soysunna, "an itu wek kaya maaa pe sikoye" a.

kir kaya m-a-a-a-a nappaki kwicisunnat.   15

kep nipa mecarsunto immmaysat KOT-TOK-TAC-CAK kayapa.

(Laughter.)

aaai o-i-co-may-ti-kus.

a

nai nai nai iki sao?

us aite aite aite aite aite   sateparto.   20

otalisa nekoetpali a.

napir soke.

Fifth episode

kep palimayteparsunto, nak kaaate.

takkarku naynu saalet ukakki karmaytii.

ai   us karmaytipinparto.

"emiskinoye" kotte "nataet" a.

karmaytipinpar.   5

naynu saar nay-nu tum-mat sa-ar so-ke a.

pippirmaynai.

kep katapku kar soysunto "emiskin kep anse parna" kar soysunto a.

"emiski pe anse nono kullekoye.

anse perkus takken" kar soke.   10

"ittosa we maci?"

(Big laughter.)

napir soke.

untaraa   kep natparsunto.

nattepalirpini.

And he climbed up.

To the very top.

"I got you I picked you a hard one" ah.

Then he says to Uncle, "you sit there in front of me with your mouth wiiide open" ah.

Uncle stands up on the ground with his mouth w-i-i-i-de open.   15

Then from above he threw it down he diiid it to him KOT-TOK-TAC-CAK in the mouth.

(Laughter.)

Frieeend it-made-him-jump-up-and-down.

Ah.

Jumping jumping jumping what to do?

Agouti comes down comes down comes down comes down comes down   and he took off again.   20

[As for jaguar] He suffered and he fainted again ah.

It's true it is said.

Fifth episode

Then he [Jaguar] started chasing after him [Agouti] again, waaalking along.

So he is going about the edge of a new field.

Friend   Agouti he's already going about again.

"Now you're gonna see" he [Jaguar] shouts "you're gonna get it," ah.

He [Agouti] is already going about.   5

Its a new field a-big-new-field-it-is-said ah.

[Agouti] is circling about it.

Then when he [Jaguar] caught up with him there he said to him "now for sure then you won't get away from me again" he said to him ah.

"Now your head is really going to be eaten.

I've got you finished off see" he says to him.   10

"Did you hear boy?"

(Big laughter.)

It's true it is said.

After a moment   then he went on.

But he [Agouti] went on as well.

kep, kep wepa sokkarsunto a.   15

naynu ap-pal-lal-la kar mekitappit, appallalla wesik appallalla wesik naynu tummmat
saalet.

acuka soysunna usu.

"emispin pe an kunnoet un-tar-to-le" soke

"tekirti pin wis kammarkwelo" soysunto a.

"anmar kapkweloye.   20

kapisa pe ukku me-ca-lii.

pe anki aypittoku.

yer ittole" soysunto a.

"emiskinti anpa wis immesar takkenye a.

teysokku anmar wis k-a-m-m-a-r-kw-e-l-o-y-e."   25

kir soke "ILAKWEN" soke.

"napir pe anka soy" soysunto.

y a l a p a m e k i c u n t o a.

(Armando interjects: napiri.)

yalapa.

(Armando laughs hard.)

tek yalapa masunna.   30

takkarku kir   acu mas sanarkus kapittape tak.

ka-pi-te-ku a.

epeti   usti tarkwen pinsas mekicokku, al ipik kapo?

(Armando interjects: kammayop imaymasunte.)

kammayop.

a-s-u t-a-r k-o-l-e-m-a-s-u-n-to.   35

nappis kir sa-te-mo it-to-le soke.

nuutayna sunna tukkinmakkar nuuu.

takkar nue kapit.

(Armando interjects something unintelligible.

Muristo responds: yeo.)

kep wepa epunasunna a.

epua, takkarku nue imas merema, aaa, "kuspin" soke.   40

kep eti ar-pak-ke kwiskucunnatte a.

Then, then he began to speak ah.   15

In-the-cen-ter of the field there he lay down, there in the very center there in the very center of the big new field.

Agouti says to Jaguar.

"Right now you're going to eat me, it's-just-not-pos-si-ble" he says.

"Well if we just took a little nap first" he said ah.

"Let's sleep first.   20

After you've slept you'll-be-staaarved.

You'll make a meal out of me.

It will taste good" he said ah.

"Right now you're still a little too full see ah.

Therefore we s-h-o-u-l-d f-i-r-s-t t-a-k-e a l-i-t-t-l-e n-a-p."   25

Uncle says "ACCEPTED" he says.

"It's the truth what you say to me" he said

S i d e   b y   s i d e   t h e y   l a y   d o w n   a h.

(Armando says: It's true.)

Side by side.

(Armando laughs hard.)

Well side by side they are lying.   30

So Uncle   Jaguar always falls right to sleep see.

When he-fell-as-leep ah.

This guy   Agouti thought to himself because he [Jaguar] was lying there, how could one sleep?

(Armando interjects: He made as if he were lying sleeping.)

As if he were lying sleeping.

H-e l-a-y t-h-e-r-e s-n-o-r-i-n-g.   35

Right away Uncle did the same thing it is said.

Carefully he [Agouti] is truly looking real close caaarefully.

So he fell sound asleep.

(Armando interjects something unintelligible.

Muristo responds: yeo.)

Then he is touching him ah.

Touches, so well done he's sleeping, aaah, "it's already done" he says.   40

Then he sec-ret-ly got up ah.

AR-PAK-KE.

kep tikkarkine   soo okaarsunto.

soo > eppir eppir eppir eppir eppir eppir eppir eppir eppir okacunto, per pir.

per pe epilis so, pe aparki pe mekicunnatte a.   45

kep tikkarki koormakkarsunna, e   uste.

"Y-O-O-O.

t-u-l-e w-i-l-e-s-m-a-r" s-o-k-e.

tikka pat eti tikkarki noskwici.

"pe-ra-tar-so-tar-kwa-pun-ye-me-kis-ku-man-tur-na-pet"-so-ke, "pia pe par noota?   50

par pe noeculitteta."

(Laughter.

Brief joking conversation with field worker.)

teki   kep   napir soke a.

kammai emi kapet opurar pe kwiskuarku   pe takke taska pe itu, aaa o-i-co-may-ti-

sun-to.

pia pe parnaoe?

sotar kataniku inpa inpaki pe pe parnaet taylesulitteta.   55

(Laughter.)

ittos!

aaa.

pia pe parnaota?

napir soke.

peece.   60

IMMAYTESUNNA, pia wis tattarasar tanikki a?

apa IMM-MAY-TE-SUNTO.

IMMMAYTEKU tikkarmosku.

oete   palittocula acu.

oete.   65

napir   PEEEkwace.

n-e-k-a-t-a-r w-i-s-i-k-u-a-r, kammukka > YAS YAS yas yas.

usti tikka ka naynu tikkarpa ka alletii.

SEC-RET-LY.

Then all around   he started a fire.

The fire > goes around goes around goes around goes around goes around goes
around goes around goes around goes around the fire caught, all over.

It circled around you, you were lying right in the middle ah.   45

Then from the outside he shouted, this   Agouti did.

"Y-O-O-O

W-e'-r-e i-n t-r-o-u-b-l-e" he says.

But he's already standing far outside.

"E-ve-ry-thing-is-flam-ing-up-in-a-big-fire-its-in-cre-di-ble"-he-says, "where can
you get out?   50

You really can't get out again."

(Laughter.

Brief joking conversation with field worker.)

Well   then   it's true it is said ah.

Sleeping now drunk with sleep you got up   you see everything closed in front of
you, aaah he-made-you-jump.

Where will you go again?

The big fire is coming toward you there are no spaces no spaces in between for you
for you to go out again.   55

(Laughter.)

Did you hear?

Aaah.

Where are you going to go again?

It's true it is said.

After a moment.   60

WHAT TO DO, where is there a little clearing to come out ah?

Over there HE-DIIID-IT.

HE DIIID IT he got outside.

He passed out   he completely lost consciousness Jaguar did.

He passed out.   65

It's true   THEEERE he remained.

H-e c-a-m-e t-o, his neck was > SCARRED SCARRED scarred scarred.

And Agouti was far from him outside the field laughing at him.

napir soke.

auna we acu, ukka matta matta kus soysunto.   70

(Laughter.)

ittos!

auna we kumaysatpa tekkus takken soke.

(Armando interjects: kakkula sip sip sii.)

kakkula sip sip SIII soke weki malat weki malace pakkar   pelatar nakucunto

nAA-TE apkan ukakka.

w e a i u s p e e c e k i r k i t o t o s t a k k e n s o k e a.

napir soke.   75

Interlude: Jaguar at home with his wife

kep omese nacunto.

omese oarmakkar nue kummaysat, pia pe par parraosunna?

omey soysunna "pe an takken" soke.

"nik anki totos" takken soysunto.

"napir" soysunto.   5

"pe kekekwa saal unnil itto karmaytitteee."

omete kirka soymosunto.

"niy wekipi pey tototiku takkenye.

emite, pey yartaspinpa,

(Muristo seems to make a mistake and correct himself, says tule kwen maceret, then continues.)

tule maceret an peki kwen attaysulitteta."

(Much laughter.)

a.   10

ome kar soymosunto a.

"unnila an suika kus an pe takketteta.

(Laughter throughout line.)

kwen maceret an pe taysur takken." (Laughter throughout line, unintelligible comments at end.)

soysunto a.

"emiskino" soysunto, "anse pelaye."   15

(Armando interjects comments relating to current Mulatuppu events.)

It's true it is said.

That's how Jaguar, got his skin all stained.   70

(Laughter.)

Did you hear!

Because of these burns he got that way see it is said.

(Armando interjects: His lips are ash white ash white.)

His lips ARE ash White ash white it is said all over here all over there   they got
all over his body they WENT.

This friend Agouti really made fun of Uncle see it is
said ah.

It's true it is said.   75

Interlude: Jaguar at home with his wife: translation

Then he [Jaguar] went home to his wife.

He got home to his wife well burned, where else can you really go again?

He says to his wife "you see me" he says.

"Nephew made fun of me" see he said.

"It's true" he said.   5

"You're such a stupid oaf always going about this way."

That wife said back to Uncle.

"Nephew that same one has always been making fun of you see.

Now, he tricked you again already, as far as I'm concerned you're not a man."

(Much laughter.)

Ah.   10

His wife said to him ah.

"I've only got a husband that's how I see you.

(Laughter throughout line.)

I don't see you as a man see."

(Laughter throughout line, unintelligible comments at end.)

She said ah.

"Right now" he said, "I'm gonna really finish him off."   15

(Armando interjects: he gets going with a six horsepower motor.)

soysunto.

napir soke.

teki kep   nae taylearparsunto NATTEpalirpini.

e-m-i-s-k-i-n-o nukusparsunnat a, niwala wala walakwen meymait.

Sixth episode

parsateparta.

takkarku A-A-I-I   karmaytipinpar "EET-TO" soke.

"emiskino" soysunto.

(Armando interjects something unintelligible.)

NAT-TEpalirpini okormaynaikusparto nai nai nai nai nai nai nai nai nai.

t a k k a r k u, p o r m o n e y p u p u k k w a, a u r p a u s t o y t e s u n t o.   5

pa pormo pirki nakkwicunto a.

us pi-ok soke.

achute urpa   E-P-I-R-T-I-S-U-N-T-O us nakkwer pe takke nipa a.

aur nakkwerpat usu.

us suaryapa key nakkwe pe tak.   10

(Laughter.)

mm, nipa tukku pe taysi tayleartae.

(Comments from audience.)

napir soke.

teki   untar imas.

aipirtisunto pia nate?

kep kar kwiliarsunto a.   15

kwiliarsunto.

TI ^TI ^TI TI pu-le-kol-lo-may-te-ma-ra-tar-kol-lo-may-te-yop-por-mo a.

kir NUUU kwakit apparMMAK   mmm, "pey maluarye" tule pey sokkette a.

pittosa? mmm.

i-t-t-o-s-u-l-i.   20

He said.

It's true it is said.

Well then   he went off once again he LEFT again.

R-e-a-l-l-y n-o-w he was cured again ah, he spent a month here a month there a month everywhere.

Sixth episode:

He took off again.

So T-H-E F-R-I-E-N-D   was going about already again "ALL RIGHT" he says.

"Right now" he said.

(Armando interjects something unintelligible.)

And he left again shouting as he went along again going going going going going going going going going.

S o , t h e r e a m o n g a b u n c h o f t i n h o u s e s , A g o u t i e n t e r e d b e l o w.   5

There he climbed up on top of the tin ah.

Agouti s-u-d-d-e-n-l-y it is said.

And Jaguar below   T-U-R-N-I-N-G A-R-O-U-N-D Agouti is a great climber you see above ah.

Because he is a great climber Agouti.

You see that Agouti can't climb a pole.   10

(Laughter.)

Mm, above at the top you always see him sitting.

(Comments from audience.)

It's true it is said.

Then   after a moment.

He's turning about where did he go?

Then he started dancing ah.   15

He started dancing.

TI ᵀᴵ ᵀᴵ TI the-tin-it-roared-loud-ly-it-roared-like-thun-der ah.

Uncle got REEEALLY scared he RAN AWAY   mmm "it will fall down on you" people tell you ah.

Did you understand? mmm.

H-e d-i-d n-o-t u-n-d-e-r-s-t-a-n-d.   20 mucup icok.

aparmayteto.

kir sorpa attaysunna takkarku kwen akkar patto.

AP-PAR-MAY-MA-PIN, WEE e yartaytipali, parrasitto.

Seventh episode

nai nai nai nai nai nai nai parsoket   takkarku   suaryap toytap soket.

pittos, pormo warakkwasaar nate ittole soke ayap toytap soke.

ayapa toytapkua   wek ittoarsunto weki a.

arkanki, acute ittoar ittolesunto.

arkanti   key sorpa pe pe tak.   5

(Armando laughs.)

napir soke.

tek arkanki sorpa, weki, ittonaku   wekit e san katappitte wekitki e sor a, e sor wek

katap ittolesunto MOK.

(Armando interjects something unintelligible.)

akikinnarsunto us H H H.

"toa an ko pippi ittonai," soysunto.

(Laughter.)

kir kwakkitto.   10

"ko pippikwatte, pule sanatar tummat."

(Much laughter.)

"wekitte pule   e ko ko ko sappi tule ani, toa an ko sappi ittonai?"

soysunto.

ittosunna, wek ittoma, "e-ko-sap-pi-tu-le-ip-tum-mat-to-le-e-san-pur-sun,"

kwakkitto.

(Laughter.)

mmm aparmaysi.   15

al ati suli tule sanki pe kasatwa.

(Comments from audience.)

He jumped the other way.

And the other one [Agouti] ran away.

When Uncle looks behind so he's already gone.

AL-REA-DY-RUN-NING-A-LONG, HE was tricking him again, so he goes on again.

Seventh episode

Going going going going going going going again it is said again   so   he entered inside a pole it is said.

Did you hear? feeling his way as he went into it it is said he entered into a narrow hole it is said.

Inside when he entered   here he [Jaguar] began to touch here ah.

With his paws, that Jaguar began to touch he touched.

The paws   not your behind you see.   5

(Armando laughs.)

It's true it is said.

Well with his paws, here, he was touching his behind   here he grabbed his body right here his ass ah, he grabbed his ass here he felt it MOK.

(Armando interjects something unintelligible.)

Agouti rumbled H H H.

"Who is touching my little finger?" he said.

(Laughter.)

And Uncle got scared.   10

"This little finger, it sure has a lot of big meat."

(Much laughter.)

"Right here   this finger this finger this pinky finger of mine, who is touching my pinky finger?"

He said.

He [Jaguar] feels, here he feels, "what-an-e-nor-mous-thing-this-pin-ky-fin-ger-is-his-bo-dy-must-be-e-nor-mous," he got scared.

(Laughter.)

Mmm he went running.   15

But it wasn't really that [a finger] you really grabbed the guy by his body.

(Comments from audience.)

te-ki, tayleku   ai uste   acu epok yartaynaikucunto.
tese pey sokkolo pittoku an ai.

We-ll, indeed   that's how friend Agouti   and Jaguar the two of them went about tricking each other.

That's it up to here I could tell you more you've heard it my friend.

An aerial view of the island of Sasartii-Mulatuppu

Chief Muristo Pérez performs a ritual greeting with three other chiefs

8. THE GRAMMAR OF POETRY AND THE POETRY OF MAGIC: HOW TO GRAB A SNAKE IN THE DARIEN

This chapter explores the relationship between grammar and poetry and poetry and magic in Kuna ritual discourse. I examine in detail a magical chant used to raise a dangerous snake in the air, *nakpe ikar* (*The way of the snake*). My investigation of the chant involves all aspects of linguistic structure – phonological and morphological details, syntactic and semantic structures, metaphors and other forms of figurative language, and narrative organization. It also reveals a constant and dynamic interplay of structure and function. Attention to this interplay is crucial to an understanding of each of the devices in the chant, the meaning of the chant as a whole, the role of the chant in the event in which it occurs, and the significance of the chant in Kuna culture and society more generally.

The title of this chapter combines the titles of two classic papers in the study of language use, Roman Jakobson's (1968) discussion of the intimate interrelationships of grammar and verbal art: "Poetry of grammar and grammar of poetry" and Charles O. Frake's (1964) ethnographic analysis of drinking encounters among the Subanum: "How to ask for a drink in Subanum." My approach in this chapter, as throughout this book, involves an intersection of linguistic, literary, and ethnographic perspectives.

Interpretation of *The way of the snake* depends crucially on an analysis of the interaction of its grammatical, stylistic, poetic, rhetorical, and magical properties. Its fuller significance emerges from placing this chant within a web of cultural and symbolic associations, including the importance of snakes, the relationship between verbal magic and curing, the role of the spirit world in human life, and the power of narrative discourse.

Since *The way of the snake* contains a narrative as one of its central features, I will set the scene for my analysis with an overview of the types of Kuna narrative. (See also chapters three through seven.) One useful way to classify Kuna narratives is as either first person narratives or third person narratives. First person narratives can in turn be grouped into, on the one hand, new information narratives, characteristic of informal occasions and especially informal conversations and greetings, and, on the other hand, retellings, in which personal experiences are retold in a formal and often ritual language and style, characteristic of the speaking and chanting of the Kuna gathering house, the public, political, and social meeting place. Third person narratives are also quite common and appreciated among the Kuna. They are the form used for the performance, in a ritual language, of tribal traditions, myths, legends, history, and stories. Public performances of these tribal traditions in third person narrative form are typically used as models of good or bad behavior by narrators. They are part of the exhortative rhetoric of Kuna public politics and oratory. In a certain sense, then, these third person narratives are understood to be embedded within a first person form: "I exhort you to do X."

Another type of third person narrative is the magical *ikar* (way), which is the central and crucial act in curing and magical events. Magical ways are memorized chants in the esoteric ritual language of the spirit world.[1] They are performed by specialists, *wisikana* (knowers) of them, and addressed to particular representatives of the spirit world. Kuna magic operates in the following way. The spirit addressees of a magical chant are convinced by means of the chant that the performing specialist is able to control them, that he knows their language and every aspect of their essence and existence – the location and nature of their origin, their present abode, their physical and behavioral characteristics, and their names.

After the demonstration of this potential to control, the chant describes precisely what action the specialist wants to occur, for example, the curing of a disease or the grabbing and raising of a snake. Ideally, the spirits, upon hearing and understanding the narrative, and because of hearing and understanding the narrative, do what is described in it. Kuna magical chants are thus dramatic scripts for action performed by a live narrator and played out by spirit actors.[2] Because the spirit world underlies and

---

[1] In the performance of magical chants for curing and disease prevention, slight variations of an essentially nonreferential nature occur, involving very superficial aspects of phonology and morphology. (See below.) The magical chants performed for Kuna girls' puberty rites by contrast are completely fixed. Not the slightest variation is tolerated. The degree to which Kuna puberty rites texts are fixed in form is reflected in a personal experience. In 1970 I made a tape recording of a puberty rites specialist teaching a chant to several students. Between 1970 and 1978 I never discussed this chant with him. In March of 1979, nine years after the original recording, I brought him a transcription I had made of it, in order to translate it into ordinary colloquial Kuna, from which it differs considerably. Since he does not read or write, he asked me to read him the text. I did so line by line and he translated each line into colloquial Kuna. Typically, I barely began a line and he finished it, never missing a morpheme or even a phoneme from my transcription. In a few cases where I misread a tiny detail of my own writing, he corrected me. The Kuna thus provide still another counter example (for many others see Finnegan 1977) to the view (see Goody 1977, Lord 1960, Ong 1977) that there is no pure, verbatim memorization of fixed texts in nonliterate, oral societies.

[2] I am indebted to Chapin (1981) for the comparison of Kuna magical texts with dramatic scripts.

animates the real, actual physical world, what occurs in the spirit world is subsequently played out in the actual world. In this sense, the third person narratives of Kuna magic can be understood to be embedded within a first person command of the form: "I tell you, that is, I command you X." Magical chants are performative in the sense that their performance is essential to the successful completion of a magical action; saying is doing in that correct narration not only describes an action or event, but actually accomplishes it by causing it to occur.

The way of the snake is one of a set of magical chants known as *kaeti*, literally "grabber." Other chants in this set are used to attract bees and wasps and to grasp a hot iron rod. More generally, grabbers are members of the class or genre of chants performed by specialists to representatives of the spirit world. Many of these chants are performed in association with curing rituals and are intended specifically for such purposes as lowering high fever, alleviating headaches, aiding childbirth, strengthening blood, and improving eyesight. Others are used for the acquisition of abilities and the achievement of particular goals, such as hunting, fishing, or learning traditional knowledge. Grabbers, like all magical chants, are performed in a variety of contexts. They are performed in the actual act of control, for example, raising the snake. And they are performed for practice, for learning and teaching, for pleasure, and to remind the ever present and listening spirits that the specialist has the potential to control them. The public, verbal display of knowledge and potential power, to both the human and spirit worlds, is as important as, if not more important than, the physical act of grabbing the snake. The particular performance of *The way of the snake* that I discuss here was a practice session by a specialist-knower, Pranki Pilos of Mulatuppu. It took place on March 2, 1971.

Why snakes? The Darien jungle in which the Kuna walk, farm, and hunt is the site of some of the most dangerous snakes in the world. This is reason enough to be worried about snakes and to want to be able to control them. In addition, according to Kuna belief, snake spirits are among the most evil of spirits and, like other animal spirits, have the potential to cause serious disease, without the actual, physical animal necessarily biting or even coming into contact with the victim.[3] It is no wonder that

---

[3] Such quasi-metaphorical disease causation theories, involving animal spirits, are found in other societies, for example, the Ainu (see Ohnuki-Tierney 1977). For the details of Kuna theories and practices in relation to disease and curing, see Chapin (1981).

there is a complex of magical chants, including *The way of the snake*, whose purpose is to calm and control various snakes and snake spirits.

The interplay of structure and function

Grabbers are shorter than magical chants used in curing rituals, which typically last one hour or more. Pranki Pilos's performance of *The way of the snake* lasts eight minutes. It describes a specialist's encounter with a snake and his use of language to control it. The general structure is as follows. First there is the setting of the scene: As the specialist is working in his jungle farm, the snake appears (lines 1-20). The snake is described (lines 21-30). The snake verbally challenges the specialist (lines 31-33). The specialist responds to the challenge (lines 34-38). The snake prepares himself for the contest (lines 39-43). The specialist in turn prepares himself by applying special medicines (lines 44-57). Then comes the verbal display of power. The specialist shows that he knows the snake intimately by listing the parts of the snake's body in a series of verses (lines 58-106). Then there is a description of the desired magical action itself, the raising of the snake (lines 107-114). The uttering of the performative formula (line 115). And the act is done (lines 116-119). The snake admits defeat (lines 120-122). And he expresses fear (lines 123-125). Having won the contest and controlled the snake, the specialist shows himself to be friendly and compassionate (lines 126-129).

The story is in many ways quintessentially Kuna. The specialist is an agriculturalist and like all Kuna men, almost every day, he finds himself in the Kuna mainland, working his fields, with all the pleasures and dangers that such work in the tropical forest involves. The snake spirit is very human, almost comically so, complete with a necktie, such as that worn by Kuna chiefs. The spirit world, like the animal world, is anthropomorphized in the Kuna literary imagination. The snake is not killed but rather overpowered. This is quite in keeping with the Kuna verbally potent but physically nonviolent approach to the world.

The way of the snake is in a linguistic variety and style which is shared by Kuna magical specialists and the spirit world and differs from everyday colloquial Kuna along several dimensions. The most salient and diagnostic phonological characteristic of this magical language is that many vowels which are deleted in everyday, colloquial speech are not deleted in ritual magical chants. As a result, various consonantal assimilation processes that are an automatic consequence of vowel deletion do not occur in these chants. (See chapter two and Sherzer 1983: 36-39.) Thus *palitakkekwiciye* "is looking over" (line 4), from underlying *pal(i)takk(e)-kwic(i)-ye* (where parentheses surround potentially deletable vowels and dashes separate morpheme boundaries), would be *partaykwisye* in colloquial Kuna. *Osamakkenaiye* "he is clearing" (line 17), from underlying *osamakk(e)-na(i)-ye*, would be *osamaynaye* in colloquial Kuna. *Onakkwesikwisaye* "raises" (line 21), from underlying *onakkw(e)-sikwi-s(a)-ye*, would be *onaysikwisye*. And *sokekwiciye* "is saying" (line 85), from underlying *sok(e)-kwic(i)-ye*, would be *sokkwisye*. The presence of these underlying vowels is basic to the creation of melodic shapes in the chant, a salient aspect of the marking of its poetic line structure, as well as to its incantatory effects. The vowels and the melodic patterning are essential elements in the phonological marking, in a sociolinguistic sense, of this ritual magical variety and style, as well as its esthetic, verbally artistic quality.

With regard to morpho-syntactic structure, *The way of the snake*, like all magical chants, is marked by the use of a particular set of nominal and verbal prefixes and suffixes. These forms have several functions, which operate simultaneously. They are part of the structural apparatus of the grammar of the magical linguistic variety, serving as nominalizers, stem formatives, and tense-aspect markers. They are sociolinguistic markers of this particular linguistic variety, distinguishing it from other Kuna linguistic varieties and styles. They contribute to the esthetics of magical chants in three ways – they increase the length of words, especially in terms of the number of morphemes per word; they are ornamental embellishments; and they are one of the devices used to mark poetic lines.

There are morphemes which occur exclusively or almost exclusively in the ritual language of magical chants. For example, there are the prefixes *ipe-*, *ulu-*, *ak-*, *man-*, and *olo-*, as in *ipetinikki* "field" (line 1), *ulukwaapala* "halfway" (line 3), *aktetemakkesikwisaye* "salivates" (line 27), *manansuelupi* "silver hooks" (line 40), and *oloputi* "golden blowgun" (line 52). *Ipe*, *ulu*, and *ak* have no specific translatable meanings. *Man* and *olo* signify "silver" and "golden" respectively and I have translated them as such. Non-referential, non-translatable morphemes characteristic of the ritual language of this chant are *tar* (lines 2, 4, and elsewhere), *kwa* (line 15), and *ini* (lines 48, 57, and elsewhere).

There are also morphemes which, while they occur in colloquial Kuna, have a greater frequency and a different and wider range of meanings and functions in magical chants such as *The way of the snake*. An excellent example is in the suffix *-ye*, which is used in colloquial Kuna as an optative and emphatic marker with verbs and an emphatic and vocative marker with nouns. It is also used as a quotative marker. It occurs with great frequency in the language of magic, perhaps stressing the optative mood of magical chants. But it is also a place filler, giving the performer time to remember the next line of these memorized chants. *-Ye* can be viewed as a verbally artistic embellisher as well; it is sometimes repeated two or three times. And, since it often occurs at the ends of lines, it serves, along with other devices, as a poetic line marker. Another example is the nominal suffix *-pi*, which in colloquial speech has the meaning "only," as in *macerkanpi* "only boys." It is used in lines 40 to 42 of *The way of the snake* with a more generalized focusing or emphatic meaning. Its repetition in the first word of three consecutive lines also contributes to the overall poetic rhythm of the chant.

Morphological structure is directly involved in the magical functioning of *The way of the snake*. A set of four verbal suffixes are used in Kuna, in conjunction with the progressive aspect, to specify the position of the subject of the verb, as either *-kwici* "standing, in a vertical position," *-sii* "sitting," *-mai* "lying, in a horizontal position," or *-nai* "hanging, in a perched position, as if in the air." (See chapter four, in which metaphorical uses of these positional suffixes are discussed.) Examples from this chant are *nuptulusaekwiciye* "he is sharpening-standing" (line 7) and *ittimienaiye* "he is cutting-perched/crouched" (line 16). In lines 55 and 56, *-kwici* "standing" somewhat figuratively describes the position of the specialist's *purpa* (soul).

The grammatical category of position is crucial to the climactic moment of *The way of the snake*, the actual raising of the snake in the air. In this section of the chant, the snake is first described as dragging and turning over in a *-mai* "horizontal" position, that is, free on the ground (lines 108-109). After the performative formula, " 'Simply indeed I raise you' I am saying" (line 115), during which the snake is raised in the air, it is again described as dragging and turning over, but this time in a *-nai* "hanging" position (lines 118-119). That is, while the chant never explicitly and specifically states that the specialist has actually succeeded in grabbing and raising the snake, the simple, economic shift in verbal suffixes, from *-mai* "horizontal" to *-nai* "hanging," on the same pair of verbs, dragging and turning over, quite poetically and powerfully signals that the snake is in the air, on the specialist's hand.

The process of moving from *-mai* to *-nai* involves the projection of a paradigm syntagmatically, the classic Jakobsonian definition of poetry. And this occurs as the magical, powerful climax of the chant, addressed to the spirit of the snake itself, and thus precisely convincing it that it has been controlled, grabbed, and raised, and causing all of this to occur in actuality. This is a true case of poetry in action.[4] The poetic-magical potential of Kuna grammatical structure is actualized in these crucial lines of *The way of the snake*, in which grammar becomes poetry and poetry becomes magic.

Another salient aspect of *The way of the snake* is lexicon. Like all magical chants, *The way of the snake* uses the vocabulary of the linguistic variety particular to the spirit world. In fact, vocabulary is the most diagnostic marker of this linguistic variety. Many words in *The way of the snake* are entirely different from the corresponding words in colloquial Kuna. These are presented in table I.

TABLE I.   **Lexical Differentiation in Colloquial Kuna and** *The way of the snake*

The way of the snake	Colloquial Kuna	English
ipetinikki	*pula*	grass
tata nakipe nele	*tata*	sun
ipetintuli	*esa*	knife
totokkwa	*pippikwa*	small
nuptulumakke	*es nukar sae*	sharpen
ipeirkiirki	*mima*	file
kan apisua	*wisit*	specialist
ittimie	*sikke*	cut
osamakke	*nek turwie*	clear
ipeakmuanapa	*pula*	grass cuttings
pulamakke	*yoke*	prepare
tikkinmakke	*sikkirmakke*	move up and down

---

4   It is interesting to compare this case of poetry in action with the sequence of increasingly powerful sounds (ritual insults) reported by Labov for a group of Harlem Blacks (Labov 1972a: 349):
Junior: I'll take your mother.
Rel: I took your mother.
Both the Kuna magical text and the Harlem sounding bring about their results with what Labov terms the "minimax" solution: "striking semantic shifts with minimal changes of form."

unnimakke	*meloe*	fortify
akselewala	*arkan*	hand
tuki	*ituki*	in front of
kwakwa	*mattarre*	flat
yalumakke	*tipamakke*	wag
kunnukke	*iploe*	kill

In addition, there are words in *The way of the snake* which have a different meaning in colloquial Kuna, resulting in a figurative, metaphorical effect. These are presented in table II.

TABLE II. Figurative Vocabulary in *The way of the snake*

English	Colloquial Kuna	*The way of the snake*
move	*nae*	*akpanne* "swing back and forth"
dark blue	*arratikki*	*koka nisa* "koka plant juice"
fangs	*nukar* "teeth"	*manansuelu* "silver hooks"
fangs	*nukar* "teeth"	*olosiku* "golden arrow"
tongue	*kwapin*	*oloputi* "golden blowgun"

This comparison of colloquial Kuna and the language of spirits reveals a metaphorical structure in the lexicon of *The way of the snake*. According to Kuna belief, however, personal, creative metaphor is not involved here, although such metaphor is highly developed in other styles of Kuna discourse, most notably in political oratory. (See chapter four.) Rather, in the spirit world, snakes, like humans, have arrows, hooks, blowguns, and neckties (line 89). This knowledge, and especially its expression in the text of *The way of the snake*, is an important aspect of the specialist's verbal demonstration to the snake spirit that he knows all there is to know about snakes, and especially, snake spirits. In addition, the associated metaphorical effect, like all the other poetic features in the chant, is pleasing to and appreciated by the spirit world and plays a significant role in the magical, controlling power of the text.

Related to the lexical structure of *The way of the snake* and also essential to its magical power is the use of names. A crucial element in controlling an object is knowing its spirit name. Constantly labeling the snake *Maci oloaktikunappi nele*,[5] its spirit name, is another aspect of the specialist's demonstration to the spirit that he has intimate knowledge of it and can thus control it. It is interesting that at the climactic moment of the raising of the snake, the snake is no longer labeled *Maci oloaktikunappi nele*, but rather by the colloquial metaphorical euphemism *kali* "vine" (lines 108, 109, 112, 118, 119). This is an intriguing insertion of everyday language into a magical chant. The names of the medicines used by the specialist to protect himself against the snake involve still another type of verbal magical power. Like the snake's name, they are the medicines' spirit names and knowledge of them is essential to being able to control and thus use them. But in addition, the chant, by means of the creation of names, endows the spirit medicines with properties which are encoded in these names. Thus, *oloputi nolomakke tule* (literally: "weak blowgun medicine") renders the snake's fangs ineffective and *oloputi nupyasae tule* (literally: "double up blowgun medicine") takes the strength out of the fangs. To describe an action in the spirit language causes that action to occur; to name an object causes the object to exist and to have the properties encoded in the name.

Another feature of the language of *The way of the snake*, which is very characteristic of Kuna magical chants in particular and all Kuna discourse more generally, is a reflexive and meta-communicative focus and orientation. *The way of the snake* is constantly pointing inward to itself, situating itself as a communicative event, and specifying what is happening within this event at the very moment that it occurs. In particular, the chant is literally punctuated by the verbs *uanae* "counsel" and *soke* "say," as the performer-specialist insistently informs the snake's spirit that he is counseling it and telling it to do certain things. In addition to their intersecting referential and metacommunicative function, these two verbs, *uanae* and *soke*, occurring as the last word in a line, contribute to the formal marking of poetic lines and structured groups of lines. And they are also place fillers and holders, giving the performer time to think of his next memorized line.

I turn how to a pervasive feature of the structural organization of *The way of the snake* and indeed of all Kuna magical chants, which is also extremely common in both oral and written ritual and poetic discourse around the world, syntactic and semantic

---

5   The ordinary Kuna word for this snake is *tappa*, a small pit viper.

parallelism. There are various types of parallelism operating in *The way of the snake*.

There are certain crucial lines which are repeated identically or almost identically[6] throughout the text, punctuating it by marking the boundaries of sections within it. Examples are:

> *Maci oloaktikunappi nele* is present (lines 20, 28, etc.).
> He is counseling *Maci oloaktikunappi* (lines 49, 58, etc.).
> The specialist is saying (lines 63, 66, etc.).
> The specialist knows well (lines 65, 70, etc.).
> *Maci oloaktikunappi nele* sticks out the point of his tongue.
> He sticks out the point of his tongue (lines 24-25).

Two lines differ in nonreferential morphemes (and the possible deletion of a word):

> The specialist is sharpening (*nuptulu-makke-kwiciye*) his little knife.
> He is sharpening (*nuptulu-sae-kwiciye*) his little knife (lines 6-7).

in which the verb stem formative *-makke* of the first line is replaced by the verb stem formative *-sae* of the next line.

Two lines are identical except for the replacement of a single word, the two words being slightly different in meaning and within the same semantic field:

> He is cutting small bushes.
> He is clearing small bushes (lines 16-17).

> The specialist moves.
> The specialist advances (lines 11-12).

Another parallelistic pattern involves not single pairs of lines, as in the preceding examples, but rather an entire set of lines, a stanza-like frame which is repeated, each

---

6   I include identical repetition as a type of parallelism here, although other students of parallelism might not, because of its role in the overall parallelistic patterning and structuring of Kuna magical chants.

time with a change in the word used to fill a particular slot. In the long section of the chant in which the specialist demonstrates his intimate knowledge of the parts of the snake's body (lines 60-106), the following frame is repeated:

> "How your [body part] was formed, put in place.
> The specialist knows well."
> The specialist is saying.

In this way, all of the body parts of the snake are listed. It seems worth noting here, since Goody (1977) and others have pointed to the list as a characteristic of written discourse, that this example of the use of parallelism to perform orally a list of items is but one of the many such cases in Kuna and other nonliterate societies. In fact, one of the functions of this kind of frame-parallelism in oral discourse seems to be precisely the memorization and performance of lists.

Parallelism thus serves a set of intersecting and overlapping functions in *The way of the snake*. It often involves the syntagmatic projection of a paradigm or taxonomy (of body parts, medicines, or movements). In addition to its poetic function (in the sense of Jakobson), this process of projecting taxonomies onto a fixed line, verse, or stanza enables the generation of a long text or portion of text. Length is an important aspect of the power of magical chants. The more recalcitrant the snake, the longer the specialist will make the text, precisely by generating more lines by means of parallelistic structures. At the same time, the performer's intimate knowledge of the nature of the spirit world, especially its parts and taxonomic classification, is also displayed by parallelistic structures and processes. And since specialists must memorize these texts, parallelistic line, verse, and stanza frames seem to provide mnemonic aids to memorization. Finally, this extensive parallelism aids in actual performance, providing both time and procedures for moving from line to line, narrative description to narrative description. It is no wonder, given these various functions, that parallelism is so pervasive in *The way of the snake*.

Another aspect of *The way of the snake* is the interplay of first, second, and third person within the narrative and the relation of this interplay to the use of quoted dialogue. *The way of the snake*, like all Kuna magical chants, is a third person narrative. Although the actual performer is the specialist who will raise a snake, the chant describes the spirit world in which both specialist and snake are third persons.

But at various points, the dialogue between the specialist spirit and the snake spirit is quoted. This direct quotation of speech, of others as well as of oneself, is a salient feature of Kuna discourse. (See chapter five, as well as Sherzer 1983: 201-207.) In the dialogues quoted in *The way of the snake*, the pronouns "I" and "you" are used. "You" is used in many lines of quoted dialogue to refer to the specialist spirit and the snake spirit, and "I" is used in several lines of quoted dialogue to refer to the snake spirit. However, "I" is used to refer to the specialist spirit in only one line, the climactic moment of the text, the performative formula within the performative chant, the actual moment of the grabbing and raising of the snake, the crucial line (115), " 'Simply indeed I raise you' I am saying," in which the single quotation marks within double quotation marks indicate that the actual specialist is quoting the specialist spirit who is quoting himself.[7] In this climactic moment of *The way of the snake*, the grammatical category of person, like other features in the structure of the text, serves several functions, including especially poetic and magical ones. Once again, grammar becomes poetry and poetry becomes magic.

The poetics of performance

These then are the textual properties of *The way of the snake*. Pranki Pilos learned this chant by listening to it performed by a specialist-teacher and by repeating it line by line. In this sense it can be said that Pranki has memorized *The way of the snake* and indeed its referential content and basic structure is identical in each performance. At the same time Pranki manipulates this basic structure and creates his own, unique version of *The way of the snake*, his own unique poetics of performance.

The parallelistic patterns which permeate the chant provide an example. In parallel lines certain words can either be repeated or deleted. Thus in the quite parallel lines 16 and 17, *ipetiniki* and *purwikan* are repeated identically as are the verbal suffixes *-nai* and *-ye*. Only the verb stem changes. On the other hand in the parallel lines six and seven the subject *apisuati* (the specialist) is not repeated. I have translated the absence of this word in line seven as "he." In Kuna the form of the third person pronoun is zero, so it is actually ambiguous whether line seven means "he is sharpening his little

---

[7]   I have placed "I" within brackets in other lines within the text where I felt that the English translation required it. The brackets are intended to indicate that the original Kuna version did not have the Kuna word *ani* "I".

knife" or "is sharpening his little knife." It is also possible for repeated words to be changed in form in certain ways. *Apisuati* occurs in line one with the suffix *-ye* and in line two without it. In lines 11 and 12 it appears in the form *kan apisu*. These lexical alterations and alternations, presences and absences, have a patterning of their own. They are created by Pranki and are an aspect of his own personal structuring of this text, his own poetics of performance.

With regard to the grammar of the ritual language of *The way of the snake*, especially the prefixes and suffixes characteristic of this grammar, there are also choices available to the performer. *-Ye* is a frequent line-final marker. But there are lines in which it does not occur. Sometimes these create an unexpected counterpoint to the presence of *-ye*, as in lines 20, 23, 33, and 56. Sometimes the absence of *-ye* sets up a parallelistic pattern of its own as in lines 29 to 30 and lines 35 to 38. *-Ye* itself might intrude contrapuntally in a series of lines without it, as in line 41 (within lines 40-43) and line 46 (within lines 44-47). *-Ye* can also occur line internally, as in lines one, 87, 92, 116, and 127. And, as we have seen, it can alternate with its absence within a parallelistic structure, as in lines one and two.

Tar is a referentially meaningless form, a kind of a vocable, which occurs only in the ritual language addressed to spirits. Pranki inserts it here and there, as in lines two, four, 12, 22, 100, 106, 122, and 125.

The ritual forms are sometimes alternated in a patterned way with their colloquial counterparts, as in the parallel lines six-seven, nine-ten, and 14-15, in which the first occurrence of the verb uses the ritual stem formative suffix *-makke* while the second occurrence uses the colloquial stem formative suffix *-sae*.

A final and most interesting aspect of Pranki Pilos's performance of *The way of the snake* is his structuring of lines and verses. The 129 lines are grouped into 45 verses. Four-line verses predominate. There are 13 four-line verses. Four is the most salient symbolic, magic number in Kuna, reflected for example in the fact that curing chants are performed on four consecutive afternoons. But verses consisting of other numbers of lines are found as well. There are twelve one-line verses, five 2-line verses, eleven three-line verses, two five-line verses, and two six-line verses. Four-line verses dominate in the presentation of the ten body parts (lines 60-106); but there are some one-line verses, one three-line verse, one five-line verse, and one six-line verse in this section as well. The metacommunicative lines "The specialist is saying" and "He is counseling *Maci oloaktikunappi nele*" sometimes occur alone, sometimes combined with others. Here and elsewhere the one-line verses provide breaks in the rhythm of the chanting. The three-line verses are used in the dramatic, climactic conclusion of the performance (lines 107-109, 117-119, 120-122, 123-125, and 127-129). With regard to the structuring of lines and verses in addition to other aspects of his performance, Pranki Pilos uses the expressive resources of language and the voice, musicality and silence, as well as sociolinguistic variations to create a unique and personal version of *The way of the snake*, against the backdrop of a memorized text with fixed semantic, referential, and narrative content.

Unlike curing and magic in other traditional societies, in particular many North and South American Indian groups, Kuna curing and magic involve no drugs, no trances, and no spectacular tricks or sleight of hand. Rather, Kuna magical actions are achieved solely by means of verbal communication between humans and spirits. Like all Kuna the spirits have a great appreciation of verbal artistry and verbal play.

While Kuna magic is verbal, it does not involve abracadabra, hocus-pocus, unintelligibility, or weirdness which Malinowski (1935) thought should be everywhere characteristic of magic.[8] Rather, it is based on a highly intelligible language. This language is intelligible in two senses. First, although it is not understandable to most human nonspecialists, it is completely and necessarily understandable to the spirit addressees. Second, as I have shown here, it is analyzable, in the sense of linguistic analysis, phoneme by phoneme, morpheme by morpheme, word by word, line by line, and verse by verse.

While figurative-metaphorical language is clearly an aspect of Kuna curing and magical chants, it is not as crucial to the functioning of these chants as it is in the political discourse of the gathering house, where metaphors are creatively adapted and manipulated. (See chapters three, four, and six.) Kuna magical language cannot be productively analyzed by focusing exclusively on metaphors and metaphorical relationships, as Tambiah has analyzed Trobriand magical language or Rosaldo Ilongot magical language. Rather, as I have demonstrated through this close reading of the text of *The way of the snake*, grammar, speech play, narrative, parallelism, metaphor, and

---

[8]   That is, the magical chants I have discussed here. Another form of discourse sometimes used in magic is the *sekretto*, a short verbal charm which involves a considerable amount of nonintelligible, nonanalyzable language. (See the text in chapter five which discusses the learning of such forms.)

counsel intersect. In the verbal mediation among humans, nature, and the world of spirits, grammar becomes poetry and poetry becomes magic.

My approach to the performance and structure of *The way of the snake* is quite analogous to the linguistic analysis of a poem. This is because understanding of this chant requires recognition of its poetic properties. At the same time, examination of this magical narrative is an illustration of my ethnographic approach to discourse and a discourse approach to the relationship between language and culture. Attention to the constant and dynamic interplay of structure and function in *The way of the snake* reveals a complex web of relations within Kuna language, culture, and society, which involves the strategic importance of snakes in Kuna culture; the relationship between humans and animals and plants; the use of language and speech to display knowledge, respect, and control; the relationship between the world of humans and the world of spirits, mediated by the poetic-rhetoric of memorized oral chants; the role of grammar, parallelism, metaphor, and narrative structure in this poetic rhetoric; and the belief in the power and ability of language to solve specific problems.

The text

In my representation of Pranki Pilos's performance of *The way of the snake*, lines are determined by melodic shape, including falling pitch, lengthened final vowels, and pauses. A slightly audible tightening of the glottis, followed by a long pause, separates verses. I have indicated this with an extra space between lines. The translation is relatively literal. I have used brackets to fill in anaphoric references that are not overtly expressed in the Kuna text but are needed in English [I, you] and to translate the meaning of a crucial grammatical category [in horizontal position, in hanging position]. Those few words I felt necessary to leave in Kuna are explained in notes. Otherwise the translation is accessible to English readers, who should be able to appreciate the figurative vocabulary, the pervasive parallelism, and the line and verse patterning.

apisuatiye, ipetinikki tana ukakka ukakkase.
apisuati neka tar palitakkekwicitarkuaye.

tata nakipe nele ulukwaapala kusattikiye.
apisuati neka tar palitakkekwiciye.
ipetinikki tana ukakka ukakkakiye.   5

apisuati ipetintuli totokkwapi nuptulumakkekwiciye.
ipetintuli totokkwa nuptulusaekwiciye.
ipeirkiirkikineye.

ipetintuli totokkwapi nuptulumaktetikineye.
ipetintuli nuptulusatetikineye.   10
kan apisu akpatteye.
kan apisu tar seleteye.

tata nakipe nelekwa uluapala tar kusattikineye.

apisuati ipetintuli totokkwapi opinyamakkenaiye.
ipetintuli totokkwapi opinyakwasaekwanaiye.   15

ipetiniki purwikan ittimienaiye.
ipetiniki purwikan osamakkenaiye.

ipetiniki purwikan ittimienaittikineye.
ipetiniki purwikan osamakkenaittikineye.
maci oloaktikunappi nele neka ipekue.   20

maci oloaktikunappi nele akkukar onakkwesikwisaye.
akkukala tar takulekesikwisaye.
ipeakmuanapa ulupa.

maci oloaktikunappi nele kwapina tukku tipamakkesikwisaye.
kwapina tukku tipamakkesikwisaye.   25

The specialist, is at the edge of his field.
The specialist is looking over his farm.

When the sun is halfway up in the sky.
The specialist is looking over his farm.
At the edge of his field. 5

The specialist is sharpening his little knife.
He is sharpening his little knife.
With a file.

When he finishes sharpening his little knife.
When he finishes sharpening his knife. 10
The specialist begins to move.
The specialist begins to advance.

When the sun if halfway up in the sky.

The specialist is working with his little knife.
He is working with his little knife. 15

He is cutting small bushes.
He is clearing small bushes.

While he is cutting small bushes.
While he is clearing small bushes.
Maci oloaktikunappi nele is present. 20

Maci oloaktikunappi nele raises his chin.
The chin appears white.
Under the grass cuttings.

Maci oloaktikunappi nele sticks out the point of his tongue.
He sticks out the point of his tongue. 25

pela koka nisa takketiyopi.
e kwapina tukku aktetemakkesikwisaye.
maci olo aktikunappi nek ipekue.

naka maci oloaktikunappi neleti, neka tar ipekue.
kalu akmuanapa ulupa.   30

maci oloaktikunappi nele tar kolesikwisaye.
"pule pan kalu saklati nue wisirpatipaye."
maci oloaktikunappi tar kolesi.

apisuati maci oloaktikunappi uanaeye.

"na pe kalu saklati wisikusakupinne.   35
na pe kalu saklapa totoketanikki.
na pe kalu sakla epiryetanikki."
maci oloaktikunappi uanae.

maci oloaktikunappi neleti.

manansuelupi pulamakkesikwisa.   40
manansuelupi opiesikwisaye.
manansuelupi tikkinmakkesikwisa.
maci oloaktikunappi nek ipekue.

naka apisuati na purpa unnimakkali.
na purpa meloali.   45
akselewala ka nika takkaliye.
akselewala ka ina nisa matta tar naisikkali.

apisuati maci oloaktikunappiti na tar penekuiniye.

It looks like the dark blue of the *koka* plant juice.
The point of his tongue salivates.
Maci oloaktikunappi nele is present.

Indeed *Maci oloaktikunappi nele* is present.
In his abode under the grass cuttings.   30

Maci oloaktikunappi nele calls.
"How well do you know the abode of my origin?"
Maci oloaktikunappi is calling.

The specialist counsels *Maci oloaktikunappi*.

"Indeed [I] know already the abode of your origin.   35
Indeed [I] have come to play in the abode of your origin.
Indeed [I] have come to encircle the abode of your origin."
He counsels *Maci oloaktikunappi*.

Maci oloaktikunappi nele.

He prepares his silver hooks.   40
He moves his silver hooks across his mouth.
He moves his silver hooks up and down.
Maci oloaktikunappi is present.

Indeed the specialist fortifies his *purpa*.[9]
Indeed he augments his *purpa*.   45
He gives *nika*[10] to his hand.
He puts a lake of medicine on his hand.

The specialist competes with *Maci oloaktikunappi*.

[9]   soul
[10] strength

maci oloaktikunappi uanaekwiciye.

apisuati maci puna olotuktutili nikkolekwiceye.   50
puna olotuktutili nikkolekwiciye.
oloputi nolomakke tule nikkolekwiciye.
oloputi nupyasae tule nikkolekwici.

naka apisuati maci oloaktikunappi tukiye.
na purpati melokwiciye.   55
na purpati tar kannokekwici.
maci olo aktikunappiti na tar penekuiniye.

maci oloaktikunappi uanaekwici.

naka maci oloaktikunappi nele nek ipekuekwasikuainiye.

"apisuati pe purpati wisikusarpa."   60
kana tar sokekwiciye.
"pe purpati palamisaye."
kan apisu tar sokekwici.

"naka pe kakkulapilli mekwitemalatti.
kana wisikusarpaye."   65
kanati sokekwicikuaye.

kan apisuati sokekwiciiniye.

"pe akkukala yoletemalatti.
pe akkukala samattar kutemalattiye.
kana tar wisikusarpaye."   70
kanati tar sokekwicitarkuaye.

naka tar kan apisuati sokekwicikusainiye.
"pe ipiyakwakwakana kuttusikwitemalatti.

He is counseling *Maci oloaktikunappi*.

The specialist is calling to *Puna olotuktutili*.　　　50
He is calling to *Puna olotuktutili*.
He is calling to *Oloputi nolomakke tule*.
He is calling to *Oloputi nupyasae tule*.

Indeed the specialist is ready for *Maci oloaktikunappi*.
Indeed his *purpa* is augmenting.　　　55
Indeed his *purpa* is strengthening.
He indeed competes with *Maci oloaktikunappi*.

He is counseling *Maci oloaktikunappi*.

Indeed *Maci oloaktikunappi* is present.

"The specialist knows well your *purpa*."　　　60
The specialist is saying.
"He captured your *purpa*."
The specialist is saying.

"Indeed how your lips were placed on.
The specialist knows well."　　　65
The specialist is saying.

The specialist is saying.

"How your chin was put in place.
How your lower chin was formed.
The specialist knows well."　　　70
The specialist is saying.

Indeed the specialist is saying.
"How your pupils were formed.

kanati wisikusarpa."
kana sokekwici.   75

kan apisuati sokekwicikusainiye.

"pe kwapina tukku yoletemalatti.
kana wisikusarpaye."
kanati sokekwici.
maci oloaktikunappiye uanae.   80

naka tar kan apisuati.
"pe olosiku tukku yoletemalatti.
pe olosiku tukku tikletemalattiye.
kana wisikusarpaye."
kanati sokekwiciye.   85
maci oloaktikunappiye uanae.

naka maci oloaktikunappiye uanae.

naka maci oloaktikunappi neleye.
"pe mussue tukku naikutemalattiye.
kana wisikusarpa."   90
kanati sokekwiciye.
maci oloaktikunappiye uanae.

naka kan apisuatinaye.

"pe olosiku kici sikwitemalattiye.
kana wisikusarpaye."   95
kanati sokekwiciye.
maci oloaktikunappiye uanae.

kana apisua neleti.
"pe nono kwakwakana samattarekutemalatti.

The specialist knows well."
The specialist is saying.　　　　　　　　　　　　　　　　　75

The specialist is saying.

"How the point of your tongue was put in place.
The specialist knows well."
The specialist is saying.
He counsels *Maci oloaktikunappi.*　　　　　　　　　　　　80

Indeed the specialist.
"How your golden arrow was put in place.
How your golden arrow was buried in.
The specialist knows well."
The specialist is saying.　　　　　　　　　　　　　　　　　85
He counsels *Maci oloaktikunappi.*

Indeed he counsels *Maci oloaktikunappi.*

Indeed *Maci oloaktikunappi nele.*
"How your necktie was hung on.
The specialist knows well."　　　　　　　　　　　　　　　　90
The specialist is saying.
He counsels *Maci oloaktikunappi.*

Indeed the specialist.

"How the venom of your golden arrow was put in place.
The specialist knows well."　　　　　　　　　　　　　　　　95
The specialist is saying.
He counsels *Maci oloaktikunappi.*

The specialist.
"How your flat head was formed.

kana tar wisikusarpaye."   100
kanati sokekwici.

naka kana apisua neletina.

kana apisuati sokekwicikusainiye.
"pe yarkikala mekwitemalatti.
pe yarkikala ururukutemalattiye.   105
kana tar wisikusarpa tar kana."

maci oloaktikunappi nele ipeakmuanapa ulupaliye.
kali mokimakkemaiye.
kali piknimakkekwamaiye.

apisuati akselewalapilliti seoyokekwiciye.   110
akselewalapillipali.
kaliti mamaksale mamaksale.
oloputi tar yalumakkesikwisa.
naka apisuati oloakselewalapillipaliye.
" 'unni na pe onakko' anti sokekwiciye."   115

maci oloaktikunappiye uanae.

ipeakselewalapillipaliye.
kaliti mokimakkenaiye.
kali piknimakkenaikusaye.

maci oloaktikunappiti tar kolekuiniye.   120
"ani kan apisuati ani purpati wisikusarpa," sokekuiniye.
maci oloaktikunappiti tar kole.

naka maci oloaktikunappiti tar kole naikusainiye.
"ani kana apisuati iki ani satotipa ani kunnuktotipaye."
maci oloaktikunappiti tar kolenai.   125

The specialist knows well."   100
The specialist is saying.

Indeed the specialist.

The specialist is saying.
"How your spinal cord was put in place.
How your spinal cord was made flexible.   105
The specialist knows well the specialist."

Maci oloaktikunappi nele is under the grass cuttings.
The vine is dragging [in horizontal position].
The vine is turning over [in horizontal position].

The specialist is signalling toward his hand.   110
Toward his hand.
The vine has almost arrived almost arrived.
He wags his golden blowgun.
Indeed on the specialist's golden hand.
" 'Simply indeed I raise you' I am saying."   115

He counsels *Maci oloaktikunappi*.

On his hand.
The vine is dragging [in hanging position].
The vine is turning over [in hanging position].

Maci oloaktikunappi calls.   120
"My specialist [you] know well my *purpa*," he says.
Maci oloaktikunappi calls.

Indeed *Maci oloaktikunappi* is calling [in hanging position].
"My specialist whatever will [you] do to me would [you] kill me?"
Maci oloaktikunappi is calling [in hanging position].   125

naka apisuati maci oloaktikunappi uanaeye.

"kati na pe kunnukkewaliye? patto aya nueti na satepinnemalaye.
kati na pe kunnukkewaliye."
maci oloaktikunappiye uanae.

Indeed the specialist counsels *Maci oloaktikunappi.*

"How indeed could [I] kill you? we have just indeed already become good friends.
How indeed could [I] kill you?"
He counsels *Maci oloaktikunappi.*

9. SOME FINAL WORDS

A theorist of literature, Thomas Pavel, in a book entitled *Fictional Worlds* (1986), cites a student of myth and oral literature, Mircea Eliade, in an article entitled "Littérature orale," who in turn cites inhabitants of a particular village in Rumania for whom a true story had become a myth, an actual event had crossed the border into legend. Pavel is fascinated by this process and calls it mythification. In very Kuna fashion, by quoting Pavel quoting Eliade quoting Rumanian villagers, I want to recast briefly for you, the readers of this book, my understanding of the import of what I have been trying to convey in the previous eight chapters.

All reality, natural, physical, cultural, social, linguistic, and artistic, is always presented and represented to and by natives and to and by us through the filter of discourse. This is true for all historical times and all societies and situations, from nonliterate and traditional to literate, modern, and complex. To make this point, I have chosen the Kuna, a South American lowland tropical forest mainly island society fragilely on the edge of the modern complex world. This is where I have focused most of my research. What I study here is a set of speech events, significant and crucial moments through which the Kuna world is conceived, shaped, and transmitted. By means of the voices and texts represented here, the Kuna envisage, organize, and interpret their world and we, their other in this case, perceive it as well.

Translating the experience of the anthropological other, the primitive, the nonliterate has been the traditional objective of the anthropologist. Some recent publications have questioned this enterprise from a variety of independent yet intersecting perspectives. They have pointed to the political-economic chasm that exists between the investigator and the native, a chasm which is both a reflection and an instance of a macro-sociological situation (i.e. the rich and the powerful vs. the poor and the weak) and an interactional encounter involving power relationships. Somewhat related, they have noted that field research methods, and especially participant observation as conventionally conceived, are inadequate for getting at the realities of the people we aim at studying. Furthermore, they have accused anthropology of tending to idealize the people it studies, treating societies as isolated and traditional, rather than placing them in the actual world system which is their complex reality. Finally they have stressed that the investigator is as much if not more writer-author than scientist-transmitter of facts and therefore transforms the other, the people she or he studies, because of her/his own stylistic conventions. This situation has been discussed, with a perhaps overabundance of rhetorical flourish, in such terms as "the crisis in contemporary anthropology," "the predicament of culture," "the politics and poetics of ethnography," and "ethnography as text," in which authors take obvious pleasure in celebrating the impossibility of describing, analyzing, or representing the other.[1]

Each of these perspectives, in its own way, turns attention away from doing field research, the central and significantly crucial moment of anthropology, and especially from ethnography, which involves interacting with and interpreting the thoughts, words, and actions of others. They focus instead on things one could find out or thought one already knew without carrying out field research as well as on the product of the fieldwork experience, the ethnographic text. My own position, expressed through extended illustration in the chapters of this book, is more hopeful, some would call it traditional. While recognizing the value of these excursions away from and challenging of anthropology's valid objectives, namely the description of social and cultural experience, I would argue that we surely not abandon the possibility of serious and scholarly descriptions of the languages and cultures of other societies, but rather take up the challenge of finding more accurate and creative ways of doing so. The aim of my approach, in which language and especially discourse is front and center, is to tell the Kuna story as the Kuna tell it, a story in which Kuna voices are presented, appreciated, and valued. These Kuna voices are not just quoted here and there to demonstrate that I the author have really been there, but are made the centerpieces of a series of chapters so that the Kuna view of their own lives, their own culture, their own society, their own language, their own esthetics, their own natural environment, and their own personal selves gradually emerges until it is expressed fully.

In all of this I am not absent and I am not naive. Of course I have had a role, and a quite significant one. I have interacted with the Kuna, I have included certain of their voices and certain of their events here and have not included others, I have represented their words with a writing system of my own choosing, I have created texts and segmented them in particular ways, and I have offered my own interpretations of the world of Kuna verbal life. But at the same time, the Kuna, that not so elusive other, if

---

[1]   A representative selection of works in this vein would include Clifford (1988), Clifford and Marcus (1986), Fabian (1983) Geertz (1988), Marcus and Cushman (1982), and Marcus and Fischer (1986). They all have predecessors, as anthropology has always had a healthy self-critical tendency.

one takes the linguistic, ethnographic, and folkloristic endeavor seriously, are fully present and represented.   Not only do I describe events in full, but the verbal performances which are centerpieces of these events are represented here as full texts, in their original language and in translation.   I claim that this discourse-centered approach, while not overcoming all of the obstacles to studying the other, an impossible goal, takes us a long and meaningful way along the path of this goal and in ways that no other current anthropological approach does.

I first entered the Kuna world in 1968 from the perspective of the ethnography of speaking. My approach has always involved studying actual speech events and making recordings of performances within them – a continuous process of transcription, translation, and interpretation. In my exploration of Kuna ways of speaking, I have become increasingly aware of and impressed by the verbal artistry which is at the center of Kuna life. This book, in which my theory and my methodology meet, is at the intersection of the ethnography of speaking and ethnopoetics.

The Kuna have been, are today, and always will be at a major crossroads of the world's social, political, and economic systems. They have suffered from this, benefited from this, adapted to this, and played with this. And they have successfully maintained their individuality, integrity, and ecology in remarkable ways. The study of discourse is an excellent way into the Kuna's dynamic and constantly changing relationship with the world around them just as it is an excellent way into their most ongoing traditions. For discourse proposes and indeed enacts in performance new ways of thinking and doing, emergent individual, social, cultural, and esthetic responses to the struggles of orientation and reorientation. I hope that I have been able to demonstrate some of this, and especially the verbal beauty that the Kuna themselves so much appreciate.

As successful as the Kuna have been in maintaining their verbal traditions, we must keep in mind that they, like so many other native groups, in both North and South America, lead a most delicate and fragile existence. We do not know how many verbal art traditions have died out, have been pushed aside, or have been brutally slaughtered. My foremost goal in this book is to record one tradition that is still very much alive and in a modest way contribute to its being appreciated and, at least on the printed page, maintained.

I end, I believe appropriately, in a very Kuna way, by quoting the endings with which performers represented in this book have ended their performances, thus creating my ending out of their endings.

Now indeed up to here.
I have given you a few words.
We are many more speakers don't you hear.
Up to here indeed I have told you a little, you have heard.
(Muristo Pérez, from chapter four.)

YOU HAVE HEARD, up to here.
(Olowitinappi, from chapter five.)

The ancestors chant this see.
Up to here I have told you a little.
(Mastayans, from chapter six.)

That's it up to here I could tell you more you've heard it my friend.
(Muristo, from chapter seven.)

REFERENCES

Apte, Mahadev L.
  1985 *Humor and laughter: An anthropological approach.* Ithaca: Cornell
      University Press.
Arrowsmith, William
  1961 The lively conventions of translation. In William Arrowsmith and Roger
      Shattuck (eds.), *The craft and context of translation*, pp. 122-140.
      Austin: University of Texas Press.
Basso, Ellen
  1985 *A musical view of the universe: Kalapalo myth and ritual performances.*
      Philadelphia: University of Pennsylvania Press.
  1987 *In favor of deceit: A study of tricksters in an Amazonian society.* Tucson:
      University of Arizona Press.
Basso, Keith
  1979 *Portraits of "the whiteman": Linguistic play and cultural symbols among the
      Western Apache.* Cambridge: Cambridge University Press.
Bauman, Richard
  1977 *Verbal art as performance.* Rowley, Mass.: Newbury House.
Beidelman, T. O.
  1961 Hyena and rabbit: A kaguru representation of matrilineal relations. *Africa*
      31: 61-74.
Bloch, R. Howard
  1983 *Etymologies and genealogies: A literary anthropology of the French middle
      ages.* Chicago: University of Chicago Press.
Bloch, Maurice
  1975 Introduction. In Maurice Bloch (ed.), *Political language and oratory in
      traditional society*, pp. 1-28. London: Academic Press.
Bloch, Maurice (ed.)
  1975 *Political language and oratory in traditional society.* London: Academic
      Press.
Blount, Ben G.
  1975 Agreeing to agree on genealogy: A Luo sociology of knowledge. In Mary

Sanches and Ben G. Blount (eds.), *Sociocultural dimensions of language use*, pp. 117-135. New York: Academic Press.

Brenneis, Donald L., and Fred B. Myers (eds.)

1984 *Dangerous Words: Language and politics in the Pacific.* New York: New York University Press.

Bright, William

1979 A Karok myth in "measured verse": The translation of a performance. *Journal of California and Great Basin Anthropology* I: 117-123. [Also in Bright 1984.]

1984 *American Indian Linguistics and Literature.* Berlin: Mouton Publishers.

Burke, Kenneth

1957 Literature as equipment for living. In *The philosophy of literary form.* Rev. ed., pp. 253-262. New York: Vintage Books.

Burns, Allan F.

1980 Interactive features in Yucatec Mayan narratives. *Language in Society* 9: 307-319.

1983 *An epoch of miracles: Oral literature of the Yucatec Maya.* Austin: University of Texas Press.

Calame, Claude

1987 Spartan genealogies: The mythological representation of a spatial organisation. In Jan Bremmer (ed.), *Interpretation of Greek mythology*, pp. 153-186. London: Crook Helm.

Carne-Ross, D.S.

1961 Translation and transposition. In William Arrowsmith and Roger Shattuck (eds.), *The craft and context of translation*, pp. 3-21. Austin: University of Texas Press.

Chapin, Mac

1970 *Pab igala: Historias de la tradición kuna.* Panama City: Universidad de Panamá.

Chapin, Norman Macpherson

1981 Medicine among the San Blas Kuna. Ph.D. dissertation. University of Arizona.

Clifford, James

1988 *The predicament of culture: Twentieth-centure ethnography, literature, and art.* Cambridge, Massachusetts: Harvard University Press.

Clifford, James, and George E. Marcus, (eds.)

    1986 *Writing culture: The poetics and the politics of ethnography.* Berkeley: University of California Press.

Curtius, Robert Ernst

    1953 *European literature and the Latin Middle Ages.* Princeton: Princeton University Press.

Cushing, Frank Hamilton

    1901 *Zuni folk tales.* New York: Putnam.

Douglas, Mary

    1968 Jokes. *Man* 3: 361-376. [Also in Douglas 1975.]

    1970 *Natural symbols: Explorations in cosmology.* London: Barrie and Rockliff.

    1975 *Implicit meanings: Essays in anthropology.* London: Routledge and Kegan Paul.

Eggan, Fred

    1950 *Social organization of the Western Pueblos.* Chicago: University of Chicago Press.

Fabian, Johannes

    1983 *Time and the other: How anthropology makes its object.* New York: Columbia University Press.

Finnegan, Ruth

    1977 *Oral poetry.* Cambridge: Cambridge University Press.

    1988 *Literacy and orality: Studies in the technology of communication.* Oxford: Basil Blackwell.

Fock, Niels

    1963 *Waiwai: Religion and society of an amazonian Tribe.* Copenhagen: National Museum.

Fox, James J. (ed.)

    1988 *To speak in pairs: Essays on the ritual languages of eastern Indonesia.* Cambridge: Cambridge University Press.

Frake, Charles O.

    1964 How to ask for a drink in Subanun. *American Anthropologist* 66 (6): 127-132.

Freud, Sigmund

1905 Jokes and their relation to the unconscious. In J. Strachey and A. Freud (eds.), *The standard edition of the complete works of Sigmund Freud.* London: Hogarth [1974].

Friedrich, Paul

1979 *Language, context, and the imagination.* Stanford, California: Stanford University Press.

Geertz, Clifford

1960 *The religion of Java.* Glencoe, Illinois: The Free Press.

1973 *The interpretation of cultures.* New York: Basic Books.

1988 *Works and lives: The anthropologist as author.* Stanford, California: Stanford University Press.

Goody, Jack

1977 *The domestication of the savage mind.* Cambridge: Cambridge University Press.

Gossen, Gary

1974 *Chamulas in the world of the sun: Time and space in a Maya oral tradition.* Cambridge, Mass.: Harvard University Press.

Gumperz, John

1971 *Language in social groups.* Stanford, California: Stanford University Press.

Hickerson, Nancy Parrott

1978 The "natural environment" as object and sign. *The Journal of the Linguistic Association of the Southwest* 3: 33-44.

Holmer, Nils M., and S. Henry Wassén

1947 *Mu-Igala, or the way of Muu, a medicine song from the Cunas of Panama.* Göteborg: Göteborgs Ethnografiska Museum.

1958 *Nia-ikala: Canto mágico para curar la locura.* Etnologiska Studier Series 23. Göteborg: Göteborgs Etnografiska Museum.

1963 *Dos cantos shamanísticos de los indios Cunas.* Etnologiska Studier Series 27. Göteborg: Göteborgs Etnografiska Museum.

Howe, James

1977 Carrying the village: Cuna political metaphors. In J. David Sapir and J. Christopher Crocker (eds.), *The social use of metaphor*, pp. 132-163. Philadelphia: University of Pennsylvania Press.

1986 *The Kuna gathering: Contemporary village politics in Panama.* Austin: University of Texas Press.

Howe, James, and Joel Sherzer

1975 Take and tell: A practical classification from the San Blas Cuna. *American Ethnologist* 2: 435-460.

1986 Friend Hairyfish and Friend Rattlesnake or keeping anthropologists in their place. *Man* 21: 680-696.

Howe, James, Joel Sherzer, and Mac Chapin

1980 *Cantos y Oraciones del congreso Cuna.* Panama City: Editorial Universitaria.

Hymes, Dell

1959 Myth and tale titles of the Lower Chinook. *Journal of American Folklore* 72: 139-145.

1965 Some North Pacific Coast poems: A problem in anthropological philology. *American Anthropologist* 67: 316-341.

1974 Studying the interpretation of language and social life. In *Foundations in Sociolinguistics,* pp. 29-66. Philadelphia: University of Pennsylvania Press.

1977 Discovering oral performance and measured verse in American Indian narrative. *New Literary History* 8(3): 431-457.

1981 *"In vain I tried to tell you" : Essays in Native American ethnopoetics.* Philadelphia: University of Pennsylvania Press.

Jakobson, Roman

1959 On linguistic aspects of translation. In Reuben A. Brower (ed.), *On translation,* pp. 232-239. Cambridge, Mass.: Harvard University Press.

1960 Closing statement: linguistics and poetry. In Thomas A. Sebeok (ed.), *Style in language,* pp. 350-377. Cambridge, Mass.: MIT Press.

1966 Grammatical parallelism and its Russian facet. *Language* 42: 398-429.

1968 Poetry of grammar and grammar of poetry. *Lingua* 21: 597-609.

Jung, Carl G.

1964 *Man and his symbols.* New York: Dell Publishing Company.

Kramer, Fritz W.

1970 Literature among the Cuna Indians. Etnologiska Studier Series 30.

Göteborg: Göteborgs Etnografiska Museum.

Kroeber, Karl (ed.)

1981 *Traditional literatures of the American Indian: Texts and interpretations.*
Lincoln: University of Nebraska Press.

Labov, William

1972a Rules for ritual insults. In *Language in the inner city: Studies in the Black
English vernacular*, pp. 297-353. Philadelphia: University of
Pennsylvania Press.

1972b The Transformation of Experience in Narrative Syntax. In *Language in the
inner city: Studies in the Black English vernacular*, pp. 354-396.
Philadelphia: University of Pennsylvania Press.

Langer, Susanne K.

1942 *Philosophy in a new key: A study in the symbolism of reason, rite, and art.*
Cambridge, Mass.: Harvard University Press.

Lévi-Strauss, Claude

1949 L'efficacité Symbolique. *Revue de l'histoire des religions* 135: 5-27.

1964 *Le Cru et le cuit.* Paris: Plon.

1964, 1966, 1968, 1971 *Mythologiques.* Paris: Plon.

Lord, Albert B.

1960 *The Singer of Tales.* Cambridge, Mass.: Harvard University Press.

Mackensen, Lutz

1923 *Der singende Knochen.* Helsinki: Folklore Fellows Communication No.
49.

Malinowski, Bronislaw

1935 *Coral gardens and their magic, volume 2: The language of magic and
gardening.* London: Allen and Unwin.

Marcus, George E., and Dick Cushman

1982 Ethnographies as texts. *Annual Review of Anthropology* 11: 25-69.

Marcus, George E., and Michael M.J. Fischer

1986 *Anthropology as cultural critique: An experimental moment in the human
sciences.* Chicago: University of Chicago Press.

McLendon, Sally

1981 Meaning, rhetorical structure, and discourse organization in myth. In
Deborah Tannen (ed.), *Analyzing discourse: text and talk.* Georgetown

University Roundtable on Language and Linguistics 1981, pp. 284-
305. Washington, D.C.: Georgetown University Press.

Mitchell, W.J.T. (ed.)

1981 *On narrative.* Chicago: University of Chicago Press.

Moore, Sally Falk

1987 Explaining the present: Theoretical dilemmas in processual ethnography.
American Ethnologist 4: 727-736.

Nordenskiöld, Erland

1938 *An historical and ethnological survey of the Cuna Indians.* Etnologiska
Studier Series 10. Göteborg: Göteborgs Etnografiska Museum.

Oberg, Kalervo

1953 *Indian Tribes of Northern Mato Grosso, Brazil.* Washington, D.C.:
Smithsonian Institution, Institute of Social Anthropology, Publication
No. 15.

Ohnuki-Tierney, E.

1977 An octupus headache? A lamprey boil? Multisensory perception of
"habitual illness" and world view of the Ainu. *Journal of
Anthropological Research* 33: 245-257.

Ong, Walter J.

1977 *Interfaces of the word.* Ithaca: Cornell University Press.

Paine, Robert (ed.)

1981 *Politically speaking: Cross-cultural studies of rhetoric.* Philadelphia: ISHI.

Paredes, Américo

1977 On ethnographic work among minority groups: A folklorist's perspective.
New Scholar 6: 1-32.

Parkin, David

1984 Political language. *Annual Review of Anthropology* 13: 345-365.

Pavel, Thomas

1986 *Fictional worlds.* Cambridge, Mass.: Harvard University Press.

Philips, Susan

1974 Warm Springs "Indian time": How the regulation of participation affects the
progression of events. In Richard Bauman and Joel Sherzer (eds.),
Explorations in the Ethnography of Speaking, pp. 92-109. Cambridge:
Cambridge University Press.

1975 Teasing, punning, and putting People on. *Working Papers in Sociolinguistics* 28. Austin: Southwest Educational Development Laboratory.

Prince, Gerald

1973 *A grammar of stories: An introduction.* The Hague: Mouton.

Radcliffe-Brown, A. R.

1940 On joking relationships. *Africa* 13: 195-210.

1949 A further note on joking relationships. *Africa* 19: 133-140.

Rosaldo, Michelle

1975 It's all uphill: the creative metaphors of Ilongot magical spells. In Mary Sanches and Ben G. Blount (eds.), *Sociocultural dimensions of language use*, pp. 117-203. New York: Academic Press.

Sahlins, Marshall

1981 *Historical metaphors and mythical realities: Structure in the early history of the Sandwich Islands kingdom.* ASAO Special Publications No. 1. Ann Arbor: The University of Michigan Press.

1985 *Islands of history.* Chicago: University of Chicago Press.

Sapir, J. David, and J. Christopher Crocker (eds.)

1977 *The social use of metaphor: Essays on the anthropology of rhetoric.* Philadelphia: University of Pennsylvania Press.

Sherzer, Dina

1986 *Representation in contemporary French fiction.* Lincoln: University of Nebraska Press.

Sherzer, Dina, and Joel Sherzer

1976 *Mormaknamaloe*: The Cuna mola. In Philip Young and James Howe (eds.), *Ritual and Symbol in Native Central America*, pp. 21-42. University of Oregon Anthropological Papers 9.

Sherzer, Joel

1970 Talking backwards in Cuna: The sociological reality of phonological descriptions. *Southwestern Journal of Anthropology* 26: 343-353.

1977 Cuna *Ikala*: Literature in San Blas. In Richard Bauman, *Verbal art as performance*, pp. 133-150. Rowley, Mass.: Newbury House Publishers.

1983 *Kuna ways of speaking: An ethnographic perspective.* Austin: University of Texas Press.

1987 A diversity of voices: men's and women's speech in ethnographic
      perspective. In Susan U. Philips, Susan Steele, and Christine Tanz
      (eds.), *Language, sex, and gender in comparative perspective*, pp. 95-
      120. Cambridge: Cambridge University Press.

1989 The Kuna verb: A study in the interplay of grammar, discourse, and style.
      In Mary Ritchie Key and Henry M. Hoenigswald (eds.), *General and
      Amerindian Ethnolinguistics: In remembrance of Stanley Newman*, pp.
      261-272. Berlin: Mouton Publishers.

Sherzer, Joel, and Greg Urban (eds.)

1986 *Native South American discourse*. Berlin: Mouton Publishers.

Sherzer, Joel, and Sammie Ann Wicks

1982 The intersection of music and language in Kuna discourse. *Latin American
      Music Review* 3: 147-164.

Sherzer, Joel and Anthony Woodbury (eds.)

1987 *Native American discourse: Poetics and rhetoric*. Cambridge: Cambridge
      University Press.

Stanek, M.

1983 Sozialordnung und Mythik in Palimbieri. *Basler Beitrage zur Ethnologie*
      23: 174-182.

Stolz, Benjamin A., and Richard S. Shannon (eds.)

1976 *Oral literature and the formula*. Ann Arbor: Center for the Coordination of
      Ancient and Modern Studies, University of Michigan.

Swann, Brian (ed.)

1983 *Smoothing the ground: Essays on Native American oral literature*.
      Berkeley: University of California Press.

Swann, Brian, and Arnold Krupat

1987 *Recovering the word: Essays on Native American literature*. Berkeley:
      University California Press.

Tambiah, S. J.

1968 The magical power of words. *Man* 3: 175-208.

Tedlock, Barbara

1986 Crossing the sensory domains in Native American aesthetics. In Charlotte
      J. Frisbie (ed.), *Explorations in ethnomusicology: Essays in honor of*

David P. McAllester. Detroit Monographs in Musicology Number 9, pp. 187-198. Detroit: Information Coordinators.

Tedlock, Dennis

1978 *Finding the center: Narrative poetry of the Zuni Indians.* Lincoln: University of Nebraska Press.

1983 *The spoken word and the work of interpretation.* Philadelphia: University of Pennsylvania Press.

1987 Hearing a voice in an ancient text: Quiché Maya poetics in performance. In Joel Sherzer and Anthony Woodbury (eds.), *Native American discourse: Poetics and rhetoric,* pp. 140-175. Cambridge: Cambridge University Press.

Tedlock, Dennis (translator)

1985 *Popol Vuh: The definitive edition of the Mayan book of the dawn of life and the glories of gods and kings.* New York: Simon and Schuster.

Thompson, Stith

1961 *The types of the folktale.* Helsinki: Folklore Fellows Communication No. 184.

Turner, Victor

1966 Color classification in Ndembu ritual: a problem in primitive classification. In M. Banton (ed.), *Anthropological approaches to the study of religion.* ASA Monograph No. 3, pp. 47-84. London: Tavistock Publications. [Also in Turner 1967.]

1967 *The forest of symbols: Aspects of Ndembu rituals.* Ithaca: Cornell University Press.

Urban, Greg

1986 Ceremonial dialogues in South America. *American Anthropologist* 88: 371-386.

Wassén, S. Henry

1938 *Original documents from the Cuna Indians of San Blas, Panama, as recorded by the Indians Guillermo Haya and Ruben Pérez Kantule.* Etnologiska Studier Series 6. Göteborg: Göteborgs Etnografiska Museum.

Waterman, T. T.

1914 The explanatory element in the folk-tales of the North American Indians. *Journal of American Folklore* 27: 1-54.

Wolf, Eric R.

    1982 *Europe and the people without history*. Berkeley: University of California Press.

Woodbury, Anthony C.

    1985 The functions of rhetorical structure: a study of Central Alaskan Yupik Eskimo discourse. *Language in Society* 14: 153-190.

    1987 Rhetorical structure in a Central Alaskan Yupik Eskimo traditional narrative. In Joel Sherzer and Anthony Woodbury (eds.), *Native American discourse: Poetics and rhetoric*, pp. 176-239. Cambridge: Cambridge University Press.

Yates, Frances

    1966 *The art of memory*. Chicago: University of Chicago Press.

INDEX

Bright, William, 28

change, 74-5, 82-3, 171
chanting, 24-5, 37-8, 163-4, 204
chief, 37-8, 48, 66-8, 71-4, 164
  chief's spokesman, 37-8, 47, 49-50, 164
conflict, 73-5, 82-3, 212-3
counsel, 64-7, 84
curing, 119-22, 240-1

discourse, 1-2, 6-7, 164-5, 266

ethnopoetics, 5

figurative language, 20, 42, 246, 252
  see also metaphor
formulaic language, 42-3, 172

gathering house, 3, 36-7, 64, 162, 203
  discourse, 20, 22, 119, 177
Geertz, Clifford, 81
grammar, 16-8, 71-2, 79, 125, 210, 244, 251
  morphology, 17-8, 243-5
  phonology, 16-7, 242-3

humor, 9, 21-2, 47, 124, 163, 205-9, 212,
  214-5
  see also speech play
Hymes, Dell, 28

ideology, 7, 41-2, 70-1, 82-3

learning, *see* teaching
Lévi-Strauss, Claude, 11-12, 50, 174-6
line, 22-6, 29, 44-6, 51, 75-6, 84, 126, 178,
  215, 251-3
literary language, *see* poetic language, verbal art

magic, 240-1, 245, 246-7, 252
McLendon, Sally, 28
memory, 48-50, 240, 249
metacommunication, 69, 125, 247
metaphor, 67-8, 76-84, 246
molas, 1, 3, 80
myth, 11, 39-40

names, 205, 246-7
narrative, 21-2, 80, 124-6, 239-40
  see also stories

oral discourse, 9-10, 44, 49, 84, 124, 126, 215,
  240, 249
oratory, *see* speech making

parallelism, 18-20, 43-4, 48-9, 75-6, 248, 250-1
poetic language, 4-5, 18, 44, 75, 244-5, 249
  see also verbal art
politics, 7
  political discourse, 82

quotation, 30, 44, 76, 124-7, 250

report, 119
ritual dialogue, 23, 37, 162, 164, 203-4
ritual speech, 46-7, 164-5, 251

snakes, 120-1, 241-2
speech making, 25, 64, 83, 119
speech play, 9, 204-8
spirits, 65, 120, 164, 240-2, 245, 252
  communication with, 3, 65, 120, 165, 240-1
stories, 25, 163, 203-4
symbolic anthropology, 81

teaching, 120, 122
Tedlock, Dennis, 28
transcription, 27-30
translation, 27, 30-3, 36-9, 47-8, 84-5, 127, 178-9,
  215, 253
tricking, 206-8
trickster tale, 203, 208, 212-3

verbal art, 2-3, 204-5
  see also poetic language
verse, 24-5, 44-6, 51, 251-3
vocabulary, 20, 166, 245-6

Woodbury, Anthony, 28
women's speech, 3
writing, 123

281